New Directions in German Studies
Vol. 38

Series Editor:

IMKE MEYER
Professor of Germanic Studies, University of Illinois at Chicago

Editorial Board:

KATHERINE ARENS
Professor of Germanic Studies, University of Texas at Austin

ROSWITHA BURWICK
Distinguished Chair of Modern Foreign Languages Emerita, Scripps College

RICHARD ELDRIDGE
Charles and Harriett Cox McDowell Professor of Philosophy,
Swarthmore College

ERIKA FISCHER-LICHTE
Professor Emerita of Theater Studies, Freie Universität Berlin

CATRIONA MACLEOD
Frank Curtis Springer and Gertrude Melcher Springer Professor in the
College and the Department of Germanic Studies, University of Chicago

STEPHAN SCHINDLER
Professor of German and Chair, University of South Florida

HEIDI SCHLIPPHACKE
Associate Professor of Germanic Studies, University of Illinois at Chicago

ANDREW J. WEBBER
Professor of Modern German and Comparative Culture, Cambridge University

SILKE-MARIA WEINECK
Grace Lee Boggs Collegiate Professor of Comparative Literature
and German Studies, University of Michigan

DAVID WELLBERY
LeRoy T. and Margaret Deffenbaugh Carlson University Professor,
University of Chicago

SABINE WILKE
Joff Hanauer Distinguished Professor for Western Civilization and
Professor of German, University of Washington

JOHN ZILCOSKY
Professor of German and Comparative Literature, University of Toronto

A list of volumes in the series appears at the end of this book.

France/Kafka
An Author in Theory

John T. Hamilton

BLOOMSBURY ACADEMIC
NEW YORK • LONDON • OXFORD • NEW DELHI • SYDNEY

BLOOMSBURY ACADEMIC

Bloomsbury Publishing Inc
1385 Broadway, New York, NY 10018, USA
50 Bedford Square, London, WC1B 3DP, UK
29 Earlsfort Terrace, Dublin 2, Ireland

BLOOMSBURY, BLOOMSBURY ACADEMIC and the Diana logo are trademarks of
Bloomsbury Publishing Plc

First published in the United States of America 2023

Copyright © John T. Hamilton, 2023

Cover design: Andrea F. Busci
Cover image: *Au rendez-vous des amis, 1922: Aragon, Breton, Baargeld,
De Chirico, Eluard, Desnos, Soupault, Dostoyevsky, Paulhan, Perst, Arp, Ernst,
Morise, Fraenkel, Raphael* by Max Ernst (1891–1976), Museum Ludwig, Cologne,
Germany. Public domain

All rights reserved. No part of this publication may be reproduced or transmitted in any form or by any means, electronic or mechanical, including photocopying, recording, or any information storage or retrieval system, without prior permission in writing from the publishers.

Bloomsbury Publishing Inc does not have any control over, or responsibility for, any third-party websites referred to or in this book. All internet addresses given in this book were correct at the time of going to press. The author and publisher regret any inconvenience caused if addresses have changed or sites have ceased to exist, but can accept no responsibility for any such changes.

Library of Congress Cataloging-in-Publication Data
Names: Hamilton, John T., author.
Title: France/Kafka : an author in theory / John T. Hamilton.
Description: New York : Bloomsbury Academic, 2023. | Series: New directions in German studies ; vol. 38 | Includes bibliographical references and index. | Summary: "Explores Kafka's influence on French intellectual history and theory in the 20th century and therefore on a central strand of modern literary criticism and philosophy"–Provided by publisher.
Identifiers: LCCN 2022031372 (print) | LCCN 2022031373 (ebook) | ISBN 9798765100363 (hardback) | ISBN 9798765100370 (paperback) | ISBN 9798765100387 (epub) | ISBN 9798765100394 (pdf) | ISBN 9798765100400 (ebook other)
Subjects: LCSH: Kafka, Franz, 1883-1924–Influence. | France–Intellectual life–20th century. | France–Civilization–German influences. | France–Civilization–Czech influences. | France–Civilization–Jewish influences.
Classification: LCC PT2621.A26 Z7461927 2023 (print) | LCC PT2621.A26 (ebook) | DDC 833/.912—dc23/eng/20220913
LC record available at https://lccn.loc.gov/2022031372
LC ebook record available at https://lccn.loc.gov/2022031373

ISBN:	HB:	979-8-7651-0036-3
	PB:	979-8-7651-0037-0
	ePDF:	979-8-7651-0039-4
	eBook:	979-8-7651-0038-7

Series: New Directions in German Studies

Typeset by RefineCatch Limited, Bungay, Suffolk

To find out more about our authors and books visit www.bloomsbury.com
and sign up for our newsletters.

One does not reach one's full development until after death, when one is all alone.

—*Franz Kafka*

Contents

Abbreviations   x

I Gradus ad Parnassum   1
The Writer and the Author in Theory 3 • Through a Glass, Darkly 6 • To the Louvre 10 • An Improbable Apparition 15 • A Second Life 19

II Metamorphoses   23
Naturalization Papers 25 • Amid Intimacy and Exoticism 29 • Universal Man 36 • Dreams, Rivers, Snow 42 • Translative Decisions 45 • Bifurcations 49

III Trials   55
Paratexts 57 • The Adventurer 59 • The Saint 67 • A Certain Plume 70 • Extremism 74 • Non liquet 79

IV Contingencies   83
Preoccupations 85 • Nothing but Nothing 87 • Seasickness on Land 90 • Phantom War 96 • Homo absurdus 100 • Impossible Hope 105 • Objective Style 108

V Judgments   113
Upside Down, Right Side Up 115 • Disengagement 118 • Incendiaries 126 • The Child 133 • The Author in Theater 137

VI Labyrinths   141
Signs of Change 143 • The New New 150 • Rhizomes 152 • Primal Scenes 157 • Derrida's Pharmacy 164

   Works Cited   169
   Index   177

Abbreviations

B   Franz Kafka, *Briefe 1902–1924*, ed. Max Brod. Frankfurt am Main: Fischer, 1958.
BF   Franz Kafka, *Briefe an Felice und andere Korrespondenz aus der Verlobungszeit*, ed. Erich Heller and Jürgen Born. Frankfurt am Main: Fischer, 1967.
C   Franz Kafka, *The Castle*, tr. Anthea Bell. Oxford: Oxford University Press, 2009.
CS   Franz Kafka, *The Complete Stories*, ed. Nahum N. Glatzer. New York: Schocken, 1983.
D   Franz Kafka, *Diaries, 1910–1923*, tr. Joseph Kresh and Martin Greenberg. New York: Schocken, 1975.
KGW   Franz Kafka, *Gesammelte Werke*, 12 vols., ed. Hans-Gerd Koch. Munich: Fischer, 1994.
L   Franz Kafka, *Letters to Friends, Family, and Editors*, tr. Richard and Clara Winston. New York: Schocken, 1977.
LF   Franz Kafka, *Letters to Felice*, tr. James Stern and Elisabeth Duckworth. New York: Schocken, 2016.
T   Franz Kafka, *The Trial*, tr. Mike Mitchell. Oxford: Oxford University Press, 2009.

Standard English translations have been used throughout and occasionally modified. Unless otherwise noted, all translations are mine.

I Gradus ad Parnassum

THE WRITER AND THE AUTHOR IN THEORY

The fate of Kafka in twentieth-century France constitutes an exemplary case of a writer becoming an author in theory. No doubt, Kafka's work always elicits some manner of theorization. His literary approach—the plotting, the characterization, and the modes of presentation—betrays a proclivity towards the kinds of ambiguities, conundrums, and paradoxes that seem to demand philosophical reflection. Even the fact that the texts evade full comprehension, that they constitute, as Theodor Adorno notes, "a parabolic system the key to which has been stolen," seems only to solicit more speculation.[1] If the term *theory* can be said to have retained the initial sense of *theōros* as a foreign emissary sent to consult the notoriously ambivalent oracle, every reader is a theorist, one who arrives from afar seeking the axiom that governs the work and realizing, sooner or later, that the decisive law exists only insofar as it remains forever out of reach. Why, then, focus on the French?

To begin, it is not uncommon to regard the development of twentieth-century French philosophy as constituting, however diversely and complexly, an identifiable moment, analogous, say, to the continuous discourse that defines Ancient Greek philosophy from Parmenides to Aristotle or German idealism from Kant to Hegel, each circumscribed by time and place and characterized by specific questions and methods of inquiry.[2] The narrative that would be baptized in the United States as *French Theory* ostensibly stretches from Sartre to Deleuze, a period that is coeval with a concentrated engagement with Kafka. As a consequence, in addition to generating a profusion of literary scholarship, commentary, and interpretation, Kafka's writings were contemplated and debated by nearly every major French thinker, most of whom were trained as academic philosophers. Over this period of roughly five decades—from the appearance of the first translation in 1928, four years after the writer had been laid to rest in Prague, to 1983, when the Centre Pompidou celebrated the centennial of his birth—Kafka's literary corpus was metamorphosed, processed, and judged, justly or not, to provide a sustained focal point for reflection on the key theoretical issues that comprise twentieth-century French intellectual history.

This narrative developed in close relation to the social and political upheavals that marked the era. Kafka's reception in France began

---

[1] Theodor W. Adorno, "Notes on Kafka," in *Prisms*, tr. Samuel and Shierry Weber (Cambridge: The MIT Press, 1967), 246.
[2] Cf. Alain Badiou, *The Adventure of French Philosophy*, tr. Bruno Bosteels (New York: Verso, 2012), li–lii.

within the context of the lingering optimism of rapprochement during the post-Armistice decade, then developed alongside the ideological entrenchment that confronted the economic crises, the menace of fascism, and the futility of appeasement. While Kafka's work was suppressed in Germany under the Nazi regime, the author's reputation spread across the French capital. He whetted the surrealists' appetite for a revolution of the world through a revolution of the word. He nourished the patriots and the dissidents, the communists and the aesthetes, who were desperate for texts that would endorse their programs either to recharge or to eliminate a parliamentary system deemed incompetent and corrupt. He filled the populace to the point of nausea. Having gone underground during the Occupation, Kafka became a hero of the Resistance and emerged triumphant after the Liberation. He was touted by the existentialists as the clairvoyant who had foreseen the entire disaster: The alienation suffered in a bureaucratized society, the oppression under the yoke of totalitarianism, the arrests of thousands upon thousands who were unaware of having done anything wrong, the deportations to death camps run with factory efficiency, where victims would be slaughtered like a dog. Kafka gave voice to the world's absurdity. He was celebrated as the modern poet of nothingness and contingency, as the preacher of the death of God and the leap of faith. Accordingly, his texts held ground amid postwar tensions between Gaullism and Marxism, between cautious individualism and troubled collectivism, as the nation slid into a reckoning with its colonial past, straight into the civil unrest of 1968 and its dispersed aftermath.

Throughout, the two major endeavors, Kafka reception and French philosophy, progressed side by side, hand in hand, so closely allied that it is difficult to decide on questions of causation: To what extent was French thinking responsible for producing theoretical constructions of Kafka and to what extent did Kafka's works contribute to the articulation of French conceptions? To what extent did reception reshape the text and to what extent did the text transform its recipients?

To insist on the uniqueness of the French Kafka—Kafka as an *object of theory*—does not mean to suggest that the author has not also been treated as a *writer* among French scholars and readers on par with other major cultures, or that non-French interpreters have refrained from theoretical conclusions, or that the discourse I am singling out did not benefit from or build upon more standard methods of literary study. Nor am I proposing that the terms and theorems of the French Kafka failed to participate in the broader scholarship and reception worldwide. Exchanges were many and profoundly significant, triggering a feedback loop of mutual development and mutual limitation. I would especially discourage the idea that French philosophical involvement should be regarded as definitive or authoritative. On the contrary, the present study, in the course of delineating and evaluating this national-historical moment, attempts to assess what separates the two images of Kafka—Kafka the writer and Kafka the theoretical object. Where do they conflict and where do they overlap? How do they converge and how do they diverge? Can one—should one—strive to ransom the writer from his fate as an author in theory?

For the moment, the simple fact is indisputable: From Phenomenology and Existentialism to Structuralism and Poststructuralism, Kafka's presence was persistent. The list of theorists who directly engaged with the Prague author speaks for itself: Jean Paulhan, Bernard Groethuysen, André Breton, Jean Wahl, Jean-Paul Sartre, Albert Camus and Maurice Blanchot, Pierre Klossowski and Georges Bataille, Roland Barthes, Jean-François Lyotard, Jacques Derrida, Hélène Cixous, Gilles Deleuze, and Félix Guattari. Parallel to this legacy are the many creative endeavors that prompted or responded to the philosophical labor, works that tended to side more with Kafka the writer than with the author in theory, at times confirming or enhancing, at times critically challenging the premises and concepts at hand: The idiosyncratic prose of Henri Michaux, the dream-texts of Michel Leiris, the novels of Sartre, Camus, and Blanchot, André Gide's theatrical production of *The Trial*, Eugène Ionesco's Theater of the Absurd, and the *nouveau roman*.

Circa 1960, as existentialist readings started to fade, Kafka powered a network of readings assignable to Marxist critique, sociology, structuralism, and semiotics, as well as materialist, deconstructive, and feminist approaches. "French theory," in turn, would have far-reaching effects on how literature in general would be examined or extorted to address fundamental questions regarding ontology and epistemology, subjectivity and language, social and political reform.[3] It is no exaggeration to claim that the French theoretical engagement with Kafka during the latter half of the twentieth century instigated much of how we understand and grapple with culture in the twenty-first, from reflection on the performativity of gender—Judith Butler credits Derrida's reading of Kafka's "Before the Law" as having ignited her *Gender Trouble* (1990)[4]—to the abuses of power that take advantage of a socially networked, post-factual, hyper-mediatized world.

---

[3] For a critical history, see François Cusset, *French Theory: How Foucault, Derrida, Deleuze & Co. Transformed the Intellectual Life of the United States*, tr. Jeff Fort (Minneapolis: University of Minnesota Press, 2008).

[4] Judith Butler, *Gender Trouble: Feminism and the Subversion of Identity*, 2nd ed. (New York: Routledge, 1999), xiv.

6   France/Kafka

THROUGH A GLASS, DARKLY

Ever since Thales was reported to have tripped into the proverbial well, theory has been subjected to ridicule.[5] Just as this fabled astrologer from Miletus purchased his knowledge of the distant heavens with ignorance of what lay at his feet, so have literary theorists, especially of the Parisian variety, been charged with disseminating pronouncements of such prolixity that they detract from the artistic merits of the work. The more difficult and jargon-ridden the expositions appear, the more they seem to distance us from the texts presumably under discussion. Thus, *theory* is often judged to be at loggerheads with its traditional complement, *practice*. The theorist is vilified for discounting the practical exercise of understanding and taking pleasure in the text that lies in front of our eyes. Although *theōria* derives from the Greek verb for beholding (*theaomai*), the insight it supplies seems haunted by blindness. For what theory sees is invisible, that which exceeds and threatens to supplant what ought to be visibly discernible in the text itself. Why struggle with the enigmas of Blanchot, Deleuze, or Derrida, when we could engage directly with the enigma that is Kafka?

A man from Bohemia who passed away quietly at the age of forty, a German-Jewish author who published but a handful of stories that attracted limited attention, a writer who began three novels yet finished none, would nonetheless, within a decade of his death, become the favored candidate for philosophical election in Paris. What would account for this outcome?

The process might be viewed as a case of gross naturalization, appropriation, and universalization, an unchecked scheme on the part of French theorists to take a foreign author hostage and compel him to speak on behalf of their native cause. In this regard, the case of Kafka might simply be another episode in a long history of the French adoption of German writers and artists: Schiller during the Revolution of 1789, Hoffmann at the height of French Romanticism, Heine, Wagner, Nietzsche, and so forth. Yet these moments are relatively diffuse and belong to broader trends of the cross-cultural exchange. Moreover, they

---

[5]   The episode concerning Thales of Miletus is recounted, not without typical irony, by Socrates in Plato's *Theaetetus* 174a, in Plato, *Complete Works*, ed. John M. Cooper (Indianapolis: Hackett, 1997), 93. For a comprehensive and engaging investigation of this anecdote across the centuries, see Hans Blumenberg, *The Laughter of the Thracian Woman: A Protohistory of Theory*, tr. Spencer Hawkins (New York: Bloomsbury, 2015).

fail to feature the continuity and specificity that make Kafka's role in French thought strikingly singular.

Certainly, Kafka is not the sole author in theory. Other instances are analogous, including cases of German thinkers who have nominated French authors for their ruminations. Walter Benjamin's Baudelaire and Theodor Adorno's Proust readily come to mind. Yet, while the respective *Arcades Project* and *Notes to Literature* have stimulated a good deal of philosophical discussion, they ultimately give rise to a distinct line of discourse that lacks the diversity and interrelatedness that obtain with the French Kafka. That said, the joint development of Kafka and French theory took place with a constant eye on German philosophical and literary-critical interventions. French Phenomenology and Existentialism, for example, are unthinkable without the foundational inspiration of Edmund Husserl, Karl Jaspers, and Martin Heidegger, just as Poststructuralism cannot be understood apart from Marx, Nietzsche, and Freud. Two-way streets abound, directing the intellectual traffic from East to West, Present to Past.

As for the charge of appropriation or even extortion—that Kafka may have been violently abducted from his eastern German-Jewish-Czech context for the sake of theoretical generalizations—one would have to consider, again, the extent to which the author's work is amenable to this manner of speculation. The parabolic nature of Kafka's narratives, the frequent absence of geographical, national, or cultural markers, as well as the minimalist portrayal of his protagonists, would appear to encourage universal applicability. The abbreviated K. could well function as a cipher for anyone, like an algebraic variable to be factored into an axiomatic equation. The near anonymity, the erasure of national or ethnic determinations, arguably primed Kafka's texts to serve as a representative of Everyman.

Still, the story of the French Kafka cannot be reduced to representativeness. That would limit the texts to a function that many of the thinkers under discussion would reject. The alliance between Kafka and contemporary French thought instead demonstrates a special coalition of literature and philosophy that for the most part invests in fresh philosophical-literary ventures. If literature is thought to be grounded in the particularity of lived experience and philosophy in the universality of the concept, then Kafka's prolonged residency in French theory constitutes a dynamic synthesis of the vitalist and formalist poles, a site where life and concept may reflect each other.

The motif of reflection is explicit in Claude David's introductory essay in the 1976 Pléiade Edition of Kafka's *Œuvres complètes*:

[Kafka] is felt to be an enigma, but at the same time an image of ourselves to which each of us would like to bring a personal touch or alteration. It has been said that he reflects, like a mirror, all the anxieties and problems of those who read or comment on it.[6]

David enlists the Pauline trope, "we now see through a glass and in an enigma [*per speculum et aenigmate*]" (1 Corinthians 13:12), which from Augustine on has authorized scriptural openness, the text's capacity to afford multiple meanings and interpretations. Astutely, however, David neither emphasizes the Christian implication nor includes the messianic hope contained in Paul's verse: "now . . . in an enigma, but then face to face," an allusion to the Final Judgment when all shall be revealed. The omission is pertinent, as if to endorse Kafka's equally well-known aphorism: "The messiah will come only when he is no longer necessary, he will come only on the day after his arrival; he will come, not on the last day, but on the very last" (KGW 6, 182). Time itself would have to end for conclusive understanding to emerge. Full revelation will obtain only when there will be nothing left to say. Blanchot, whose literary reflections obsessively turned to Kafka, recognized instead how the finitude of the work is negated by the infinitude of writing. In his final essay on Kafka, aptly titled "The Very Last Word" (1968), Blanchot ends by affirming that Kafka provides "the last word that only proposes to simulate and dissimulate the expectation of the very last."[7] The simulation and dissimulation, the likeness and concealment, comprise the visual mirror and verbal enigma proposed by my title: *France/Kafka*. It stresses the mutual reflection and refraction that should help us appreciate how Kafka's work specifically accommodated French speculation.

The specular, enigmatic relationship is persistent. Together with accounts of Kafka in France stand images of France in Kafka. Both those who denounce theory as impotent prattle and those who uphold its capacity to illuminate what would otherwise be overlooked may be perceived as forming a clear antithesis, yet they share at least one common feature: Both regard theory as extraneous to the works they contemplate. The presupposition is that Kafka's writing consists of surface events that are symptomatic of some ideational depth that

---

[6] Claude David, "La Fortune de Kafka," in Franz Kafka, *Œuvres complètes*, Bibliothèque de la Pléiade, 2 vols., ed. Claude David (Paris: Gallimard, 1976), 1, x.
[7] Maurice Blanchot, "Le tout dernier mot," in Blanchot, *De Kafka à Kafka* (Paris: Gallimard, 1981), 244 ["The Very Last Word," in Blanchot, *Friendship*, tr. Elizabeth Rottenberg (Stanford: Stanford University Press, 1997), 265–88; here, p. 284 (trans. modified)].

theory is at pains to reveal, in ways that either beneficially expand or detrimentally reduce the literary value of the texts. Whether one evaluates theory as obfuscating or enlightening, one often presumes that the explicative model subsists independently, that theory relates to the text from without. Yet, rather than discount Existentialism or Deconstruction as autonomous models applied *a posteriori* to Kafka's writing, it may just as well be the case that these and other modes of theorization have developed their signature methods through direct engagement with the work, that the theories articulate a response to specific themes and concepts, tensions and structures in the literature itself. From this perspective, contrary to theory's detractors and supporters alike, interpretive models are engendered by the material they ponder. Camus' existentialist reading of Kafka, for example, may not necessarily entail fashioning the text into the Procrustean bed of readymade theorems, but instead demonstrate to what extent these ideas are already embedded in the work.

Locked within the circuit of a perpetual mirror stage, *France/Kafka* attends to a genealogy through which the literature and its theoretical responses mutually form, inform, and transform each other, a projection of reflections whereby each side acquires its countenance and cogency. As Michel Foucault has argued, the concept of genealogy denotes a genetic relationship that depends on receptive processes and contingencies which evade teleological control: Genealogy "opposes itself to the search for 'origins.'"[8] Every theoretical intervention, as well as every one of Kafka's texts, can thus be regarded as singular events that appeal to a general law while remaining irreducible to it. In this regard, Kafka's scriptural evidence does not serve as the origin that would validate or invalidate a theoretical thesis, for it is only when theory is understood as autonomous that verifiability comes into play. Instead, the reciprocal, chiastic relationship that the present study explores should demonstrate that no original truth can be recovered, that we are caught in a *mise-en-abyme*. Accordingly, the series of theoretical engagements with Kafka does not merely comprise a history of failed attempts to attain the original sense of the texts. Like the messiah, the truth of Kafka's works and therefore the truth of any theory will only come on the day after arrival. *France/Kafka* offers one story, if not about the second coming, then at least about the second life that was to be the writer's destiny.

---

[8]   Michel Foucault, "Nietzsche, Genealogy, History" [1971], in Foucault, *Language, Counter-Memory, Practice: Selected Essays and Interviews*, ed. Donald Bouchard (Ithaca: Cornell University Press, 1977), 139–64; here, p. 140.

TO THE LOUVRE

In recounting "Kafka's Fortune" (1976), Claude David admits to being utterly confounded:

> Nothing seemed to destine Kafka to the fame he received: neither this miserable life, nor this strange, rough, apparently impenetrable work. Nor the environment in which he had lived: this Prague, which was little known in France, this almost exotic Bohemia, with its fields of snow and its sleds.[9]

From the cathedra of the self-styled capital of the World Republic of Letters, from this vantage point of French *civilisation*, Kafka's work might be regarded as a piece of exotic *Kultur*, "strange" and "rough," yet how valid is the claim that *nothing* predisposed this corpus for a smooth welcome?

Prague might not have been a frequent destination point for early twentieth-century French tourists, but as a major Central European capital, it was by no means isolated from the continental culture of which Paris was a part. However singular and solitary it may appear, Kafka's style developed vis-à-vis an intimate familiarity with much of the literature and philosophy that was being read and discussed among the French intelligentsia at the time. In addition to a humanist-classical education, which he shared with most *lycéens*, Kafka avidly engaged with the modern canon: Goethe, Hoffmann, Dickens, Dostoevsky, Gogol, Tolstoy, Strindberg, Knut Hamsun, and above all Flaubert, whom Kafka recognized as a "blood relative."[10] Without delving into the murky waters of possible influence, one could surmise that the shared literary inheritance would have positioned Kafka's work to meet his French readership at least halfway.

Certainly, Kafka's protracted and intense study of Kierkegaard and Nietzsche would have connected him with the existentialist generation and beyond. Hermeneutic coercion is not at all needed to recognize in Kafka's stories and novels many points of contact: The anguish, despair, and paradoxes of faith; the contingency of existence, the moral consequences of the death of God, and the drive towards self-overcoming—all voiced from the perspective of a bachelor's solitude.

---

[9] David, "La Fortune de Kafka," ix.
[10] Kafka, Letter to Felice Bauer, Sept. 2, 1913 (BF 460/LF 315–16). On Kafka's reading, see Monika Schmitz-Emans, "Kafka und die Weltliteratur," in *Kafka-Handbuch: Leben—Werk—Wirkung*, ed. Bettina von Jagow and Oliver Jahraus (Göttingen: Vandenhoeck & Ruprecht, 2008), 271–92.

Already adrift in a postmodern condition, the Danish ironist and the Zarathustran prophet come across as kindred spirits with a man "as lonely as Franz Kafka."[11] With this common repertoire of themes, problems, and premises in view, theoretical conjectures appear less as an imposition and more as a reciprocal dialogue. That the writer from distant Prague so readily became an author in French theory cannot, therefore, be immediately discounted as a perversion or as the effect of speculative overreach, even if the latter interpretations should prove to be inadequate or misleading.

Another significant source that irrigated Kafka and his theorists alike was Franz Brentano. The author of *Psychology from an Empirical Standpoint* (1874) and one of the most prominent philosophers at the University of Vienna, Brentano played a substantial role in the development of European intellectual history, having advised a roster of students who would set many of the terms of engagement for the twentieth century: Sigmund Freud, Edmund Husserl, Rudolf Steiner, Carl Stumpf, and Christian von Ehrenfels, to name the most illustrious. Thus, the foundation of psychoanalysis, modern phenomenology, anthroposophy, experimental psychology, and Gestalt psychology owe some measure of debt to Brentano's seminal theory of consciousness. By the time Kafka entered the German University of Prague in 1901, Brentano's concepts and descriptive method had long held sway across the Austro-Hungarian Empire, not only in philosophy and psychology, but also in ethics, politics, religion, and law. Although registered in jurisprudence, Kafka enthusiastically attended seminars taught by Ehrenfels and by Anton Marty, one of Brentano's staunchest disciples and university rector. It was Marty who inspired a group of young acolytes to congregate at the Café Louvre in Prague to discuss and propagate Brentano's work. At the invitation of his friends, Hugo Bergmann, Emil Utitz, and Oskar Pollak, Kafka began joining these meetings around 1903 and would remain a regular participant until 1906. Max Brod also counted himself as a member of the so-called Louvre Circle until the group expelled him after he published two stories that satirized the Brentanists as sterile and disingenuous. Although Kafka apparently sided with Brod and quit the gatherings, he would soon resume contact.[12]

---

[11] The reference is to Marthe Robert's psychological biography *As Lonely as Franz Kafka* [1979], tr. Ralph Manheim (New York: Harcourt Brace Jovanovich, 1982).

[12] For an overview of Kafka's connection to the Louvre Circle, see Reiner Stach, *Kafka: The Early Years*, tr. Shelley Frisch (Princeton: Princeton University Press, 2017), 255–63.

Biographers vary on how much weight to accord this episode in Kafka's life. Whereas Klaus Wagenbach insisted that Brentano's thought substantially informed Kafka's burgeoning literary approach, Brod dismissed any suggestion of influence, either because of his mistreatment by the Louvre conclave or because of his firm belief that Kafka wrote purely intuitively and had no deep interest in theory.[13] More recently, scholars have turned to textual analysis to demonstrate that Kafka's early experiments in fiction do in fact exhibit features specifically related to Brentano and his followers. Arnold Heidsieck's diligent study, for example, outlines the theorems discussed by the Louvre Circle and shows in detail how "Kafka embeds them almost serially in his developing themes and paradigms."[14] Again, regardless of how one might judge the ultimately evasive matter of influence, the main point is incontestable, that for a prolonged, particularly formative period of time, Kafka engaged with a body of conceptual work that would also feed directly into French theory.

Brentano's legacy cannot be overstated. His notion of intentionality and intentional objects, which warrants exclusive attention to the structures of mental states, provided the basis for Husserl's phenomenological method, which in turn developed into Heidegger's ontology and thus inspired Sartre's existentialist account of consciousness. Subsequently, it was an intense scrutiny of Husserl and his Brentano-inflected discussion of auto-affection that occasioned Derrida's concept of *différance*, while Freud's theories of the Unconscious and the Oedipal Complex not only supplied the paradigms for Hélène Cixous's psychoanalytic readings of literature, but also furnished the target for Deleuze and Guattari's "schizoanalysis." Moreover, Anton Marty's contribution to the Prague School of linguists, including Roman Jakobson and Nikolai Trubetzkoy, would allow Russian formalism to bear on French structuralism and semiotics. It is also worth noting that Bernard Groethuysen, who wrote his dissertation in Berlin under Brentano's student Carl Stumpf, composed the first major French essay on Kafka for the translation of *The Trial* in 1933.

The main thrust of Brentano's descriptive psychology concerns the primacy of inner "perception" (*Wahrnehmung*) over external "observation"

---

[13] See Neil Allan, *Franz Kafka and the Genealogy of Modern European Philosophy: From Phenomenology to Post-Structuralism* (Lewiston: Edwin Mellen Press, 2005), 11–13.

[14] Arnold Heidsieck, *The Intellectual Contexts of Kafka's Fiction: Philosophy, Law, Religion* (Columbia: Camden House, 1994), 48; cited in Barry Smith, "Brentano and Kafka," *Axiomathes* 8 (1997), 83–104; here, p. 83. Heidsieck's and Smith's readings build upon the seminal work of Peter Neesen, *Vom Louvrezirkel zum Prozess: Franz Kafka und die Psychologie Franz Brentanos* (Göppingen: Kümmerle, 1972). The thesis is further pursued by Allan, *Franz Kafka*, 16–57.

(*Beobachtung*). Unlike sensory objects, which are transcendent to the mind, mental objects are fully immanent to consciousness. As in Husserl's *epochē*—the negative gesture of bracketing out the world, the skeptical disposition of withholding assent—and in line with Descartes's hyperbolic doubt, it is Brentano's sole task to analyze and pass judgment on the structures of these internal manifestations, without regard for external reality. In fact, for Brentano, reality can only be ascribed to intentional objects of consciousness and not to unintentional objects in the world, which he would therefore qualify as "non-real." The result could be viewed as a radical subjectivism if not pure solipsism, which even rejects introspection insofar as it distances mental states as stable objects of observation, as quasi-physical rather than purely psychical objects.[15] As a corollary, the self cannot be conceived as a substantive entity detached from the intentional phenomena of consciousness; rather, the unity of the self is like "a flowing stream in which one wave follows another and imitates its movement."[16]

To discern traces of Brentano's descriptive psychology in Kafka, literary critics have analyzed his early narrative, *Description of a Struggle*, which dates from 1904–5, that is, at the height of Kafka's participation in the Louvre Circle. Tellingly, near the beginning of the story, the protagonist and his new acquaintance turn onto the Ferdinandstraße, where the Café Louvre was located. Although this work has been relatively neglected by commentators, it is important to stress that Kafka was sufficiently satisfied to publish several excerpts of the first and second versions of the text: "Conversation with the Supplicant" and "Conversation with the Drunk" in Franz Blei's journal *Hyperion* (March–April 1909), as well as shorter pieces in his 1913 collection, *Betrachtung* (*Meditation* or *Contemplation*).

The episodic story shifts from one narrator to the next in a kaleidoscopic, nearly schizophrenic dispersion of subjectivity. Throughout, the descriptions give literary form to Brentano's central thesis, that the self is nothing but the site of shifting phenomena in consciousness. Kafka exaggerates this notion by describing reality as an arbitrary product of subjective will, for example, in the section titled "A Walk":

> I walked on, unperturbed. But since, as a pedestrian, I dreaded the effort of climbing the mountainous road, I let it become gradually flatter, let it slope down into a valley in the distance. The stones vanished at my will and the wind disappeared. [. . .] I caused to

---

[15] Franz Brentano, *Psychology from an Empirical Standpoint*, tr. Antos C. Rancurello, D.B. Terrell, and Linda McAlister (New York: Routledge, 1995), 22.
[16] Brentano, *Psychology*, 130; also cited with discussion in Allan, *Franz Kafka*, 19.

> rise an enormously high mountain whose plateau, overgrown with brushwood, bordered on the sky. [...] This sight, ordinary as it may be, made me so happy that I, as a small bird on a twig of those distant scrubby bushes, forgot to let the moon come up.
>
> (KGW 5, 62–3/ CS 22)

As we shall see, this early text approximates Sartre's 1938 novel, *Nausea*, which was in part inspired by Husserl's elaboration of Brentano's method. "Is it not this fever," one of Kafka's narrators exclaims, "this seasickness on land?" (KGW 5, 126/CS 33). The resemblance of the two works is all the more striking insofar as it is unlikely that Sartre was aware of Kafka's fragmentary story, which would first appear in French translation in 1946. The shared provenance—Kafka and Sartre as initiates in Brentannian concepts—would alone account for the common approach.

Uncannily, in the section entitled "Conversation with the Drunk," Kafka turns to a depiction of Paris, which he had not yet visited in person. At this point, the narration falls to the histrionic "Supplicant" (*Beter*), who was introduced in the preceding section and now interrogates an inebriated nobleman.

> I ask you, much-decorated sir, is it true what I have been told? Are there people in Paris who consist only of ornate dresses, and are there houses that merely have portals, and is it true that on summer days the sky over the city is a fleeting blue embellished by little white clouds glued onto it, all in the shape of hearts?
>
> (KGW 5, 85–6/CS 42)

The French capital is presented as pure façade, a metropolis of flat surfaces without depth, a society of the spectacle. Interpretation is impossible because there is no interior space, no subjectivity directing the show, nothing that would function as the guarantor of meaning. In the view of one recent scholar, Kafka here shows himself as a poststructuralist *avant la lettre*: "Kafka seems to construct little more than a decentered assemblage of free-floating signifiers whose unreadability subverts traditional expectations of mimetic representation, symbolic modes of narration, and hermeneutic quests for determinate meaning."[17] In this phantasmagoria, accident and disorder proliferate in an endless stream of traffic.[18]

---

[17] Rolf Goebel, "Paris, Capital of Modernity: Kafka and Benjamin," *Monatshefte* 90 (1998), 445–64; here, p. 461.

[18] Cf. Mark Anderson, *Kafka's Clothes: Ornament and Aestheticism in the Habsburg Fin de Siècle* (Oxford: Clarendon Press, 1992), 42–4.

These Paris streets [...] they suddenly branch off, don't they? They're turbulent [*unruhig*], aren't they? Things are not always in order, how could they be, after all? Sometimes there's an accident, people gather together from the side streets with that metropolitan stride that hardly touches the pavement; they are all filled with curiosity, but also with fear of disappointment; they breathe fast and stretch out their little heads.

(KGW 5, 86/CS 42)

Written towards the end of Kafka's participation in the Louvre Circle and near the start of his engagement with Flaubert, the text relishes in Paris as a literary construction, a figment of a mental state, which for Brentano is the only real reality. Before he became an object of French theory, Paris had been an object of Kafka's theory. Three years later, he would have the opportunity to test this real unreal city against the concrete experience of these restless streets. The relation between what the theorist envisioned and what consciousness actually perceives constitutes one of the fundamental tensions that generates Kafka's texts just as it will steer their reception—that is, when Kafka's unreadable Paris reads the unreadable Kafka.

AN IMPROBABLE APPARITION

L'homme n'est rien, l'œuvre—tout.

—Gustave Flaubert

The trip to Paris was set for October 1910, intended to trace the itinerary of Frédéric Moreau, the protagonist of Flaubert's *L'Éducation sentimentale*, which Brod and Kafka regarded as the author's masterpiece, equal only to the works of Plato and Goethe.[19] The friends' high opinion of the 1869 novel would persist. To Felice Bauer, Kafka would later confess: "*Education sentimentale* is a book that for many years has been as dear to me as are only two or three people; whenever and wherever I open it, I am startled and succumb to it completely, and I always feel as though I were the author's spiritual son, albeit a weak and awkward one" (Nov. 15, 1912; BF 95–6/LF 42). The spiritual son of a bachelor father.

---

[19] See Brod's essay, "Gustave Flaubert: 'Erinnerungen eines Narren'" ("Memoirs of a Fool"), published in *Neue Freie Presse*, February 16, 1908, 36; cited in Hartmut Binder, *Kafka in Paris: Historische Spaziergänge mit alten Photographien* (Munich: Langen Müller, 1999), 11. I have taken most of the details in this section from Binder's comprehensive account, 11–116.

16   France/Kafka

Having postponed his vacation to autumn, Kafka spent most of the summer preparing for the pilgrimage, taking private French conversation lessons and re-reading Flaubert's text in the original. To experience Paris itself, to walk where Frédéric Moreau walked, would be as if literature itself had come to life. But then, a few days prior to departure, Kafka wrote a worried note to Brod. His foot was "enormously swollen." One cannot help but recall the plight of Oedipus. As a consequence, Kafka feared he might have to call everything off. "If the wish for a trip can be strong enough to make me well, I'll be well by Saturday, I assure you" (L 67).

The mind-over-matter strategy clearly worked, for on the morning of October 8 Kafka boarded the train with Max and Otto. They traveled to Nuremberg, where they stayed the night, and continued on to Paris the following morning. All seemed to go smoothly. Yet, as their train pulled into the Gare de l'Est, a new ailment cropped up: A cluster of pus-filled abscesses had formed across Kafka's upper back. The new affliction hindered Kafka's ability to join his friends on their walking tour. He would manage to take in a few sights but invariably had to return early to his hotel to reapply the plaster.[20] There is no evidence of the excitement one would expect from a man who long dreamed of Paris and was visiting the city for the very first time. Kafka's body was now overriding his wishful spirit. By Sunday evening, he bid his friends farewell and the following morning boarded the train for home, the three-week holiday curtailed to a mere seven days.

Once back in Prague, Kafka sent three postcards to Brod in Paris, detailing his ongoing torment. In addition to the abscesses, the skin on his back broke out into a horrible rash.

> I am very pale only because everybody regards me as an improbable apparition. [. . .] My idea, which of course I did not reveal to the doctor, is that the international pavements of Prague, Nuremberg, and above all Paris have caused this eruption. And so, I am now sitting at home in the afternoon as in a tomb.
> (L 67/B 82)

Kafka depicts himself as an "apparition" or "appearance" (*Erscheinung*)—a *phainomenon*, in the strictest sense—improbable because still a living creature, however pale. Fittingly, he proffers an

---

[20] See Max Brod's travel notes in *Max Brod, Franz Kafka: Eine Freundschaft*, vol. 1, *Reiseaufzeichnungen*, ed. Hannelore Rodlauer and Malcolm Pasley (Frankfurt am Main: Fischer, 1987), 37–8.

improbable etiology, that the pavement, above all in Paris, was the cause of abscesses. The concern with how he appears to others—or the fact that he is but an appearance to others—evokes the shame that will haunt much of his work.

Kafka's desire to follow in the footsteps of Flaubert's Frédéric correlated with the aspiration to become literature itself, to disappear into the work. The wish had been articulated by Flaubert, something Kafka would have come across in the study Brod had given him years before, *Flaubert: Son hérédité—son milieu—sa méthode* (1903) by René Dumesnils, a physician also from Rouen who would one day publish a novel entitled *L'Absence* (1919). In Paris, Kafka had perhaps longed to metamorphose his shameful human frame into a literary corpus, but the body protested. While his friends were living it up in Paris, coordinating their Flaubert with what was taking place on the boulevards, Kafka resigned himself to his home in Prague, trapped in a sickly body as if in a tomb.

Throughout the period around 1910 and essentially for the remainder of his life, Kafka regarded his body as an obstacle. The headaches, the stomach pain, the insomniac's exhaustion, all seemed to impede his creative progress; yet physical ailments were not the sole problem. Even the healthy body posed a serious distraction. Months before he left for Paris, Kafka confessed: "Have I not even the resolution to take this penholder, this piece of wood, in my hand every day? I really think I do not. I row, ride, swim, lie in the sun" (May 17–18, 1910; KGW 9, 17/D 14). The noun for "resolution"—*Entschlossenheit*—is constructed from the root term *Schloss*, "lock," and the prefix *ent-*, which denotes a separation or removal. A decision to act is thus figured as a mind that is no longer "locked" or "closed" (*geschlossen*). Here, Kafka, wittingly or not, alludes to his body as a *Schloss*, as a "lock" to be broken or even as a "castle" from which he must escape in order to write freely. His bodily enclosure, perceived as a worrisome source of debility or as a tempting site of pleasure or simply as an organism whose livelihood demanded working in an office, consistently struck Kafka as that which prevented him from achieving his ideal of liberation, of immersing himself fully in creative writing—again, of disappearing into literature à la Flaubert. The image of the fasting artist who desires to waste away for the sake of his art starts here.

Kafka would express these views in a well-known letter to Felice Bauer from 1913. Having showed an example of his writing to a Berlin graphologist, Felice reported the diagnosis, which elicited Kafka's protest:

> I am no means 'extremely sensual,' but have a magnificent inborn capacity for asceticism . . . Even 'artistic interests' is not true; in

fact, of all the erroneous statements, that is the most erroneous. I have no literary interests, but am made of literature, I am nothing else, and cannot be anything else.

(Aug. 14, 1913; BF 244/LF 304)

Becoming indistinguishable from the writing would be the greatest achievement, something that Kafka believed he had attained, perhaps for the first and only time in his life, after writing *The Judgment* the year before: "Only in this way can writing be done, only with such coherence, with such a complete opening out of the body and the soul" (Sept. 23, 1912; KGW 10, 101/D 213). It was a Sunday night, on the eve of work, when Kafka set himself at his desk and composed, in one fit of continuous inspiration, the story he would henceforth regard as his breakthrough. The creative fire had vanquished bodily exhaustion. He had written straight through the night until he had to wash up and go to the office. As he left his room, he took notice of the "undisturbed bed" (KGW 10, 101/D 213). From that point forward, there would be many narratives that would break out from the place where one normally satisfies the body's need for rest: The bed that Georg Bendemann's father rejects, the bed on which Gregor Samsa finds himself mysteriously transformed, the bed on which Josef K. is unexpectedly arrested, the bed that K. seeks in crossing the bridge to the grounds of the *Schloss*. All these cases point to the idea that literature begins with the author's resolution or *Entschlossenheit* to distance himself from his weary body and thereby become literature and nothing else.

The motifs of the 1912 breakthrough already started to coalesce in late 1910, after he returned, unsuccessful, from the streets of Paris.

When I sit down at the desk, I feel no better than someone who falls and breaks both legs [*beide Beine bricht*] in the middle of the traffic of the Place de l'Opéra. All the carriages, despite their noise, press silently from all directions in all directions [*von allen Seiten nach allen Seiten*], but that man's pain keeps better order than the police, it closes [*schließt*] his eyes and empties the square and the streets without the carriages having to turn about. The great commotion hurts him, for he is really an obstruction to traffic, but the emptiness is no less sad, for it unshackles his real pain.

(December 15, 1910; KGW 9, 103/D 29)

The passage could serve as an allegory of writing. Kafka sits at his desk or "writing table" (*Schreibtisch*) in Prague and envisions the distant capital as the site of self-distancing that appears to be prerequisite for writing. He conjures the dangerous traffic at the Place de l'Opéra, the site of artistic works (*opera*), where the body breaks and intervenes. The pain (*Schmerz*) is real, but so is the resultant ordering of the traffic, the ordering that is literature—the imagined triumph that literalizes the common wish for success: "Break a leg!" (In German, *Hals- und Beinbruch!* "Break a leg and your neck!"). The pain "closes [*schließt*] his eyes" to the present as if to unlock the imagination or resolve upon (*entschließen*) a future readership, one that moves "from all directions to all directions," "from all sides [*Seiten*] to all sides [*Seiten*]," or across all the "pages" [*Seiten*]. The productive breaking of the body anticipates the opening of the soul that will give birth to *The Judgment*, his creative breakthrough. Kafka will come to live for these moments, for the resolution to write continuously, to return to Paris, so to speak, where the "traffic" or "communication" (*Verkehr*) might be steered by his literary endeavors, where nameless readers might attend to the painful "scream" (*Schrei*) of the body in pain still discernible in the "writing" (*Schreiben*), where they might hear the *cri* in *écriture*, where they might trace the writing that marks the author's absence or death. We are but one step away from the sentence that will conclude the breakthrough story itself. After Georg Bendemann let his body fall to its demise, we read: *In diesem Augenblick ging über die Brücke ein geradezu unendlicher Verkehr*—"At this moment an unending stream of traffic was just going over the bridge" (KGW 1, 52/CS 88). After the work is finished, readers are invited to traffic with the words left in the writer's wake.

A SECOND LIFE

Le rêve est une seconde vie.

—Gérard de Nerval

On February 21, 1911, Kafka reflected on his present prospects.

> My life here is such as if I were entirely certain of a second life, in the same way, e.g., I got over the pain [*verschmerzte*] of my unsuccessful stay in Paris with the view that I will strive to go there again very soon. With this, the sight of the sharply divided light and shadows on the pavement of the street.
>
> _____
>
> For a moment I felt clad in armor.
>
> _____
>
> How far from me are, e.g., my arm muscles.
>
> (KGW 9, 117/D 39)

The notebook entry sets up an antithesis between the capital of the Kingdom of Bohemia, where Kafka currently lives and works, and the capital of the French Nation which he visited four months earlier with the hope of returning soon. The contrast between the two capitals or headings or even chapters (*capitula*) is not only geographical but also temporal: Kafka's "life here" in Prague is set in the positivity of the present tense, while his time "there" in Paris is placed first in the past and then in the future, tenses that negate the present: The no-longer and the not-yet. The general sense is easy to discern and concurs with other passages written around the same time, which grapple with the difficulty of becoming a literary artist. Present conditions in Prague, where office work frustrates his aspirations to write literature, correspond to a rather disappointing visit to Paris; yet, just as he sees himself traveling again to France, so he can entertain the likelihood of attaining a second life as a creative writer. The Paris episode functions as an example of his resilience, his will to succeed, taken here as metonymy for a literary future.

The framing of the entry is keenly etched, almost too schematically, underscoring the nearness of Prague to present time and the distance of Paris to past and future times, all from the situated perspective of the writing subject. This coordination of the three basic tenses, however, is disturbed by the fragment that follows, a sentence without a finite verb: *With this, the sight of the sharply divided light and shadows on the pavement of the street.* While fragments of this sort are perfectly ordinary in diary style, in this particular context, the usage is striking. Is the vision a recollection of a past scene or the projection of something to come? The statement is open to interpretation. In the absence of a finite verb, the image can only implicitly be assigned to a determinate time or to a determinate subject. Strictly speaking, the fragment is subjectless and timeless, without a definite marker of person or tense, as if the time-bound subject, Kafka, has evanesced into the words he inscribes, at least for a moment. The grammatical indeterminacy contaminates the content of the passage. While the sharp division between the lit and shadowy parts of the pavement would seem to reinforce the antithetical construction of the first sentence, the aperçu instead causes everything to blur.

One might rashly conclude that Paris, set under the rubric of the negative (not here, not now), would fall on the side of darkness, if only because shadows are the negation of light, but that is evidently not the case, for both capitals are portrayed in chiaroscuro. Prague is gloomy yet also enlightens; it invites Kafka to surmise that he is capable of vanquishing the present darkness, just as he overcame the dismal pain or *Schmerz* of his "unsuccessful stay" by looking forward to revisiting the Ville Lumière. The blurring accounts for the ambivalence previously expressed in the subjunctive clause: His present accomplishment of getting over the former pain makes him feel "as if [he] *were* entirely certain of a second life." The future is possibly bright, which is also to say, possibly dark.

As Head of the Appeals Department at the Workmen's Accident Insurance Institute in Prague, Kafka was accustomed to looking into the future. His chief responsibility was to address employers' concerns regarding the risk classification of their factories, which required observing present vulnerabilities and calculating likely consequences and their impact.[21] The notebook entry adopts the same method. Trained to determine probabilities on the basis of the evidence at hand, Kafka envisions "a second life" dedicated to literature. Like many burgeoning authors, Kafka often viewed his day job as a hindrance to realizing this dream. Two days earlier, on the Sunday before another workweek would begin, he had complained in a separate notebook: "If I did not have to go [to the office], I could live calmly for my own work and should not have to waste these six hours a day which have tormented me to a degree that you cannot imagine . . . it is a horrible double life from which there is probably no escape but insanity [*Irrsinn*]" (Feb. 19, 1911; KGW 9, 26/D 37–8). Now, on Tuesday, despite being burdened by office obligations, he at least feels as if he were absolutely sure he would have this second life and leave the other life behind. The thought of having once conquered pain encourages his mind "to wander" (*irren*) towards a future that might be successful. Insanity or *Irrsinn* is no longer the only probable escape from his "horrible double life"; there is now the conviction of his artistic promise, unless, of course, he "is mistaken" (*irrt*) and the two lines of flight are, as the word suggests, the same.

The subjunctive mood not only beclouds certainty but can also express what is contrary to fact. Kafka's life here in Prague is such as if he *were* entirely certain but he *is* not, or at least not entirely. The caution is well grounded, and not merely because the future is inscrutable. Given that the first visit to Paris was painfully unsuccessful, how could he be perfectly sure the second trip would be better? And, by the extension he sets up, how could he know, without the shadow of a doubt, that his artistic talents would ever come to light? Regardless, Kafka senses some strength, a newfound measure of invulnerability, albeit fleetingly: "For a moment [*Augenblick*] I felt clad in armor. / How far from me, e.g., are my arm muscles."

---

[21] Cf. Franz Kafka: *The Office Writings*, ed. Stanley Corngold, Jack Greenberg, and Benno Wagner (Princeton: Princeton University Press, 2009), 120.

Another statement, followed by another illuminative example. While Kafka derived vague assurance from the example of having once overcome pain, he now illustrates the sense of being armored with the example of being distanced from his body. The second instance, formulated in the indicative mood, comes across as stronger, despite its momentary nature. Here, the form accords with the content: An expression of strength strongly expressed. The potency is clearly not corporeal: He detaches himself from his muscles. The motif of distance is crucial. His consciousness of being "far" (*fern*) from the arms before him correlates to Paris, which lies faraway, *in der Ferne*. Detached from his body, which is empirically situated in Prague, his mind is somewhere else. The vision offers a foretaste of a second, stronger life, one that will be emancipated from the workaday world, a new chapter posited in the not-yet of literary achievement, set in a future which may be bright or may be dark.

Before Gérard de Nerval left his apartment to greet his afterlife, he inscribed a note to his aunt: "Do not wait for me this evening, for the night will be black and white." Without necessarily realizing it, Kafka's French readership would be waiting for him.

II Metamorphoses

NATURALIZATION PAPERS

On New Year's Day 1928, the *Nouvelle Revue Française* upheld its reputation as one of Paris's most prominent literary journals in presenting contributions from well-recognized authors and poets, including several luminaries whose names had been firmly installed into the pantheon of modern French culture: André Gide, Paul Valéry, and Marcel Proust. Tucked in amid this distinguished roster was a piece by a writer few had ever heard of beyond the German-speaking realms, the first installment of a work entitled *La Métamorphose* by one Franz Kafka, translated by one Alexandre Vialatte.[1]

Neither an editorial introduction nor any biographical information was provided, save for a brief bibliographic notice appended at the chapter's end, which tersely stated that the text was written in German under the title *Die Verwandlung* and that it first appeared in *Der jüngste Tag*, a series published by Kurt Wolff in Munich. No date was given. For even the moderately curious reader, the absence of identifying marks would have been frustrating. Was the original a recent publication? Was the excerpt taken from a short story, a novella, or a novel? And who was Franz Kafka, this German writer with a discernibly Czech surname? Where did he reside? What else did he write? Was he still alive? For the moment, *La Métamorphose* was left to speak for itself.

An unusual tale about a traveling salesman named Grégoire Samsa, who one morning awoke to find himself transformed into a "formidable vermine"—how was it first received? In the absence of any direct testimony, one can only conjecture. A conceivable impulse would have been to relate the unfamiliar example to familiar paradigms. The Ovidian title, for instance, might have encouraged some to view the narrative in an ancient mythological tradition, however estranged by the modern, realist setting. The recasting might account for the inversion of the classical plot; namely, the choice to open with the metamorphosis rather than having it occur at the climactic conclusion. For others, the omission of any concrete place names or discernible landmarks would seem to point to something akin to Christian parables or perhaps a Talmudic *mashal* or some other allegorical form in line with the medieval *Ovide moralisé*. More contemporaneously, one might have categorized the work as belonging to the genre of *la littérature fantastique*, where creaturely transformations were not uncommon. The incursion of the strange into an otherwise domestic scene could well have been taken as

---

[1] Kafka, "La Métamorphose," tr. Alexandre Vialatte *Nouvelle Revue Française* 172 (January 1, 1928), 66–84.

an implicit critique of present society—a world of anxiety and doubt, riddled by the panic of failing before one's employer, the fear of embarrassing one's family, the realization that today's mass man had been reduced to an alienated, dehumanized, verminous existence. Despite the protagonist's explicit attestation that "it was no dream," the scenario was altogether nightmarish. Perhaps, one might have concluded, it was the work of a Surrealist or an Expressionist?

One could go on. As Adorno would note regarding Kafka's works in general: "Each sentence says: interpret me, and none will permit it. Each compels the reaction, 'that's the way it is,' and with it the question: How do I know this? The ongoing déjà vu is declared permanent."[2] In 1928 Paris, the lack of background information would have only made hermeneutic endeavors more difficult. Yet, such vagueness could have just as well been regarded as liberating and fruitful, especially for more creative readers. Years after *The Metamorphosis* first appeared in French, the translator Vialatte reflected on the inaugural effect and its exciting promise: "[Kafka] landed in the world of literature like a Martian upon the banks of the terrestrial globe. No one had spotted him, except for a few lighthouse watchmen. [. . .] One was free to make things up. It was splendid."[3] Thus, at this initial stage of reception, both text and author, freed from extrinsic grounding, could easily serve as a viable projection screen for the reader's imagination and theoretical suppositions.

Kafka landed in the world of literature like a Martian—The extraterrestrial figure would also be employed by one of Kafka's earliest interpreters, Claude-Edmonde Magny, who in 1942 commented that "his tales do not give at all the impression of being a 'literary' object written by a man, but rather some kind of aerolithe, a dark mass, surprising and yet familiar, an object to meditate on. There are few works whose author is absent to this extent."[4] Like Grégoire Samsa, whose place of residence is never named, Kafka would have bordered on the non-human, with no earthly home, perhaps one of those terrifying bug-like aliens depicted in H.G. Wells' popular *The War of the Worlds*, a hidden monster hurtling meteoric work down from the sky. As an author thoroughly absent

---

[2] Theodor W. Adorno, "Notes on Kafka," 246 (trans. modified). [Adorno, "Aufzeichnungen zu Kafka," in *Gesammelte Schriften*, vol. 10.1, *Kulturkritik und Gesellschaft* I, ed. Rolf Tiedemann (Frankfurt: Suhrkamp, 1977), 255.]

[3] Alexandre Vialatte, "Introduction," in *Le Procès* [1933] (Paris: Gallimard, 1957), 32.

[4] Claude-Edmonde Magny, "Kafka, ou l'écriture objective de l'absurde" [1942], in *Les sandales d'Empédocle: Essai sur les limites de la littérature* (Neuchâtel: Baconnière, 1945), 174.

from his work, Kafka would have achieved the ideal held by Flaubert, to be in his work as God in the world, everywhere present and nowhere visible. What results is an abstract character, "surprising and yet familiar"—both a victim and perpetrator of *dépaysement*, yet in a way that still reflected and resonated with one's world. Since the author seemed to come from nowhere, his work could belong everywhere. Arriving in Paris on New Year's Day without baggage, Franz Kafka stood poised to be transformed and appropriated, naturalized and universalized into the French Kafka.

The path was well laid by the *Nouvelle Revue Française* (*NRF*). Indeed, Kafka's introduction into French letters could not have been more auspicious. Issued on the first of each month, the *NRF* had, since its founding in 1909 by André Gide and his circle, functioned as a vital organ of contemporary French literary culture, a reputation bolstered by Gaston Gallimard, whose prestigious publishing house took over production in 1911. After its re-launching in 1919, under the editorship of Jacques Rivière, the *NRF* emerged as a mighty arbiter of Parisian taste, analogous to the *Criterion* in England and *The Dial* in America or *Die neue Rundschau* in Germany, defining and influencing the shape and direction of an ever-growing, modern canon.[5] Initially conceived in opposition to Charles Maurras' far-right, ultra-nationalist *Action française*, the *NRF* maintained its moderate-liberal position, which represented the virtues of the bourgeois republican tradition. After the Armistice, as the well-established *Revue des Deux Mondes* leaned more towards political and social issues, the aestheticism of the *NRF* dovetailed with its support for French-German rapprochement and its openness to translating foreign literature, positions it shared with the acclaimed *Mercure de France* and, beginning in 1924, with the highly successful quarterly, *Commerce*, edited by Paul Valéry, Léon-Paul Fargue, and Valéry Larbaud. Yet, whereas *Commerce* was more amenable to Surrealism and the avant-garde, the *NRF* addressed a centrist audience in offering a balanced variety of authors, whose styles and aesthetics spanned a broad spectrum, from conservative-classical tendencies to progressive-modernist experiments.[6] As the historian

---

[5] For an excellent account of the influence of the *NRF* in French modernism, see Gisèle Sapiro, *La Guerre des écrivains* (Paris: Fayard, 1999).
[6] Although not an exclusively Surrealist venue, many of the contributions published by *Commerce* exhibit the journal's allegiance to the movement: Louis Aragon, "Une vague de rêves" (Autumn 1924), André Breton, "Introduction au discours sur le peu de réalité" (Winter 1924), and the opening chapter of his *Nadja* (Autumn 1927), as well as Bernard Groethuysen's translation of Friedrich

Jean Lacouture affirms: "From the beginning, what the history of the *NRF* entails, but what must be constantly re-invented, was a classicism open to all forms of modernity."[7]

For any new author, appearing in the *NRF* would have been a stroke of good fortune, an advance into legitimacy. Throughout the 1920s, as Paris developed into an inebriating hub of European modernism, the review had steadily expanded its readership and influence, moving from an average of three thousand copies per month before the outbreak of war in 1914 to printing twelve thousand copies by 1927.[8] Kafka's French debut thus acquired a substantial commendation, all the more magnified by appearing alongside the likes of Valéry, Proust, and Gide. Whatever perplexity early readings of *La Métamorphose* might have caused, the luminosity of these respected writers coupled with the authoritative imprint of Gallimard could not but redound to Kafka, granting the alien author admission into the inner circle of Parisian culture. Unlike his vagrant protagonist, K., who vainly seeks legitimation from the Castle, Kafka arrived with concrete assurance of belonging. Especially from the republican vantage point of the *NRF*, Paris was a city that prided itself as a tolerant haven for foreigners, as an asylum for refugees, or, as Henri Michaux would characterize it, as "the homeland of those free spirits who have not found a homeland."[9] Thus, Kafka was primed to have his national and biographical vagueness converted into the trans-national, trans-historical status of a classic.

Hölderlin's late fragments of madness (Autumn 1925). Cited from Eugène Jolas, *Man from Babel*, ed. Andreas Kramer and Rainer Rumold (New Haven: Yale University Press, 1998), 293 n.75. In contrast, the *NRF*, especially under Jacques Rivière's direction (1919–25), maintained a more cautious attitude towards Surrealist radicalism, with a pronounced preference for English, Irish, and American authors: Samuel Butler, Joseph Conrad, T. S. Eliot, John Galsworthy, Rudyard Kipling, George Bernard Shaw, and W. B. Yeats, including Valéry Larbaud's essays on Joyce's *Ulysses* (1922 and 1925). See Annalisa Federici, "The *Transatlantic Review* and the *Nouvelle Revue Française*—Between Tradition and Modernity: The Ford-Larbaud-Joyce Connection," *International Ford Maddox Ford Studies* 15 (2016), 115–28.

[7] Jean Lacouture, *Une adolescence du siècle: Jacques Rivière et la* NRF (Paris: Seuil, 1994), 560.

[8] See Martyn Cornick, *The* Nouvelle Revue Française *under Jean Paulhan, 1925–1940* (Amsterdam: Rodopi, 1995), 12–13.

[9] Cited in Pascale Casanova, *The World Republic of Letters*, tr. Malcolm DeBevoise (Cambridge: Harvard University Press, 2007), 29.

AMID INTIMACY AND EXOTICISM

Reception never takes place in a vacuum. Despite subsequent assertions that Kafka's *Metamorphosis* pierced the stratosphere of French consciousness like a meteor out of the blue, it is certainly possible that at least some readers had already heard of the Prague author. The many officers, soldiers and administrators occupying the Rhineland would have had opportunities to see Kafka in print—likely not the 1915 limited edition of *Die Verwandlung* in Kurt Wolff's series, but rather the posthumous novels edited by Max Brod, *Der Prozess* (*The Trial*, 1925) and *Das Schloß* (*The Castle*, 1926)—or they could have come across the name in the several book reviews and essays that started to crop up soon after Kafka's death in 1924, pieces by notable figures such as Thomas Mann, Hermann Hesse, Kurt Tucholsky, Willy Haas, and, of course, Brod.[10] Meanwhile, a Spanish translation of Kafka's story, *La metamorfosis*, had already appeared in 1925 in Ortega y Gasset's *Revista de Occidente*. Although, as was customary, the Madrid review did not provide the name of the translator, the version is identical to the translation that would be published in 1938 by the Losada house in Buenos Aires and was now attributed to Jorge Luis Borges, who claimed to have first encountered Kafka's work while studying in Geneva, sometime between 1915 and 1919.[11] It was also around 1927 when Edwin and Willa Muir discovered Kafka while residing in Weimar and began working on their translation of *The Castle*, which would appear with Secker and Warburg in London in 1930.

Kafka, in other words, had already been in circulation, however unevenly or disparately, when *La Métamorphose* appeared, even if one would assume that for the majority of the Parisian audience the author had been until then an unknown entity. Regardless, the fact that the story appeared in the pages of the *NRF* was decisive. During the heyday of European modernism, literary journals were especially effective in mediating the relationship between new works and the public; and the *NRF*, with its light beige cover and title in signature red, would have communicated that Kafka, whoever he was, should be taken as a writer of high caliber deserving serious consideration. Most responsible for this initiative were the young translator, Alexandre Vialatte, and Jean Paulhan, the review's chief editor. Both recognized something uniquely

---

[10] See Peter Beicken, *Franz Kafka: Eine kritische Einführung in die Forschung* (Frankfurt am Main: Athenäum Fischer, 1974), 27–33.
[11] See Juan Fló, "Jorge Luis Borges, traductor de *Die Verwandlung* (Fechas, textos, conjeturas)," *Anales de Literatura Hispanoamericana* 42 (2013), 215–40.

relevant and urgent in Kafka's style and themes. In addition, their sympathies for the Surrealist school, although not uncomplicated, would soften the *NRF*'s stand on literary provocations and play a significant role in directing the first phase of reception towards André Breton and his circle.

Originally from Nîmes, Paulhan earned a degree in philosophy at the Sorbonne then spent several years in the colony of Madagascar, where he taught at a lycée, prepared translations, and prospected for gold. In 1910, he returned to Paris and began to publish poetry, attracting the attention of writers and artists, including Guillaume Apollinaire, who, in 1917, would coin the term *surréalisme*. The following summer, Paulhan began a formative correspondence with Breton, who was still in active service as a medic in Verdun. Impressed by Paulhan's imaginative fluency in literary and conceptual history, Breton introduced him to Louis Aragon, Paul Éluard, and others of the Dadaist/proto-Surrealist movement, who all frequented Adrienne Monnier's bookshop, the *Maison des Amis des Livres*, in the rue de l'Odéon. A testament to Paulhan's importance to this burgeoning scene is Max Ernst's 1922 group portrait, *Au Rendez-vous des amis*, which features the young writer front and center—a depiction that demonstrates Paulhan's "role as a pathfinder, or scout, or even guru, for the avant-garde."[12]

Through Aragon, Paulhan met Gide, who arranged his employment as secretary to Jacques Rivière, then editorial director at the *NRF*. As Rivière's health waned, Paulhan took on greater responsibilities, developed a close working relationship with Gaston Gallimard, and, in the wake of Rivière's death in 1925, was promoted to the chief editor's office. Paulhan would now exercise key power in piloting new literary directions. Yet almost inevitably, the new position alienated several Surrealists, including Éluard, who remained suspicious about the *NRF*'s reputation for bourgeois moderation. They regarded Paulhan's ambition to represent a broad array of authors as equivocal and further vilified the journal's commercial success. The animosity was in part mutual, with Paulhan casting aspersion on the extremism voiced in the Surrealist Manifesto of 1924. The culminating point came three years later, when Breton was said to have threatened his former friend publicly to a duel.

---

[12] Martyn Cornick, "Jean Paulhan and the *Nouvelle Revue française*: Modernist Editor, Modernist Review?" *Romanic Review* 99 (2008), 9–26, p. 17. Cornick corroborates this view by calling attention to Éluard's piece, "Jean Paulhan le souterrain," published in the Dadaist journal, *Littérature*, in November 1919.

All the same, Paulhan was committed to the innovations afforded by Surrealist writers. Not unlike Breton, it was his explicit intention to pair writers of different sensibilities, to stage dynamic juxtapositions, and create the conditions for unforeseeable cross-fertilizations. Late in life, in an address to the Club du Faubourg in 1953, Paulhan underscored the vitality of running a journal like the *NRF*.

> You see literature being formed and invented and groping amid a thousand dangers. You take part in it. You return to it several times. A magazine is only valuable if one discovers, next to a few established authors (as one says), young writers who are restarting literature at their own risk. You see letters in their nascent state.[13]

In 1928, the placing of the essentially unknown work of Kafka amid "established authors" would become the most fruitful instance of Paulhan's editorial midwifery. Design was everything, hedging risky choices with sure bets, while also achieving an overall balance. On this basis, Paulhan's editorial practices have been compared to the art of flower arranging: "The composition of the contents of each issue, this arrangement of flowers, this Japanese-style *ikebana*, without rules, but not without rigor, was in itself a critical tour de force, renewed every month."[14] Of particular concern was the New Year's Day number. To the poet André Suarès, Paulhan later admitted that "the first *NRF* of the year is composed with more care or more love—or even observed more attentively—than the issues that follow."[15]

The January 1, 1928, edition clearly exhibits this intention. Kafka's *Métamorphose* is the fifth in a series of six pieces that together contain multiple cross-resonances on formal, thematic, and cultural levels. Granted that not every reader would go through each text in succession, the table of contents at least affords a snapshot of the sensibilities of the period, a fittingly Janus-faced record with one eye on the past and the other on what was yet to come.

The volume opens with the continuation of an epic poem by Jules Romains, *L'homme blanc* ("The White Man"). What is for us today a

---

[13] Paulhan, "Présentation de la *NRF* au Club du Faubourg," *Œuvres*, vol. 4, 377; cited in Cornick, *The Nouvelle Revue Française*, 11.
[14] Auguste Anglès, "*NRF*," *Magazine littéraire* 192 (February 1983), 21; quoted in Cornick, "Jean Paulhan," 21.
[15] Paulhan to Suarès (December 17, 1932), *Correspondence: Jean Paulhan, André Suarès*, ed., Yves Alain Favre (Paris: Gallimard, 1987), 44.

discomfiting title would have been charitably received by a contemporary audience as reflecting the poet's pacifism, which railed against nationalism and individualism. In Romains' lexicon, "whiteness" was understood as an unmarked category or non-race, which transcends ethnic provincialisms. He was best known for his collection *La vie unanime* (1908), which he published at the age of twenty. Like the Italian Futurists, he embraced the modern city and celebrated technological innovation with a youthful appeal to the single, fused soul of the masses. Romains regarded the adherence to ethnic-national difference as the obstacle to his unanimist vision and, during the Great War, quickly rose as the principal spokesman for French-German reconciliation. While acknowledging a variety of fundamental "ethnotypes"—a troubling German inclination to both order and irrationality, which he opposed to British wisdom and French elegance—Romains called for a dialectical synthesis that would integrate national diversity into a united Europe, which in turn would represent the apex of spiritual, artistic, technical, and economic achievements for the world.[16] In expansive, quasi-Whitmanesque verse, *L'homme blanc* traces humanity's progress from the African savannah to the European shores.

In heading off the January 1928 volume with Jules Romains, who now served on the supervisory committee at the *NRF*, Paulhan reinforced the journal's commitment to a pan-European ideal grounded in republican values, an ideal shared by the review's principal founder, André Gide, who had argued, in the wake of the Versailles Treaty, that peace would be maintained only by promoting a shared, trans-national literary culture.[17] Regarded either as the absence of color or the synthesis of every color, Romains' "whiteness," however naively or dubiously, functioned as a cipher for a post-racist future.

The subsequent story by Paul Morand, *Syracuse (U. S. A.)*, set in upstate New York, exposes the more insidious aspects of Eurocentrism. Whereas Romains stands for common humanity, Morand strikes an unapologetically chauvinist pose. Based on his frequent trans-Atlantic trips, he surrenders to his fascination for Black American culture while retaining his indebtedness to Arthur de Gobineau's quasi-scientific "racial demography." Morand thus depicts the Black American

---

[16] Cf. Ariane Bogain, "Jules Romains' Vision of a United Europe in Interwar France: Legacy and Ambiguities," *Modern and Contemporary France* 21 (2013), 89–105, p. 92.

[17] André Gide, "Réflexions sur l'Allemagne," *Nouvelle Revue Française* (November 1921), 513–21.

population as hopelessly regressive, genetically driven by the savagery of the African jungle. Incapable of moving past the most egregious stereotypes, the narrative follows the career of Lincoln Vamp, a well-to-do Black physician who preaches the benefits of obsequious assimilation. With optimism, Dr. Vamp travels to Brussels for the Pan-African Congress and pays a visit to the Musée de Tervuren, where he is overwhelmed by the exhibit of African masks. He plummets into bestial reveries, strips off his clothes, and is transformed into a bloodthirsty panther. In retrospect, Morand's bigotry would only confirm the suitability of his later appointment as ambassador of Vichy France during the Second World War. For now, in 1928, the savage metamorphosis, which occurs at the story's climax, anticipates the verminous transformation that triggers Kafka's tale.

For the third article, Paulhan turned to André Gide, who sustains the African theme with an excerpt from his diary account of recent visits to the Congo and Chad—*Sur le Logone* ("On the Logon River"). Gide portrays Africa in Edenic terms, indulging in the wondrous spectacle of the florescent landscape, the colorful birds and fish, and the exotic butterflies, which he avidly adds to his collection. He is entranced by the singularity of the tribal chants, which he wishes Stravinsky could hear—the voice "strangled by tears," "with suddenly hoarse accents, raucous, as if out of tune" (34). In this regard, Gide comes close to rehearsing Morand's outsider exuberance, relishing in the potential that cultural difference holds for rattling European complacency and instigating personal rejuvenation. For Gide, however, ethnic difference is not broached to confirm European superiority. If anything, an appreciation of diversity stands to reveal one's own acculturated limitations. Still, it is difficult not to discern a trace of condescension.

> The people of these primitive tribes, I am convinced more and more, do not have our way of reasoning and that is why they so often seem to us stupid. Their acts evade the control of the logic that we have learned from childhood, and which, by the very forms of our language, we are unable to do without.
>
> (40)

Particularly striking is the way Gide adheres to European poetry, as if it were ballast to stabilize his journey through the illiterate villages. The citations he selects filter his surroundings, while giving voice to his passion for his companion, Marc Allégret. For example, when Allégret is bathing in the river to alleviate a high fever, Gide quotes two lines from Goethe:

Des edlen Körpers holde Lebensflamme
Kühlt sich im schwiegsamen Krystall der Welle.[18]

The noble body's lovely flame of life
Cools itself in the silent crystal of the waves.

The lines are taken from the overwrought lyrical pronouncements of the Homunculus, the artificial man created in the laboratory of Faust's former assistant, Wagner, in the Second Act of *Faust II*. In quoting the speech of this "little man" of art, whose alchemical birth circumvents sexual reproduction, Gide unleashes a wealth of allusive meaning: Homoerotic ardor correlates Goethe's conjunction of fire and water and Allégret's feverish body in the river, and thus allows a German literary classic to penetrate the equatorial climes of the Congo, to compel a collision of contrasting mentalities, while maintaining a certain cultural superiority that keeps the population under observation at a safe distance. In another key—in a gesture that would have arguably pleased Paulhan's sense for editorial orchestration—Gide cites a passage from Milton's *Samson Agonistes* (vv. 93–7), which he explicitly imagines could have been "destined for Jules Romains":

Why was the sight
To such a tender ball as the eye confin'd?
So obvious and so easy to be quench'd?
And not, as feeling, through all parts diffus'd,
That she [the soul] might look at will through every pore.
(Cited in Gide, 51)

Following Gide's ethnographic reportage, the volume shifts gears. Whereas the first three contributions feature exoticist, neo-primitive representations of African life, the second group focuses on European literary culture, without the foil of otherness. Heading this second batch is a series of *Petits Textes* by Paul Valéry, the nation's most celebrated poet and recent inductee to the Académie Française: eleven prose poems, each limited to a single page and offered as ekphrastic descriptions on a set of engravings. Valéry's aesthetic refinement diverges from Gide's rugged notes from the sub-Saharan savannah and therefore instills a more contemplative tone. The first chapter of Kafka's *Métamorphose* appears next, followed by a selection of

---

[18] Lines 6909–10 from *Faust II*, quoted in German, *Sur le Logone*, 32.

letters by Marcel Proust to his friend, Marie Sheikevitch (*Lettres à une amie*), equipped with an introduction and explanatory notes by René Gullouin.

As usual, the volume closes with several essays and book reviews, which further convey the *NRF*'s aesthetic, philosophical, and political inclinations. For New Year's Day, one finds a reflective piece on calendrical time by Alain, the nom de plume of Émile Chartier, professor at the Lycée Henri IV, followed by an essay on Mallarmé's reception in England and Germany by Albert Thibaudet. Ramon Fernandez next provides a laudatory review of *La Trahison des clercs*, Julian Benda's scabrous critique of intellectuals who abandon the pursuit of truth in favor of political agenda. After a number of theater and film reviews by Jean Prévost, there are several brief book reviews: One on the final volume of Proust's *Recherche*; and one by Gabriel Bounoure on *Qui je fus*, the premier collection of verse and prose by the Belgian-born Henri Michaux, who will, as we shall see, make a crucial contribution to Kafka's early French reception.

My decision to spend some time detailing the context in which Kafka first appeared in French is not so much concerned with arguing for any determinative influence. My aim, rather, is to depict, in an admittedly sketchy fashion, the ideational environment from which Kafka's reception will proceed. In taking the six main pieces into consideration, one can in fact discern a telling design, a balanced arrangement of correlations, which falls into two distinct parts:

1. Romains, *L'homme blanc*—epic poetry
2. Morand, *Syracuse (U. S. A.)*—narrative fiction
3. Gide, *Sur le Logone*—personal diary

4. Valéry, *Petits Textes*—prose poetry
5. Kafka, *La Métamorphose*—narrative fiction
6. Proust, *Lettres à une amie*—personal correspondence

Whereas the first group exhibits a French penchant for exoticism, the second reverts to intimacy. Gide's diary functions as an apt threshold insofar as it combines the two themes: An intimate account inscribed in an exotic setting, with homoerotic overtones that resonate with Proust's confessional letters. It is noteworthy that Kafka, the only foreign text in the volume, is located in the second group, cozily installed between Valéry and Proust, that is, within an intimate French sphere, as if his exotic nature has been fully assimilated by means of translation. Moreover, the shared motif of both central pieces of narrative fiction—the creaturely transformation in Morand and Kafka—underscores what distinguishes them: The specificity of Black American life in *Syracuse* contrasts with the placeless and nameless vagueness of Kafka's setting. Without a trace of his Eastern European provenance, Kafka comes across as a naturalized resident. For the next two installments of *La Métamorphose*, the table of contents printed on the review's cover even forgo designating the story as a translation. The implication is that Kafka is now a French author, however strange, a writer belonging to the familiar sphere yet poised to exert a defamiliarizing effect.

UNIVERSAL MAN

Whereas Kafka's *naturalization* might have been the intention behind Paulhan's editorial practice, the motive behind Vialatte's translation could be seen as leaning more towards *universalization*. The two operatives are correlative: The editor's quasi-surrealist gesture of provocation within the frame of the familiar aligns with the translator's doctrine that the text, although derived from specific cultural and historical circumstances, can address all humankind.

When Paulhan first met him in 1921, Vialatte was still a student in the Auvergne, at Clermont-Ferrand, where he had written for the college's Nietzschean-inflected journal *Le Gay Sçavoir*. Several pieces drew Paulhan's attention, and on the basis of Vialatte's literary talents as well as his training in modern German literature, Paulhan recommended him for a translator's position at the *Revue rhénane* in French-occupied Mainz.[19] It was in this capacity, in late 1926, that Vialatte first happened upon the relatively obscure Kafka. At the time, he was finishing his first novel, *Battling le ténébreux* ("Battling, the dark one"), likely alluding to Nerval's disconsolate widower in "El Desdichado" (1854): *Je suis le Ténébreux* ("I am the Dark One," the "Obscure"). André Breton and his fellow Surrealists had adopted Nerval as one of the movement's spiritual forefathers, which is further borne out by Vialatte's treatment of his novel's plot, set in the Auvergne, relating Battling's bizarre relationship with a mysterious German woman. Paulhan was impressed with the manuscript and planned to have the novel appear with Gallimard in 1928. In the meantime, Vialatte proposed that he translate Kafka's *Metamorphosis* for the *NRF*.

It would not be a one-off project. Rather, from the start, Vialatte committed himself to longer term goals. After the first instalment of *La Métamorphose* appeared, he sent a copy to Max Brod: "I have taken on

---

[19] Alexandre Vialatte, Jean Paulhan, *Correspondance, 1921–1968*, ed. Denis Wetterwald (Paris: Julliard, 1997), 17–18.

the task of making Franz Kafka, for whom you are doing so much in Germany, known in France."[20] Vialatte goes on to express his hope "that all of Kafka will be translated, for he happens to be, as you say, one of the greatest writers of the century." Referring to Brod's essays published in his editions of the novels, Vialatte thanks him for having "shed such remarkable light on [Kafka's] work" and for having "put him at the rank he deserves."[21] From that point forward, Brod would keep Vialatte abreast on the forthcoming publication of the complete German edition of Kafka's fiction, diaries, and letters. As in the case of the Muirs, Brod's theologically tuned interpretation would leave its mark.

Vialatte, who passed away in 1971, lived to witness the role his translations had played, that the majority of readers, admirers, and interpreters in France had responded specifically to *his* Kafka. Hence, with the deflective humor and humility that are not uncommon among translators, Vialatte once described himself as "famously unknown [*notoirement méconnu*]."[22] The oxymoron conveys the sense that everyone seemed to know him as the person whom no one knew, broadly reputed for being unheard-of, a name familiar from dust jackets and flyleaves, yet someone who remained essentially unfamiliar. Everyone was acquainted with Vialatte's prose without necessarily acknowledging that it was *his* prose, his vocabulary, his stylistic choices.

Being famously unknown would seem to accord with criteria of fluency and transparency, which demand what Lawrence Venuti has called "the translator's invisibility."[23] The ideal intends to make the translation as intelligible, refined, and undisruptive as possible, creating the illusion that the original author had written the text in the target language. In this paradigm, which long predominated French translation practices, there is the pretense that the translator has relegated him- or herself to a servile role, loath to intrude and besmirch the work with the translator's personal mark. The invisible or unrecognizable (*méconnaissable*) translator is thus said to bring the foreign author to the native reader's doorstep as sleekly and noiselessly as possible. Such pretense informs much of Valéry Larbaud's reflections on the approach he assumed both in his prolific work for *Commerce* and

---

[20] Vialatte to Brod, January 29, 1928: "Je me suis donné à tâche de faire connaître en France Franz Kafka pour lequel vous faites tant en Allemagne." Vialatte/Paulhan, *Correspondance*, 38.
[21] Vialatte/Paulhan, *Correspondance*, 38–9.
[22] Cited in François Béal, *Vialatte, l'intemporel: Panorama de l'étrange échassier* (Paris: Harmattan, 2006), 11.
[23] Lawrence Venuti, *The Translator's Invisibility: A History of Translation* (London: Routledge, 1995).

in his supervision of Auguste Morel's translation of Joyce's *Ulysses* (1921–9). Tellingly, whether out of demureness or pure exhaustion, neither Larbaud nor Morel attended Joyce's launch party at Monnier's shop.[24] In describing himself as "famously unknown" or "famously unfamous," Vialatte appears to subscribe to these prevalent notions, while also pointing to the fact that mediation, however smooth it is presumed to be, invariably conditions what it transmits.

The oft-used term *domestication* connotes such conditioning. Although dressing up a foreign author to match local tastes and sensibilities is an act that aspires towards frictionless reception, it clearly wields a heavy hand. Hence, Voltaire's famous portrayal of translations as *les belles infidèles*, where beauty and elegance are purchased with unfaithfulness to the source language.[25] During the Interwar Period, such native allegiances reigned particularly in the transfers of German literature into French, where the perceived roughness of texts *outre-Rhin* was chauvinistically viewed as in need of tidying up. Jules Romains' reductive definitions of ethnotypes, mentioned above, pitting a purportedly German adherence to native culture against the elegant cosmopolitanism of the French, rehearses long-held views on the continent, articulated in 1916 by George Fonsegrive as the distinction between German *Kultur* and French *civilisation*. Whereas *Kultur* is a concept bound up with natural contingencies—where one was born, the language one spoke, the local customs that shaped one's upbringing—*civilisation* is said to be governed by a legal concept that liberates one from the "state of nature." *Kultur* is regarded as a national property that the native possesses as a birthright, while *civilisation* consists of citizens who, regardless of their home, comprise a civil society by freely pledging allegiance to a constitution.[26] The overtly schematic and problematic belief, perpetrated to some extent by both nations, was that the German *Geist* was stubbornly provincial, folksy, in a way that clashed with the cherished, self-styled *universal* values of the République. With this mindset, the only chance for German literature to succeed on French soil was for it to be properly laundered.

The contrast dates back at least to the Napoleonic Campaigns and its impact is discernible across the nineteenth century. Against this

---

[24] See Valéry Larbaud's collected essays (1929–1935) in his *Sous l'invocation de Saint Jérôme* (Paris: Gallimard, 1946).
[25] Voltaire is referring specifically to d'Albancourt's seventeenth-century translations of Latin authors.
[26] George Fonsegrive, *"Kultur" et civilisation* (Paris: Bloud & Gay, 1916), 3–4.

backdrop and specifically regarding translation, in 1836, Théophile Gautier discussed the advantages and disadvantages of domestication regarding the extraordinary posthumous success of E. T. A. Hoffmann in Paris. How is it, Gautier asks, that Hoffmann's fantastic tales are so sensationally popular in a nation driven by enlightened rationality and governed by a bourgeoisie that has little toleration for fantastic eccentricities? For Gautier, the answer must lie in the fact that Hoffmann was initially spruced up to ensure a warm welcome.

It should be said that Hoffmann has never presented himself in France with his German frock coat all adorned with frogging [*de brandebourgs*] and trimmed [*galonnée*] on all the stitching, like a savage from beyond the Rhine; before setting foot in a salon, he went to see a tailor with plenty of good taste, M. Loëve-Weimar, who made him a tailcoat of the latest fashion with which he presented himself in society and was successful with the ladies.[27]

Gautier is referring to François-Adolphe Loève-Veimars, whose translation of Hoffmann's complete works sparked a literary sensation—a heroic achievement, yet not without compromises. "Passages that [Loève-Veimars] found difficult were deleted, words were confused with others of similar graphic form, some simplifications bring Hoffmann closer to his Parisian reader, while the translator also allows himself additions to clarify this or that turn of phrase."[28] Gautier's larger point, though, is that this simplified, more approachable version—replacing the Germanic-marked "frogging" (*brandebourgs*) and "trims" (*galons*) with a fashionable and appropriately Gallic "tailcoat" (*frac*)—may have granted Hoffmann entrance into Parisian society, yet now that he has arrived, it is time to allow more of his native oddities to manifest themselves: "Perhaps with his German clothes he would have been shown the door, but now that everyone knows him and that he is an amiable fellow and only a bit original, he can, without risk, wear his national costume" (143). If domestication was needed to get Hoffmann inside, estrangement may be the way for him to stay in the room.

---

[27] Théophile Gautier, "The Tales of Hoffmann," tr. Anne E. Duggan, trans. *Marvels & Tales* 23 (2009), 138–45; here, p. 143. [Gautier, *Souvenirs de théâtre, d'art et de critique* (Paris: Charpentier, 1883), 43–50.]

[28] Michel Espagne, "La fonction de la traduction dans les transferts culturels franco-allemands aux XVIIIe et XIXe siècles," *Revue de l'Histoire littéraire de la France* 3 (1997), 413–27; here p. 425.

The pattern applies to the history of Kafka translations, but also to Brod's editorial practices. Scholars have stressed how Brod normalized Kafka's vocabulary, spelling, paragraphing, and punctuation for publication—revisions that, according to evidence, Kafka himself would have probably condoned. It is equally well known that Brod promulgated an image of Kafka that was more universal, more applicable to the human condition in general and more liable to religious and allegorical interpretations, which required bleaching the texts of any egregiously ethnic characteristics, cultural difference, and historical specificity.[29] Although it went against his convictions, Vialatte participated in this universalizing trend. Thus, over time, his translations would come to be criticized, revised, or replaced by renditions that aimed towards increasing estrangement and essentially *de-universalizing* Kafka. All the same, Vialatte's versions remained predominant, cherished for their literary qualities, even if they failed to pass academic muster. As late as 1999, Jean-Jacques Brochier remarked: "It's only necessary to look at the translations that have been tried since then, notably *The Trial*; they may be scientifically more accurate, as one says, but they fall flat; when reading *The Trial* by Vialatte, one is sure of being in front of a masterpiece."[30]

Vialatte would have contested the charge of heavy-handed domestication, which he regarded as a desideratum of his editors that he could not endorse. The translator's views were firm in the autumn of 1927, as evidenced by his correspondence with Paulhan. In reviewing the first pages of Vialatte's *Métamorphose*, Paulhan was concerned that the translation might be too foreign and therefore jeopardize the story's success: "I have the feeling that your translation is very accurate—accurate to the point perhaps that Vialatte does not appear in it enough and that he has withdrawn too much."[31] But the young translator defended his position:

> When it comes to the translation, you are a better judge than I, because the influence of the German text hinders the interpreter's judgment. But it is by design that I try to be as absent as possible from my text: the originality of Kafka's style indeed

---

[29] For a comprehensive account, see Ritchie Robertson, "In Search of Historical Kafka: A Selective View of Research, 1980–1992," *Modern Language Review* 89 (1994), 107–37.
[30] Cited in Béal, *Vialatte, l'intemporel*, 62.
[31] Jean Paulhan to Alexandre Vialatte, Nov. 25, 1927. Alexandre Vialatte/Jean Paulhan, *Correspondance: 1921–1968*, ed. Denis Wetterwald (Paris: Julliard, 1997), 28.

seems to me to reside in an excess of anonymity that becomes a personal note.[32]

Rather provocatively, Vialatte's remarks complicate the conventional ideal of the translator's *invisibility* by stressing instead the translator's *absence*. Whereas invisibility serves the function of transparency and fluency, making the translation appear as though it were not a translation at all, the translator's absence allows for opacity and foreignness to come through. Invisibility, one could say, assists domestication by refashioning the foreign author to accord with the expectations of the target culture, while absence compels the reader to venture out and approach the author on his own terms.

Vialatte opts for absence over invisibility yet does so in a curious way. In his assessment, Kafka's "style" consists "in an excess of anonymity." Kafka's "personal note" paradoxically derives from his namelessness, his own status as an unknown. Thus, in 1947, Vialatte titled his reflections on rendering Kafka *Traduit de l'inconnu* ("Translated from the Unknown"). "Who was Kafka? I have always tried not to know him, to make him mysterious to myself. Why talk about him? Why deprive him of the prestige of being known only as the author of a unique, strange, genial body of work."[33] For Vialatte, the text must take precedence over its existential source; writing itself must supplant the writer's being. One recalls the assessment of Claude-Edmonde Magny, that few authors are as *absent* from their work as Kafka. According to Vialatte, the less we know of the man the more we can admire the "unique, strange, genial oeuvre." This rather traditional view, however, is radicalized by Vialatte's concomitant premise—namely, his self-stylization as "famously unknown [*méconnu*]," which now correlates to his image of Kafka as "the unknown [*l'inconnu*]." The translator's absence thus parallels his author's absence: The Unknown rendered by the Unknown. "Kafka was a god, but an unknown god [*un dieu inconnu*] and I had made myself his prophet."[34] Like Paul preaching to Athens, Vialatte converts the unknown god into a God for everyone.

---

[32] Vialatte to Paulhan, December 9, 1927, *Correspondance*, 28.
[33] Viallate, "Traduit de l'inconnu" [1947], in *Kafka ou l'innocence diabolique*, ed. François Béal and François Taillandier (Paris: Les Belles Lettres, 1998), 27.
[34] Vialatte, "Traduit de l'inconnu," 13.

DREAMS, RIVERS, SNOW

Vialatte's insistence on the absent and the unknown is enhanced by the idea of the work's hidden provenance. The conception is indebted to a surrealist proclivity towards automatism, madness, and the *objet trouvé*, whereby poetic texts and associations are thought to derive from an unconscious, mysterious origin. For the Surrealists, the primary illustration of enigmatic origins are dreams, which, as Vialatte liked to point out, Kafka had once compared to rivers: "[Rivers] know quite a few things, only, where they come from, they don't know"—*sie wissen mancherlei, nur, woher sie kommen, wissen sie nicht* (KGW 7, 78). From the start, while working in the Rhineland, Vialatte linked his engagement with Kafka to dreams and rivers as figures that symbolize a known presence from an unknown source. Belonging to this constellation of images was the concealing snow that distinguished the German landscape.

Vialatte deploys all three figures—dreams, rivers, and snow—in his account of the day in December 1926, when he first discovered the author to whom he would devote a good portion of his professional career.

> I lived on the banks of a great river ("Dreams came up the river," writes Kafka; "You stop, you talk with them; they know many things, except not where they come from."—Mac Orlan interviewed them—). In the houses the light was yellow; outside it was gray. Snow covered the streetcars.[35]

The Rhine: A river replete with poetic resonances. For Hölderlin it is a riddle, but only for us, a river that is mindful of its Alpine source: *Ein Rätsel ist Reinentsrpungenes*, "a riddle is what has arisen purely," with the adverb [*rein*] echoing the river's name. Kafka's river, in contrast, bears dreams that are riddles unto themselves: They do not know where they come from. The Rhine might further evoke Heine, whose famous "Lorelei" opens with a similar expression of ignorance: *Ich weiss nicht, was soll es bedeuten, dass ich so traurig bin* ("I do not know what it means that I am so sad"); or perhaps the Rhine that nourished Marx's acuity and now constitutes a most contested border. In any event, it is here where Vialatte was employed as a translator for the occupying French army and for its magazine *La Revue rhénane*. Immersed in two languages,

---

[35] Vialatte, "Rencontre avec Kafka" [1957], in *Kafka ou l'innocence diabolique*, 3–12; here, p. 3.

caught between two cultures, and, as it would turn out, between two wars, Vialatte describes his situation as both isolated and populated, nestled in a snow-muffled silence that reverberates with the words of others, his ear trained on distant voices that inform, confirm, or legitimize his own thoughts: Kafka, of course, but also Mac Orlan, the pen name of Pierre Dumarchey, whose social fantasy novels would soon be compared with Kafka's work.

Writing some thirty years after the event, Vialatte recalls these other voices by setting them in brackets. On that day in 1926, he had not yet heard of Kafka, though he suggests that Kafka, along with Mac Orlan, was already present. The *parenthetical* incursion, as the term's dual prefix implies, is set both to the side of (*para-*) and within (*en-*) the reverie, a part of and apart from the translator's memory. In remembering his time in the Rhineland, Vialatte conjures the lines from Kafka's notebooks, which would only first be published in 1937, as if they were already exerting some force ten years before. The parenthesis draws Vialatte out of the recounted moment, geographically and temporally: Although he was alone in Mainz at the time, he now imagines that he was being pulled eastward to Kafka's Prague and westward to Mac Orlan's Paris, which together summoned him towards the future.

The outside in snowy gray penetrates the yellow-lit interior. The cold off to the side (*para-*) has penetrated within (*en-*). As the reminiscence proceeds, this penetration will become more concrete. The interruption registered at the time of recollection (1957) correlates to the physical disturbance experienced at the time recounted (1926).

> Snow was falling. The postman opened the door. He looked like a Christmas tree. He was a real German postman. Between his whiskers, which drooped like spruce branches, he rose, covered with snow, like a Black Forest conifer. Red things and golden things shone on the surface, and one could not tell if they were useful New Year's presents [*étrennes*] or folkloric ornaments.
>
> (3)

The depiction betrays the Frenchman's fascination for Christmas, which at the time was heavily coded as German. The snow enhances the exotic effect of this walking Christmas tree, whose appearance goes on to stimulate a rich series of associations for the memoirist, culminating in none other than Otto von Bismarck, the formidable founder of the German Empire.

> A founder, that's the thing; he looked like a founder. [. . .] A founder in a founder's uniform. In founder's boots. In a founder's belly. He put on my table, with a hairy hand, a package the size

and thickness of a brick. What monument did he want to build? What did this first stone mean? I opened it. It was Kafka's *Castle*.

(4)

Although Vialatte would not publish a full translation of *The Castle* until 1938, he accords the greatest significance to this discovery, irradiating it with a fairy-tale aura. Given what issued from this moment, one could forgive the nostalgic hyperbole: A Christmas tree bearing a unique, unexpected gift, as if to announce the advent of a new, disquieting messiah who would emerge as a literary phenomenon, the humble start of a book that would one day become the cornerstone of a monument to a century mired in bureaucracy and alienation, anxiety and fear, and hopeless hope.

As if to confirm the singularity of the event, Vialatte emphasizes how the snow falling on his street in Mainz corresponded uncannily to the novel's opening scene:

It was late evening when K. arrived. The village lay in deep snow. There was nothing to be seen of the Castle Mount. Mist and darkness surrounded it, and not the weakest glimmer of light indicated the great castle. For a long time, K. stood on the wooden bridge which leads from the road to the village and looked up into the apparent void.

(KGW 4, 9/C 5)

The gray chill, both in the novel and outside Vialatte's study, has now entered inside—*à côté de moi, pour ainsi dire* ("right beside me, so to speak" [4])—the once parenthetical voices have been realized, the external interiorized. Like K., Vialatte stands on the shaky bridge and peers into what lies ahead. The snow that concealed both without and within insulated the seeds of the future, the dark messiah's and his own.

Vialatte's metaphor is persistent: Snowfall is prerequisite for resurrection: "Time passed. The snow returned. I received *The Metamorphosis*. From the depths of his grave in the Prague cemetery, Kafka wrote more and more. Every winter the snowy wind brought a new message, enigmatic, and unfinished" (6–7). Yet unlike the evangelical Baptist, whose *auspicium* came in the form of a white dove, this twentieth-century prophet was guided by a bird blacker than the night. It bore a *dysangelium* that, from the post-1945 perspective, proved to be all too accurate.

Kafka, in Czech, is the jackdaw [*choucas*]. From the Jewish cemetery in Prague, all his little black characters, with sharp elbows, like ants, those drawings that he put in the margins, on the border of his manuscripts, those insect-shaped misgivings, those judges corseted in jackets whose flaps looked like elytra, those four-legged heroes, that army of disquiet spread over the German snow like rats.

(7)

TRANSLATIVE DECISIONS

Vialatte might have preferred to be regarded as an absent wordsmith who permitted Kafka's German peculiarity to come through in the French, yet his translations nonetheless exhibit the signs of the domestication or naturalization that Paulhan expected. The famous opening sentence of *The Metamorphosis* already reveals fundamental aspects of Vialatte's approach.

> Als Gregor Samsa eines Morgens aus unruhigen Träumen erwachte, fand er sich in seinem Bett zu einem ungeheueren Ungeziefer verwandelt.

> Un matin, au sortir d'un rêve agité, Grégoire Samsa s'éveilla transformé dans son lit en une formidable vermine.
> (Vialatte, trans. [1928])

> As Gregor Samsa awoke one morning from uneasy dreams he found himself transformed in his bed into a gigantic insect.
> (Willa and Edwin Muir, trans. [1948], CS 89)[36]

The most immediate marker of domestication is, of course, the protagonist's name—the Gallic *Grégoire* for the Germanic *Gregor*. (In subsequent editions, Vialatte will revert to *Gregor*.) Lexically, one notes how the preponderance of terms with the negating prefix *un-* (*unruhig*, *ungeheuer*, and *Ungeziefer*) is bypassed in favor of positive terms (*agité*, *formidable*, and *vermine*). The effect could be likened to a clarifying determination of what, in German, is stated by indicating what something is not: *unruhig* ("restless," astutely conveyed by the Muirs' *uneasy*), *ungeheuer* ("enormous, tremendous, monstrous" but also

---

[36] For an excellent comparative analysis of this opening line in multiple European languages, see Patrick O'Neill, *Transforming Kafka: Translation Effects* (Toronto: University of Toronto Press, 2014), 59–70.

"uncanny"—the negation of what is *geheuer*, "safe and familiar"), and *Ungeziefer* (ordinarily, a verminous pest, yet, as scholars have pointed out, originally a religious term that denotes a creature that is *not* "fit for sacrifice" [Old High German *zebar*]).[37] As for *unruhig*, Vialatte's *agité* catches Kafka's allusion to the common phrase "a restless sleep" (*ein unruhiger Schlaf*) and its manipulation into "restless dreams" (*unruhige Träume*), even if idiomatic French reduces the experience to a single dream (*un rêve agité*). Regarding the third term, *Ungeziefer*, the French *vermine* captures the more hideous social resonances of Kafka's text: In addition to designating bothersome insects and rodents, *Ungeziefer* had by 1900 become a common antisemitic slur, popularized by Hermann Ahlwardt's incendiary speech in the Berlin Reichstag in 1897, which called upon the nation "to combat the Jewish vermin [*das jüdische Ungeziefer*] and cleanse the Germanic household."[38] In comparison, the Muirs' *insect* comes across as far more innocuous.

On the level of syntax, Kafka's expansive opening temporal clause (*Als . . . erwachte*) is parceled out into distinct units: A simple temporal marker (*Un matin*) and a substantive use of the infinitive (*au sortir de*), which transfers the verb of the subordinate clause (*erwachte*) to the position of main verb (*s'eveilla*). Consequently, the vague threshold between sleep and wakefulness, conveyed by Kafka's temporal clause ("When" or "as he awoke," "as he was waking up"), is clarified by the declarative *Grégoire Samsa s'eveilla*—"he woke up," unquestionably. To be sure, Vialatte's decision is almost immediately validated further down when we learn that "it was no dream." Still, the initial effect of uncertainty and disorientation—was he still sleeping or not?—is overridden by the French preterite. Meanwhile, the reflexive pronoun for the verb "awake," required in French, appears sufficient to relieve Vialatte from rendering Kafka's own reflexive construction (*fand er sich . . . verwandelt: s'éveilla transformé* rather than the more literal choice: *se trouva transformé*). Vialatte's version thereby renders the scene more objective, eliminating the psychological perspective and the concomitant suggestion that it might only be a delusion: In French, Grégoire "awoke transformed," as opposed to the internalized sense of the German, where Gregor, "as he awoke . . . *found himself* transformed." On these points, at least, the Muirs are much more faithful to the original. Yet,

---

[37] For a summary of the scholarship, see Kafka, *The Metamorphosis*, tr. Stanley Corngold (New York: Bantam, 1972), 66–7.

[38] Cited in Andrew Barker, "Giant Bug or Monstrous Vermin? Translating Kafka's *Die Verwandlung* in its Cultural, Social, and Biological Contexts," *Translation and Literature* 30 (2021), 198–208; here, p. 204.

both the French and the English versions fail to replicate the surprising twist afforded by the German syntax: *fand er sich in seinem Bett*—"he found himself in his bed," at first a perfectly ordinary realization for someone who has been asleep—but then, *zu einem ungeheueren Ungeziefer verwandelt*—"into an enormous vermin transformed," which is most extraordinary, indeed.

What is nearly impossible to put into proper English or French is Kafka's somewhat odd usage of the verb *verwandeln* ("transform")—the final word of the opening sentence that points directly to the German title, *Die Verwandlung*. Both Vialatte and the Muirs understandably give the phrase as "transformed *into* an insect." Yet in standard German, this sense would be expressed with the preposition *in* plus the accusative case: *in ein ungeheures Ungeziefer*. But Kafka does not write *in*. Instead, rather unconventionally, he uses the preposition *zu*, which takes the dative case: *zu einem ungeheueren Ungeziefer*, transformed "*to* a monstrous insect." The distinction is slight yet significant. With the preposition *in*, the implication is that the change is continuous, that some latent quality has become manifest in the transformation; while with the preposition *zu*, the change comes across as more disjunctive, that Gregor has been altered to an entirely new shape: He has moved from a human form *to* an insect form.

Vialatte's domesticating effects are discernible throughout, for example in the following passage, close to the head of the story. Gregor appears to be less anxious about his bizarre transformation than about the fact he will be late for work, which triggers a bitterness that we presume he has harbored for some time.

> "Ach Gott", dachte er, "was für einen anstrengenden Beruf habe ich gewählt! Tag aus, Tag ein auf der Reise. Die geschäftlichen Aufregungen sind viel größer, als im eigentlichen Geschäft zu Hause, und außerdem ist mir noch diese Plage des Reisens auferlegt, die Sorgen um die Zuganschlüsse, das unregelmäßige, schlechte Essen, ein immer wechselnder, nie andauernder, nie herzlich werdender menschlicher Verkehr."
>
> (KGW 1, 94)

> "Quel métier, pensa-t-il, quel métier ai-je été choisir ! Tous les jours en voyage ! Des ennuis pires que dans le commerce de mes parents ! et par dessus le marché cette plaie des voyages : les changements de trains, les correspondances qu'on rate, les mauvais repas qu'il faut prendre n'importe quand ; à chaque instant des têtes nouvelles, des gens qu'on ne reverra jamais, avec lesquels il n'y a pas moyen d'être camarades."
>
> (1928, p. 67)

Oh God, he thought, what an exhausting job I've picked on! Traveling about day in, day out. It's much more irritating work than doing the actual business in the office, and top of that there's the trouble of constant traveling, of worrying about train connections, the bed and irregular meals, casual acquaintances that are always new and never become intimate friends.
(Willa and Edwin Muir, trans. [1948], CS 89–90)

To begin, Vialatte circumvents the mild profanity, "Oh God!", with a straightforward, secularized exclamation, repeated twice where the German gives only one instance: *Quel métier . . . quel métier ai-je été choisir!*—"What profession . . . what profession have I been choosing!" The choice to employ a colloquial iterative perfect (*j'ai été choisir*, "I have been choosing") extends the choice over time, while also dropping Kafka's modifier: *einen anstrengenden Beruf*, "an exhausting profession." Vialatte relies on the iteration and the exclamation itself to convey the sense of exhaustion, an effect he further underscores in the French by an excess of exclamation points. He also applies the principle of variation to "correct," so to speak, what may be perceived as rough redundancy. Kafka's *geschäftliche Aufregungen* ("business-related upsets") is reduced to vague *ennuis* (here, in the sense of "troubles" or "worries"), perhaps to avoid the near repetition of *im eigentlichen Geschäft zu Hause*, a phrase that is itself somewhat ambiguous. Although *zu Hause* commonly denotes "at home," in the present context, it could mean something more like "at the office." Gregor appears to be contrasting business-related travel with "actual business in the office," which is precisely how the Muirs construe it, while Vialatte contrasts "travel" with "dealing with [his] parents" (*le commerce de mes parents*). Furthermore, the French elaborates and expands where the German is succinct: "concerns about the train-connections" (*Sorgen um die Zuganschlüsse*) unfold as more objective, less psychological facts: "changing trains, the connections one misses" (*les changements de trains, les correspondances qu'on rate*).

Finally, Gregor's emotive lament, formulated in a long, exasperating attributive phrase (*ein immer wechselnder, nie andauernder, nie herzlich werdender menschlicher Verkehr* [literally: "an ever changing, never lasting, never sincerely [becoming] human acquaintance"]) is reformatted into subordinate clauses: *à chaque instant des têtes nouvelles, des gens qu'on ne reverra jamais, avec lesquels il n'y a pas moyen d'être camarades* ("at each moment new faces, people one will never see again, with whom there are no means of being friends"). Kafka's single, loaded term, *Verkehr*, which in general means "traffic" but here denotes an acquaintance one converses with, variously appears as *têtes nouvelles* ("new faces"), *gens* ("people"), and *camarades* ("friends"). Milan

Kundera has diagnosed this practice as a "synonymizing reflex" that aims to invest the text with the translator's own creativity. Since readers in the target culture have no basis for judging fidelity to the original, the translator resorts to supplying more vocabulary.[39] For the interpreter restricted to the French text alone, the effect is substantial. Each of Vialatte's word-choices belongs to distinct semantic fields with certain denotations and connotations, which steer the meaning of the passage toward particular significations and thereby complicate a text that is at once simpler and more open in the German.[40]

BIFURCATIONS

Vialatte worked not only as Kafka's translator but also as his literary agent, corresponding frequently with Brod to secure foreign rights and negotiate with publishers. As a result, Kafka's name gradually circulated among Paris's literati, though still more or less within the orbit of the *NRF*. In August 1929, the review published six of Kafka's briefer pieces translated by Félix Bertaux in collaboration with Karl Wilhelm Körner and the poet Jules Supervielle.[41] The list is noteworthy and would have conveyed a potent legitimization. Bertaux was a highly respected scholar, a friend of Heinrich and Thomas Mann, and one of the *NRF*'s chief authorities on German literature, best known for his *Panorama of Contemporary German Literature*, published in 1928, which played a key role in presenting German authors to the French public, including Stefan George, Rainer Maria Rilke, and Hugo von Hofmannsthal.[42] Bertaux had already expressed his endorsement of Kafka in a note appended to the final installment of *La Métamorphose* in March 1928, and now his decision to oversee translations of Kafka would have ratified the conviction that the work warranted a prominent place in the burgeoning canon of modern literature. Karl Wilhelm Körner was lesser

---

[39] Milan Kundera, *Testaments Betrayed: An Essay in Nine Parts*, tr. Linda Asher (New York: HarperCollins, 1995), 109.
[40] For further examples and analysis, see Manfred Schmeling, "Das 'offene Kunstwerk' in der Übersetzung: Zur Problematik der französischen Kafka-Rezeption," *Arcadia* 14 (1979), 22–39.
[41] "Bucéphale, et autres récits," Félix Bertaux, K. W. Körner, and Jules Supervielle, tr. *Nouvelle Revue Française* 191 (August 1929), 205–11. The publication also contains *Le nouvel avocat* (*The New Advocate*), *Devant la loi* (*Before the Law*), *Un message impérial* (*An Imperial Message*), *Le plus proche village* (*The Next Village*), and *Il tue son frère* (*A Fratricide*).
[42] Félix Bertaux, *Panorama de la littérature allemande contemporaine* (Paris: Éditions de Sagittaire, 1928).

known, though he would make a name for himself later on, after fleeing Nazi Germany to live in Buenos Aires, where he worked with Victoria Ocampo, associated with Borges, and served as one of the founding members of the *Deutscher Klub*, which promoted contemporary German literature in Argentina. Back in 1929, Körner's subsequent, hardly foreseeable fate in South America was uncannily presaged in that his other collaborator, Jules Supervielle, was born in Montevideo and would maintain, despite his French citizenship, an active trans-Atlantic alliance. Hailing from Uruguay, the exotic birthplace of Isidore Ducasse/ Lautréamont, Supervielle rose to prominence in Paris with his first collection of poems, *Débarcadères* (1922). The book was lauded by Gide and Valéry and thus gained him entrance into the *NRF* circuit. An outspoken critic of the Surrealists' obsession with automatic writing, Supervielle found a kindred spirit in Paulhan, who introduced him to Henri Michaux. Michaux's first collection of verse and prose, *Qui je fus* (1927), which Paulhan edited for the Éditions de la *NRF* and which received, as noted above, a substantial review in the journal's January 1928 volume, was in part dedicated to Supervielle, who had since become Michaux's close friend. All this to say that by the summer of 1929, Kafka had been fully installed among the highbrow cenacle of the Gallimard house. Broader recognition would only be a matter of time. As Paulhan remarked in early 1930, "I have the impression that, within two or three years, Kafka will be regarded as Joyce's equal: it's going to happen suddenly."[43]

In terms of translation, Bertaux, Körner, and Supervielle adhere to Kafka's pared-down language in terse, crystalline syntax, where Vialatte opts for lexical variation in a somewhat smoother presentation. Their respective versions of the opening of the parable "Before the Law" offer a good basis for comparison. For guidance, I provide my own, hyper-literal translation from the German.

> Vor dem Gesetz steht ein Türhüter. Zu diesem Türhüter kommt ein Mann vom Lande und bittet um Eintritt in das Gesetz. Aber der Türhüter sagt, daß er ihm jetzt den Eintritt nicht gewähren könne.
>
> (KGW 3, 226)

Before the law stands a doorkeeper. To this doorkeeper comes a man from the country and asks for entrance into the law. But the doorkeeper says that he cannot grant him entrance now.

---

[43] Paulhan to Vialatte, March 5, 1930. Vialatte/Paulhan, *Correspondance*, 69.

Devant la loi se dresse le gardien de la porte. Un homme de la campagne se présente et demande à entrer dans la loi. Mais le gardien dit que pour l'instant il ne peut pas lui accorder l'entrée.
(Bertaux et al.)[44]

Une sentinelle se tient postée devant la Loi ; un homme vient un jour la trouver et lui demande la permission de pénétrer. Mais la sentinelle lui dit qu'elle ne peut pas le laisser entrer en ce moment.
(Vialatte)[45]

Vialatte erases an important effect, which Kafka produced in publishing this excerpt from *The Trial* as a stand-alone piece in 1915: The phrase *before the law* serves as both the title and the incipit of the tale; it appears both *before* and *in* the story, a story, of course, that centers on being before the law and wishing to enter. Bertaux conveys this effect by beginning with *devant la loi*, while Vialatte consigns the phrase to the end of the first statement—a choice that arguably accords better with standard French syntax. Vialatte further connects Kafka's two distinct sentences with a semicolon, where Bertaux retains the telegraphic style. In terms of vocabulary, Vialatte renders *Türhüter* ("doorkeeper") with *sentinelle*, which, in addition to being grammatically gendered feminine, tends to connote a military context. Bertaux's *gardien*, in contrast, refers more generally to a watchman or guard—someone stationed at a doorway—and is therefore closer to Kafka's parabolic openness. Yet when Kafka adds specificity with "a man from the country," Vialatte opts for an unspecified *homme* ("man"). Again, Bertaux stays close to his source by giving *un homme de la campagne*. Both Frenchmen, however, appear equally averse to following Kafka's stark repetition: *Before the law stands a doorkeeper. To this doorkeeper comes a man* . . . Nonetheless, Bertaux astutely gives the emphatic *dans la loi* ("in the law"), while Vialatte glosses over it with a complementary infinitive, *pénétrer* ("enter, penetrate"). For the final sentence in this example, Vialatte again chooses a more standard, fluent French in contrast to Bertaux's version, which is slightly more estranging, as one would no doubt expect of an academic Germanist.

Although but a brief selection, the passage sufficiently represents an alternative translating practice that departs from Vialatte's domesticating approach. One recalls Gautier's comments on Hoffmann in French:

---

[44] Kafka, "Devant la loi," Bertaux, Körner, and Supervielle, tr. *NRF* 191 (August 1929), 206.
[45] Kafka, *Le Procès*, Vialatte, tr. [1933] (Paris: Gallimard, 1957), 281.

Necessarily domesticated to gain an initial audience, yet perhaps in need of becoming stranger—more German—to remain of interest. That said, Vialatte's Kafka won the day. In Claude David's 1976 Pléiade edition of Kafka's complete works, Vialatte's translations—and those by Marthe Robert—were chosen over the set prepared by Bertaux, Körner, and Supervielle. It was only in the 2018 Pléiade, edited by Jean-Pierre Lefebvre, that Vialatte was finally replaced by new translations, to match the new critical German edition based on Kafka's manuscripts and notebooks—that is, the source material prior to Brod's editorial work.

Returning to the state of affairs around 1930: Although Vialatte remained the primary translator with the publication of his versions of *The Trial* (*Le Procès*, 1933) and *The Castle* (*Le Château*, 1938), other translators, unaffiliated with the *NRF*, were active and thereby moved Kafka, however gradually, into new neighborhoods. An important instance occurred in July 1930, when Pierre Klossowski and Pierre Leyris published their translation of *The Judgment* as *Le Verdict* in the avant-garde journal *Bifur*.

Founded the year before by Pierre Lévy and Georges Ribemont-Dessaignes, *Bifur* aspired towards international collaboration, numbering James Joyce and William Carlos Williams among its editorial board members, and, together with Georges Bataille's *Documents*, loosely represented those surrealists who were dismayed by André Breton's doctrinaire commitment to communism and were therefore soundly excommunicated by the movement's leader in February 1929. Ribemont-Dessaignes was a painter, poet, and playwright who had associated with the proto-Dadaists Marcel Duchamp and Francis Picabia and participated in the early stirrings of surrealism alongside Breton and Philippe Soupault, yet distanced himself after the publication of the First Surrealist Manifesto in October 1924. After the 1929 debacle with Breton, Ribemont-Dessaignes rallied a coalition of the dissident writers and artists to prepare the pamphlet *Le cadavre*, which viciously dressed down the surrealist czar.[46] In printing a translation of *The Judgment* at the head of the July 1930 edition, Ribemont-Dessaignes consecrated Kafka before a cabal of radical artists and writers, who would represent a provocative niche in the decade to come.

The young translators, Pierre Klossowski and Pierre Leyris, would play important roles in twentieth-century culture and critique:

---

[46] For a contemporary account, see César Vallejo, *Art and Revolution* (1929–1931), in *Selected Writings*, ed. Joseph Mulligan (Middletown: Wesleyan University Press, 2015), 201–5.

Klossowski as an acclaimed novelist, visual artist, philosopher, and translator; and Leyris as the premier translator of English literature, culminating with his directorship of Shakespeare's *Œuvres complètes* (1954–61). Klossowski, brother of the painter Balthus, had reveled in a poetic childhood: his mother, Baladine, had a prolonged affair with Rilke and the family home was frequented by Gide, who initiated a passion for literature in young Pierre and would hire him, at eighteen, as his secretary to assist in the drafting of his novel, *Les faux-monnayeurs* (*The Counterfeiters*, 1925). Klossowski's first major translation project involved the late fragments of Hölderlin—*Poèmes de la folie*—which he prepared in collaboration with the erstwhile unanimist Pierre Jean Jouve, published with a preface by Bernard Groethuysen, who had long been engaged with the German poet and would soon compose the first extended philosophical essay on Kafka in French.

As for the Klossowski-Leyris translation in *Bifur*, a brief comparison with Vialatte's standard version demonstrates how the Prague author could be differently costumed.

> Es war an einem Sonntagvormittag im schönsten Frühjahr. Georg Bendemann, ein junger Kaufmann, saß in seinem Privatzimmer im ersten Stock eines der niedrigen, leichtgebauten Häuser, die entlang des Flusses in einer langen Reihe, fast nur in der Höhe und Färbung unterschieden, sich hinzogen.
>
> (KGW 1, 39)

> *It was on a Sunday pre-noon in the most beautiful spring. Georg Bendemann, a young salesman, sat in his private room in the first floor of one of low* [or *humble, menial*], *lightly built houses, which extended along the river in a long row, distinguished almost only in height and color.*

> C'était une très belle matinée de Dimanche de printemps. Georg Bendemann, jeune commerçant, était assis dans sa chambre au premier étage de l'une des maisons basses et légères qui se distinguaient seulement, dans l'égale rangée qu'elles formaient au long de fleuve, par la hauteur et la couleur.
>
> (Klossowski and Leyris)[47]

> C'était un matin de dimanche, par une année qui débutait splendidement. Georges Bendemann, un jeune négociant, se

---

[47] Kafka, *Le Verdict*, tr. Pierre Klossowski and Pierre Leyris, *Bifur* 5 (July 1930), 5.

trouvait alors dans sa chambre, au premier étage d'une de ces maisons basses, bâties de matériaux légers, uniquement différentes de hauteur ou de ton, dont la longue file s'étirait le long de la rivière.

(Vialatte)[48]

In addition to retaining the German *Georg* as opposed to Vialatte's naturalized *Georges*, the Klossowski-Leyris version estranges the French by having it adhere closely to the original's syntax: The straight declarative opening and the convoluted description that follows. Yet, despite this fidelity to the source, the translation is hardly confusing or disorienting. Rather, it produces a subtle effect by expanding standard French usage from within. In contrast, Vialatte's version is typically domesticated, beginning with the first sentence where he backpedals with a subordinate clause: *par une année qui débutait splendidement*, "in a year that started splendidly." Vialatte's *par une année* departs from standard usage yet clearly, in a somewhat Balzacian key, attempts to capture a traditional, nineteenth-century voice. That is not to discount Vialatte. On the contrary, in presenting Kafka as if he had written in French, Vialatte achieves one of Kafka's signature effects: establishing a familiar, realist setting for unnerving, defamiliarizing events. *The Judgment* is paradigmatic in this regard. It is, after all, within a *domestic* sphere, during a tense but fairly typical conversation, where the father shockingly sentences the son to death by drowning. The same, of course, holds for *The Metamorphosis*.

Despite the differences in approaches, Vialatte's Kafka in fact shares much with the author transmitted by Klossowski and Leyris, just as Paulhan at the *NRF* concurs with Ribemont-Dessaignes and Pierre Lévy at *Bifur*. Both are united in presenting a French Kafka who can accord with surrealist views and with *la littérature fantastique*, and both are equally concerned with the dogmatic turn adopted by Breton.

---

[48] Kafka, *Le Verdict*, Vialatte, tr., in Kafka, *Œuvres complètes*, David, ed., 2, 180.

III Trials

PARATEXTS

During the first years of Kafka's reception in France, though background information was scant, it was not altogether lacking. Félix Bertaux provided a brief biographical note, which was appended to the third installment of Vialatte's *Métamorphose* in the *NRF*, and Pierre Klossowski wrote the following entry, which appeared at the back of the July 1930 number of *Bifur* to supplement the translation of *The Judgment*:

> FRANZ KAFKA, died in 1924 at the age of 41 [sic]. This Czech has deepened, better than anyone, the themes that made Meyrink or Däubler's *Der Werwolf* famous. He was good like every man of genius. His *Castle*, his *Trial*, are books of such intense poetry, deep light and blinding darkness at the same time, that we always discover more in them . . . [1]

The paragraph ends with an ellipsis or *points de suspension*, leaving out (Greek: *elleipein*) more specific comments on the two novels which, for the majority of French readers in 1930, were nothing more than titles. Otherwise, the relatively unfamiliar Kafka is introduced by way of the already familiar: Gustav Meyrink and Theodor Däubler. As an author who hailed from Prague, Meyrink would have been especially pertinent. Meyrink's first novel, *Der Golem*, was first published in 1913–14, serially in *Die weißen Blätter*, the same periodical where Kafka's *Metamorphosis* originally appeared in 1915. *The Golem*, however, brought Meyrink to international fame with its eerie plot, cabalistic mystique, and depiction of Jewish life in the Prague ghetto amid antisemitic oppression, all of which were expressionistically cast in the 1920 film by Paul Wegener and Carl Boese. A French translation of Meyrink's novel had appeared the year before. Däubler's novelistic elaboration on the legend of the werewolf had also been quite popular since its appearance in French in 1921, a story of bestial transformation clearly linking up with Kafka's *Metamorphosis*. Taken together, the two works would have situated Kafka squarely in the literary genres of the fantastic and expressionism, which depict supernatural or uncanny incursions into everyday reality or display excessive attentiveness to psychological turmoil. In the absence of extensive context, such generic expectations, along with the hint of Jewish character, would have assisted in steering interpretations of *The Judgment* and Kafka in general.

---

[1]   *Bifur* 5 (July 1930), 194–5.

Vialatte's translation of *The Trial* (*Le Procès*), published by Gallimard in the early summer of 1933, provided many more directives. By that point, the Nazi Party had seized power in Germany, and within a year, Joseph Goebbels would place the Prague author's works, together with those by Brod, on the notorious *List of Damaging and Undesirable Writing*. This political action arguably stimulated even more interest in Kafka among French literati, which contrasted with Kafka's relative obscurity in England. Although the Muirs' translation of *The Castle* appeared in 1930, it did not gain much traction, having barely sold its initial run of 500 copies; and mainly because of the commercial risk, they would not find a publisher to take on their version of *The Trial* until the American Alfred Knopf agreed in 1937.

The first edition of *Le Procès* included substantial supplemental material: A prefatory essay by Bernard Groethuysen and an afterword by Brod. In framing the novel with these paratexts, the publisher clearly anticipated readers' desires for orientation. As Gérard Genette has indicated, such "allographic" pieces first emerged in France in the sixteenth century and were typically of a philological nature, supplying important information and proposing fruitful avenues of exegesis for classic texts.[2] In this tradition, the reader presumes that the framing material was produced posthumously, which sets the author in a past and in a culture that call for reconstitution, while also underscoring the work's separation from the present day. The implication is typically commendatory in that the added texts present the novel as a work warranting guidance and the novelist as deserving special recognition. For this reason, such discourses tend to exhibit the main text in an enticing light. There is also the presumption that the preface or postface writer is to be trusted, that the viewpoint expressed here is authoritative and valuable. Thus, as examples of critical interpretation, these texts are detachable from the work they discuss; and although they might be intended to elucidate, their philosophical clarity and keen erudition could, however unwittingly, threaten to outshine the stated object of attention. Like every supplement, the paratext may come dangerously close to replacing the text it serves.

As for *Le Procès*, the first intervening text was the book's advertisement, composed by Vialatte and printed on the dust cover:

> It is man who boils in Kafka's cauldron. He meticulously simmers in the dark broth of anxiety, but humor blows the lid off with a whistle and traces in the air cabalistic formulas in blue letters.

---

[2] Gérard Genette, *Paratexts: Thresholds of Interpretation*, tr. Jane E. Lewin (Cambridge: Cambridge University Press, 1997), 263.

The description rehearses the cabalistic aura evoked in Klossowski's passing reference to Meyrink's *Golem* and maintains the image of Kafka as an author with surrealist proclivities. Yet it also promises a novel that applies to human life in general: *C'est l'homme,* "it is man," who stews in this novel's cauldron. The protagonist may have originated in a distant culture; he may have been the product of foreign experience and sensibility; yet his plight is common to all, recognizable by anyone who has suffered bouts of anxiety—an affect that would have found ready resonance in a world beset by global depression with the growing threat of another world war. The description further suggests that the novel offers psychological insight and perhaps even therapeutic assistance, how anxiety can express itself in humorous outbursts and blow the lid off a life so dismally oppressed.

Vialatte's blurb makes no reference to the actual plot of the novel, which is not entirely unusual, given that cover advertisements are designed to lure the reader in. In contrast, the preface is expected to be informative, outlining the author's biography and discussing the history of the text: its conception, its composition, and its original publication, the work's position in the author's overall oeuvre as well as its relationship to the literary tradition, all with the intention of securing its place in the canon. It is therefore all the more surprising that Bernard Groethuysen's preface, which greets the reader at the gate of the text, does nothing of the sort.

THE ADVENTURER

In accord with a strategy often implemented by Gallimard, Groethuysen's preface to *Le Procès*, "À propos de Kafka," was printed in advance of the novel's publication, in the April 1933 number of the *NRF*. As such, the piece stands as the first critical endeavor in French to reflect on Kafka's significance. Rather than inform the French audience about what they are about to read, Groethuysen provides the reasons why the text must be read. This urgency will not be lost on the upcoming generation. The story of a young man who is unexpectedly arrested and must face trial for an unknown crime would soon prove its relevance. As we shall see, the philosophical musings on Kafka's import during the Nazi Occupation of Paris are to a very large degree indebted to Groethuysen's preface, which, in the assessment of Albert Camus, "offers everything and confirms nothing."[3]

---

[3] The line appears in the concluding note to the 1942 essay, "Hope and the Absurd in the Work of Franz Kafka," which Camus would append to *The Myth of Sisyphus* [1944], tr. Justin O'Brien (New York: Vintage, 1955), 138 n.7.

As mentioned, Groethuysen abstains from contextualizing the novel historically or culturally. Instead, he strives to show how Kafka broaches fundamental questions that relate to human existence in general, questions that specifically relate to discussions among German critics and scholars. For this role, he was particularly well positioned. Born in 1880 in Berlin to a Dutch father, who spoke English, and a Russian mother, who preferred French, Groethuysen embodied the cosmopolitan ideal that Gallimard cherished during the interwar period. The child's upbringing, however, was far from idyllic, darkened as it was by his father's mental illness. When Bernard was five years old, his father was institutionalized and would remain confined to an asylum in Baden-Baden until his death in 1900. The dual intimacy with multilingualism and insanity appears to have steered Groethuysen's studies in psychology and art history in Vienna, Munich, and then back in Berlin. He had the good fortune to work with several of the most inventive and probing minds of the day, with Heinrich Wölfflin and Heinrich Gomperz, with the pioneering sociologist, Georg Simmel, and with the prominent philosopher of lived experience, Wilhelm Dilthey. Especially significant was Dilthey's refined conception of "understanding" (*Verstehen*), whereby the literary and cultural historian would strive to penetrate the worldview of another thinker, epoch, or form of life to achieve empathetic identification.

This commitment to spiritual commerce with different modes of consciousness led Groethuysen to pursue a doctoral dissertation on empathy (*Mitgefühl*) with the eclectic theorist of sensation and tone-psychologist, Carl Stumpf.[4] Stumpf had studied philosophy in Vienna with Franz Brentano and would go on to direct Edmund Husserl's habilitation thesis in Halle. Subsequently, Stumpf founded the Berlin Institute of Psychology, which produced Gestalt psychology—a theoretical paradigm that derived from the work of another former Brentano student, Christian von Ehrenfels. As mentioned above, Ehrenfels was one of Kafka's philosophy professors in Prague, as well as Anton Marty, Brentano's most loyal disciple—both participants in the discussion group that met in the Café Louvre. As a student of Stumpf, Groethuysen would have arguably recognized in Kafka a kindred spirit.

---

[4] For biographical details, see Hannes Börhringer, *Bernard Groethuysen: Vom Zusammenhang seiner Schriften* (Berlin: Agora, 1978). A useful summary can be found in Michael Ermarth, "Intellectual History as Philosophical Anthropology: Bernard Groethuysen's Transformation of Traditional *Geistesgeschichte*," *Journal of Modern History* 65 (1993), 673–705.

Following his promotion in 1904, Groethuysen divided his time between Berlin and Paris as researcher and lecturer, gradually acquiring a reputation for brilliant provocation among the intelligentsia on both sides of the Rhine. Soon after war broke out in 1914, he was incarcerated as an enemy alien in a French camp near Brouges, where he was held in detention despite the public outcry headed by Henri Bergson. The harrowing experience, which could not but conjure the image of his father confined in the psychiatric ward, confirmed Groethuysen's belief in the necessity of cultivating a dialogic humanism as the antidote to the nationalistic narrow-mindedness that obstructed transcultural understanding and threatened further hostilities. After the Armistice, with a missionary's zeal, he introduced the literary works of Friedrich Hölderlin, Hugo von Hofmannsthal, and Franz Werfel as well as the writings of Husserl and Freud to France, while importing the Symbolist poets as well as Bergson, Gide, and Gabriel Marcel to the German public. In publishing with the *NRF*, Groethuysen became a close friend of Jean Paulhan, who invited him to participate every summer in the ten-day retreats to Burgundy, hosted by Paul Desjardins and Gaston Gallimard at the Cistercian abbey in Pontigny. Devoted to the unanimist theme, "The Future of Europe," these conferences served as a central hub for the intellectual elite, including Gide, André Malraux, and a young Jean-Paul Sartre. The conversations at Pontigny initiated many of the literary-political discussions that would continue to unfold around Saint-Germain-des-Prés, shuttling between the Gallimard house in the rue de Beaune (today, rue Sébastien-Bottin) and the Union pour la Vérité in the rue Visconti.[5]

True to his polyglot formation, in 1927, Groethuysen prepared separate German and French versions of his major study on the "bourgeois spirit." The German edition, pitched to academic philosophers, appeared as the first of two volumes with the Max Niemeyer Verlag in Halle, which had just published Heidegger's *Being and Time*; while the 1927 French version, published by Gallimard, was an abridgement of the two volumes and geared more towards a literary audience.[6] The variation in approach reflected the two major ethnotypes described by Jules Romains: A rigorously analytical exposition for German intellectuals and a belletristic, formally elegant presentation

---

[5] See Herbert R. Lottman, *The Left Bank: Writers, Artists, and Politics from the Popular Front to the Cold War* (Chicago: The University of Chicago Press, 1982), 32–4.
[6] *Die Entstehung der bürgerlichen Welt- und Lebensanschauung in Frankreich*, vol. 1 (Halle: Niemeyer, 1927); and *Origines de l'esprit bourgeois en France* (Paris: Gallimard, 1927). See Daniel Gordon, "Bernard Groethuysen and the Human Conversation," *History and Theory* 36 (1997), 289–311; here, p. 308.

for the French elite. That same year, 1927, together with Paulhan, Groethuysen founded a new book series, the *Bibliothèque des Idées*, for Gallimard. Five years later, he relocated to the French capital, where he frequented the casual symposia at the Malraux home on the rue de Bac, while serving as executive committee member and principal consultant on German literature for the *NRF*.

The reasons for Groethuysen's choice to abandon Germany in 1932 are self-evident. In addition to being repulsed by the mounting wave of fascism and antisemitic prejudices in the German university system, the Prussian Ministry of Science, Art, and Secondary Education interrogated him for making derisive remarks against the German nation. And so, Groethuysen would be among the first of a growing community of German writers, artists, and critics to seek refuge along the banks of the Seine. According to student accounts, in concluding his final lecture course in Berlin, he boldly declared: "Intellectuals of the world, unite!"[7] Although Groethuysen's allergy to foreordained ideologies prevented him from pledging allegiance to any political organization, his lifelong partner, Alix Guillain, a translator of Simmel, was an active member of the French Communist Party and a staunch supporter of the Soviet Union. Nonetheless, for Groethuysen, Marxism represented, as it arguably did for Gide and Paulhan, an important critical disposition, a stance immortalized in Malraux's major novel of 1933, *La condition humaine*, in which Groethuysen served as the principal model for Gisors, a professor and opium addict who "did not participate in action" and who "talked about politics only on the philosophical level," given his conviction that "there is no reality."[8]

The essay on Kafka's *Trial* is the first substantial article Groethuysen wrote after emigrating from the city of his birth and thereby puts into practice his ambition to maintain lines of Franco-German communication. In terms of form, he adopts the conversational style that he typically employed in his French philosophical writings, addressing the reader directly rather than stating a series of apodictic claims. The approach elaborates on Dilthey's method insofar as it regards the literary work as the expression of the author's soul or as an internal dialogue that the soul holds with itself. Groethuysen's governing conceit is to pose questions to the text as if it were a living individual, cross-examining the written word in order to solicit unexpected responses, all in an effort to acquire a more capacious understanding of the human psyche.[9]

---

[7] Börhinger, *Bernard Groethuysen*, 20.
[8] Cited in Gordon, "Bernard Groethuysen," 292.
[9] Cf. Jürgen Siess, "Bernard Groethuysen: Vers une anthropologie littéraire," *Raison présente* 68 (1983), 43–56; here, p. 43.

Thus, for his opening gambit, Groethuysen appeals to all human beings: *Nous ne vivons que dans un des mondes, le nôtre*, "We live in only one of many worlds, our own."[10] The placement of first-person plural pronouns in initial and final positions (*Nous . . . nôtre*) underscores the collective gesture, which should not be mistaken as some homogeneous universalization. As he demonstrates in his 1928 study, *Philosophical Anthropology*, what all humans share is a historically specific, immanent existence conditioned by constitutive otherness. We live in our own world yet often ignore the other worlds that shape and direct our existence. On the one hand, there is the world in which we live comfortably, a familiar environment that is easy to measure and navigate. This world essentially accords with bourgeois sensibility, routine, and complacency. Should we ever happen to enter another world, we should not be surprised, then, to find our senses confused and our comprehension frustrated. Although the threat of perplexity persuades most of us to remain within the reassuring limits of our experience, there are "adventurers" who risk exploring other universes, despite their inhospitable nature.

> Most of [these adventurers] lost themselves there and have had to seek refuge in the asylums, which the inhabitants of this world reserve for those who have expatriated. Nevertheless, there are also those—rare individuals, it is true—who have been able to maintain a perfectly lucid state of mind throughout their journey. They stayed awake while slumbering; they kept their eyes open while they slept. So it is with Kafka, who remained absent among us all his life and who told us of a world that necessarily seemed very obscure to us since we could only see it and think of it in our usual way.
> (11–12/397–8)

The terms are both highly resonant and deeply personal. The evocation of the asylum recalls Groethuysen's father, who spent his last decade confined in a psychiatric hospital, as well as his own wartime internment as an enemy alien and his current status as an expatriate. More generally, the description corresponds to the image perpetuated by the Surrealists,

---

10   Bernard Groethuysen, "A propos de Kafka," in Kafka, *Le Procès*, tr. Alexandre Vialatte [1933] (Paris: Gallimard, 1957), 11. Muriel Kittel published an English translation, "Apropos of Kafka," in the *Quarterly Review of Literature* 2 (1944), which was reprinted under the title "The Endless Labyrinth," in *The Kafka Problem*, ed. Angel Flores (New York: New Directions, 1946), 397–411. Citations are from these editions, with translations slightly modified.

who viewed Kafka as a precursor, a writer who bordered on madness yet remained lucent, a *voyant* like Rimbaud, who called for the "deregulation of all the senses," or a poet spiritually related to Nerval, who portrayed dreams as "a second life." One is reminded, finally, of the remarks, cited above, that would compare Kafka's arrival in France to an extraterrestrial landing, an effect that here finds a philosophical rather than a biographical explanation, that until now, Kafka had not simply been *unknown* but rather *absent* among us all, speaking of absent things.

As Groethuysen proceeds, unlike Nerval or Rimbaud, what Kafka encountered in this other world was not "the infinite," not "God," nor any "monsters." Rather, the residents of this strange universe were "creatures like you and me, speaking our language"—a world exactly like our familiar habitat yet entirely different, a place where "clocks run no longer or perhaps run otherwise," where "distances have changed and can no longer be measured." This other world is strange, "not because of a lack of reasons, but because everything is reasoned somehow backwards [*à l'envers*] and the reasoning goes on without stopping and without possible conclusion. And so, one is afraid to wake up and plays dead" (12/398). Those who return to our everyday reality suffer a *dépaysment*, a disorientation or culture shock. The adventurer is treated like a madman, much like the philosopher who returns to the recesses of Plato's cave.

To illustrate, Groethuysen tacitly reverts to his analysis of the bourgeois spirit, whose questions are never real questions since they strive only to confirm what one already knows. The bourgeois ego (*le Moi*) protects itself from otherness, it is comfortable only in the present world of familiar Being (*l'Être*) and is therefore fearful of the dream-world where it encounters the non-self (*le Non-Moi*) that resides in a transcendent realm of "non-being" (*le Non-Être*). An honest confrontation with the non-self and non-being would put one's own self into question. The encounter would reveal a truth that is difficult to bear—namely, that one's identity is constituted by non-identity, that being is conditioned by non-being, presence by absence. The ego, Groethuysen stresses, is the product of the nothingness that precedes and extends beyond one's existence, the past before one's birth and the future after one's death. In other words, this other pre- and post-existent world is our source and destination, which turns present existence into alien territory. Anguish derives from the realization that we do not belong to the world we believed was our home.

> If someone asks what you came here for, how can you respond? For after all you have not come here naturally. You are not from here. It is obvious from your worried look and the way you

apologize to everyone and act modest. You have a bad conscience. Your questions betray you. For sure, this is not your own country. Your visitor's permit? You're under arrest . . .
(13/398–9)

Although no explicit reference to Kafka's *Trial* has been made, and presumably before anyone has begun reading the novel, Groethuysen's apostrophe places the reader in the position of the work's unwitting protagonist, Josef K., who "one morning, without having done anything wrong, was arrested"—again, not unlike Groethuysen himself, the former military prisoner. The conflation of the novel's hero with both the essayist and his reader grounds Groethuysen's interpretation: *The Trial* is not simply about Josef K., it is about you and me.

The arrest exposes us to the fact that "we cannot escape the presence of others" (13/399). Any retreat into solipsistic comfort would therefore be a transgression: Faced with the other, it is no longer possible to say the pronoun *I*. "For in saying it you would declare yourself guilty" (14/399). The incomprehensibility of the law—the impenetrable otherness that constitutes one's identity—drives the search to discover the law. "You must get out of the building. But who knows its exit?" (14/400). Placed before the novel, Groethuysen's preface places us before the law.

> In the world of Kafka there is no empty space where we can take refuge. The line is drawn. You follow it.... Everything happens *more geometrico*, and everything that is, is part of an infinitely complex geometry. Learn to see without understanding. The non-self comes before the self; geometry precedes the spirit (15/400).

Cartesian rationalism, which has no difficulty speaking in the first-person singular of the *cogito*, believes that the extent of existence can be comprehended through geometric method (*more geometrico*). Yet, according to Groethuysen, in Kafka's other world, the ego itself is destabilized, doomed to follow a different geometry, a reason that operates "backwards" (*à l'envers*). A decade later, Sartre will define the fantastic universe of Kafka precisely in these terms. Indeed, in marshalling themes from Dilthey and Husserl, Freud and Bergson, Groethuysen prepares the ground for much of the discourse to come.

The essay glides into dialogic mode, with the writer now addressing the reader as *you*. You are inscribed in the text as much as you are condemned to follow the lines that have been drawn out for you.

—But you, who are you, then?

—I am the dreamer of a world where everything is perfectly ordered and where everything accuses me.

—But how is it that you are simultaneously part of this world and outside it? That you are absent and present in it at the same time? (16/401)

Then another shift, another complication, as Groethuysen presents an internal dialogue that unfolds within the consciousness of the *you*. The other is now internalized.

You say to yourself: I would like to wake up, because then I could say to him whom I see coming toward me arguing, and toward whom all my torments turn, since he is no other than myself: "Stop, I have something to say to you." What should I say to him? That we are not guilty and that everything will be explained? Obviously, this is what he expects of me, and then everything would doubtless become easy. But how to tell him this? When we met and when we were only one person, we argued, and the torment was common to both of us. You said to me: "I'm guilty" and I couldn't tell you of what.

(16–17/401–2)

One would need to find a judge to determine guilt or innocence, yet no arbitrator is ever to be found, and the hellish torment never dissipates. Groethuysen suggests that humans have invented legal codes to relieve themselves from the anguish of this indeterminate, interminable guilt. Such clarity, however, is valid only in this world and does not pertain to the absent realm. One may progress comfortably in this well-defined, well-ordered world of laws—in this insomnia between birth and death that one calls life—but the Law itself remains transcendent, lodged in the world of non-being, inaccessible and unreachable.

In neglecting to discuss *The Trial* explicitly, Groethuysen's preface would be ridiculed by later scholars averse to hyper-speculation on Kafka's philosophical import. Yet, the essay does make frequent, implicit allusions to Kafka's work: The harshness of *The Judgment*, the disorientation of *The Castle*, the frustrating claustrophobia of *The Burrow*, the humiliation of *The Metamorphoses*, the confused gazes in *The Hunger Artist*. Groethuysen thereby depicts the Kafkaesque as it would come to be understood, very much linked to the dream world from which one is exiled at birth, an utterly strange land that is nonetheless one's true home, a realm where, as exiles, we run the constant risk of being arrested.

"To be or not to be." The difficult thing is to be. It's quite simple when one is not yet born or when one is dead. No one asks you then what you are doing there. But to live is to do something, to commit oneself to something. . . . You are responsible for what you have done. You must answer . . . No one can escape his examination.

(22/406)

The existentialist theme of responsibility inheres in the dialogic mode: In questioning the text, the reader is in turn pressed to respond. Hence, the essay's conclusion prolongs the discussion between Josef K. and the priest on how to interpret the parable known as *Before the Law*, from the "Cathedral" chapter of *The Trial*. "What are you looking for? Your judgment, that is why you just prostrated yourself before the guardian so that he might let you in to the Law itself" (25/408). To experience the absent world of non-being is to encounter an imperious presence that cannot be mastered, neither by recollection nor by future planning. As Groethuysen summarizes in the final sentence: The majority "hasten to tell themselves: 'I have been dreaming, I must get back to my job.' But those who live waiting for life, hesitating to be born, have no job. Kafka was one of these; his lucid mind could tell us of that abandoned world in which he had journeyed" (29/411).

THE SAINT

Kafka's reception had begun during the author's lifetime, avidly promulgated by his close friend, self-styled agent, and future literary executor, Max Brod. The friendship dates back to the autumn of 1902, when Kafka, then a nineteen-year-old law student, rose to the defense of Nietzsche, whom Brod had denounced as a fraud.[11] However much one might question the degree of Brod's influence on Kafka's career, it is beyond question that, over the subsequent years, with indefatigable optimism, Brod not only served as an important source of advice and encouragement, but also actively used his literary connections to promote his friend's many gifts. As early as 1907, before Kafka had published a single word, Brod singled him out in a profile on young Prague painters as a "very great draughtsman [*Zeichner*]."[12] And it was

---

[11] See Peter-André Alt, *Franz Kafka: Der ewige Sohn* (Munich: Beck, 2005), 112.
[12] Max Brod, "Frühling in Prag" ("Springtime in Prague"), *Die Gegenwart* (May 18, 1907), 316–17.

through Brod that Kafka was introduced to the circle of Prague writers that included Felix and Robert Weltsch, Franz Werfel, Otto Pick, Oskar Baum, and Willy Haas.

In 1908, Brod facilitated Kafka's first publications in the inaugural issue of Franz Blei's periodical, *Hyperion*, which would form the core of Kafka's first book, *Betrachtung*, published in Leipzig by Ernst Rowohlt in 1913. In commenting on this collection, Brod celebrated the "sovereignty of the prose style," its "absoluteness [*Unbedingtheit*]" and "dialectical movement," but also a certain "immediacy, with which Kafka sets in place of reality the formal language that is peculiar to him."[13] In subsequent essays, however, attentiveness to Kafka's style shifted to matters of content, which reflected Brod's ambition to position his friend as a spokesman for modern Jewish experience. In his essay, "Our Literary Writers and the Community," published in Martin Buber and Salman Schocken's monthly, *Der Jude*, in October 1916, Brod claims that Kafka's work uniquely depicts the Jewish sense of isolation, including self-isolation, not as a cause of pain but rather as the result of sin and remorse, a profound guilt that can only be remedied through reintegration with society and with God.[14]

The thematic and formal aspects came together in Brod's essay, "Der Dichter Franz Kafka," which appeared in *Die neue Rundschau* in 1921. The title already betrays an intention to elevate Kafka to the status of "inspired poet" or *Dichter*, as distinct from the quotidian profession of "writer" or *Schriftsteller*. Accordingly, Brod praises Kafka's work for its "truthfulness, unwavering genuineness [*Echtheit*], and purity," which shine forth without the dazzling artifice that one typically finds among modernists.[15] The language is "crystal clear," like a sweet "melody," and yet contains "dreams and visions of immeasurable depth" (1210–11). Rather than provide specific illustrations, Brod enhances his claims with provocative thought-images: "If angels were to make jokes in heaven, it would have to be in Franz Kafka's language!" (1210). Here, weakness combines with strength, "the sublimity of the infinite realm" with the "convulsions of the creature"—in brief, "the profound seriousness of the religious man" (1210). Unlike other contemporary authors, Kafka describes modern decadence without lust. "He suffers degradation, while seeing and loving the good way, the determination,

---

[13] Brod, "Kleine Prosa," *Die neue Rundschau* (July 1913), 1044–5; cited in Beicken, *Franz Kafka: Eine kritische Einführung in die Forschung*, 22.
[14] See Ruth Gross, "Early Critical Reception," in *Franz Kafka in Context*, ed. Carolin Duttlinger (Cambridge: Cambridge University Press, 2017), 259–66; here, p. 261.
[15] Brod, "Der Dichter Franz Kafka," *Die neue Rundschau* (November 1921), 1210.

the cohesion, and loves nothing so much as the blue, unsullied sky above him, the eternally saving, perfect sky" (1210).

Brod places especial emphasis on hope, a theme he broaches with the now famous remark he heard from Kafka: "There is plenty of hope, an infinite amount of hope—only not for us" (1210). As Brod comments: "One can name it neither optimism nor pessimism, it is a despair that is boundless [*grenzenlos*] in depth, yet bounded [*begrenztem*] in scope, narrowly circumscribed in base." In Brod's reading, Kafka's despair is exceptional and frightening yet does not deny divine goodwill. "He does not quarrel with God, only with himself." The descent into hopelessness is but a mark of human guilt, the failure to recognize the grand and beautiful order of God's creation, which exists and persists despite our inability to grasp it.

> Then one understands that Kafka, in addition to the general tragedy of mankind, writes in particular of the suffering of his unhappy people, of homeless, ghostly Jewry, of the masses without form, without body, like no one else. Writes, without the word "Jew" appearing in any of his books. But if one wants parallels for the unconstrained meaningfulness and clarity of his dreams, one must open cabbalistic books, messianic hopes of the 16th century, blood-related books that he never read.
> (1211)

Brod thus transforms Kafka into a mythic hero, a saint, or a prophet, or even a founder of a new, modern religion, someone whose work portrays a realm of hopelessness that nonetheless whispers a hint of salvation. As for *The Trial*, Brod stresses the theological concept of original sin, relating man's search for God to Josef K.'s struggle to discover meaning in a senseless reality. The protagonist is likened to the biblical Job, who grapples with God's apparent injustice, an injustice that can be addressed only by God's merciful grace, which Brod discerns as the chief theme of *The Castle*. If Josef K. had not denied his guilt, if he did not obstinately refuse to accept the validity of the trial, he would have received the blessing of God's beneficence, rather than suffer a horrible fate.

Altogether, Brod's religious reading is highly optimistic, implying that modern humanity can be ultimately saved through the severity of God's judgment. In this way, Brod aims to reconcile the cheerful, lighthearted disposition of the friend he knew with the melancholic, guilt-ridden texts and diaries he left behind. As a result, Brod overlooks other possible interpretations of the work. He cannot, for example, consider that a life of hopelessness is much more torturous when the universe is thought to be replete with hope. Subsequent scholars and critics either rejected or expanded on Brod's theological take. In his essay "Über Franz Kafka" (1929), Walter Muschg instead reads *The Trial* as a tragic satire of our modern institutions of justice and mindless bureaucracy, while Willy Haas, writing in 1934, aligns Kafka's thought to Kierkegaard's emphases on faith over belief and love over law. Both interpretative trajectories would continue to define the general reception history.

For the moment, in the 1933 edition of *Le Procès*, Brod was given the last word: A brief "Post-Scriptum" printed at the end of the volume. The text is Vialatte's translation of the afterword that Brod included in the original German edition of 1925. Here, before indulging in the theological issues from earlier essays, Brod recounts Kafka's insistence that his uncompleted manuscripts be destroyed. "I wrested from Kafka nearly everything he published either by persuasion or by guile."[16] Brod transcribes the two notes that Kafka addressed to him yet insists that he informed his friend categorically, that he would never carry out this wish. Brod's excessive attempt at exculpation is proportionate to his heavy conscience. The universal, existential guilt described in Groethuysen's preface thus modulates into a deeply personal affair in Brod's afterword. As in Kafka's novel, and as Brod admits, the trial could go on indefinitely, "prolonged into infinity" (346/271), even if the author supplied the final execution. Without ever arriving before the highest court, all are condemned to a realm of absurdity.

A CERTAIN PLUME

As the foundation for conceptualizing Kafka's achievement was being laid across the 1930s, a poet emerged who shared the Prague author's keen awareness of the absurdity of existence as well as his profound sense of humor. The Belgian-born writer and artist Henri Michaux seemed to be coupled with the French Kafka from the start. We recall that Michaux's first semi-autobiographical collection, *Qui je fus* ("Who I was"), which was published by Gallimard under Paulhan's directorship, was reviewed by Gabriel Bounoure in the January 1928 number of the *NRF*. Moreover, Michaux dedicated a section of this work, "Énigmes," to his close friend Jules Supervielle, who collaborated with Félix Bertaux in translating the six short pieces by Kafka for the *NRF* in August 1929.

---

[16] The French translation of Brod's afterword appears on pp. 339–47. English citations are from Kafka, *The Trial*, tr. Willa and Edwin Muir (New York: Schocken, 1968), 264–71; here, p. 339 and 264, respectively.

Finally, in the July 1930 issue of *Bifur*, the Klossowski-Leyris translation of Kafka's *Judgment* was immediately followed by Michaux's *Drame des constructeurs* (*The Drama of the Constructors*), an excerpt from his collection *Un certain Plume*. As the decade wore on, the effects of this uncanny Doppelgänger would be increasingly felt.

Michaux's poem, "Encore des changements" ("Still more changes"), published in the November 1929 issue of *La Revue européenne*, features a narrator who undergoes constant metamorphoses, beginning with one that immediately calls to mind Gregor Samsa.

À force de souffrir, je perdis les limites de mon corps et me démesurai irrésistiblement.

Je fus toutes choses : des fourmis surtout, interminablement à la file, laborieuses et toutefois hésitante. C'était un mouvement fou.

Il me fallait toute mon attention.

Je m'aperçus bientôt que non seulement j'étais les fourmis, mais aussi j'étais leur chemin.[17]

By dint of suffering, I lost the limits of my body and I became irresistibly disproportionate.

I was all things: ants especially, interminably in line, laborious and yet hesitant. It was a mad movement.

I needed all my attention.

I soon realized that I was not only the ants, but I was also their path.

Michaux's narrator exhibits the same tone as Kafka's protagonist, dispassionate despite the bizarre experience, providing an evenly paced account of the consequences. Like Gregor Samsa, Michaux's narrator retains his human consciousness after human corporeal limits have been transgressed. One might even call it a liberation.

The pieces included in *Un certain Plume* (1930) likewise invite comparisons with Kafka's visions. The one-act *Drama of the Constructors*,

---

[17] Henri Michaux, *Œuvres complètes*, Bibliothèque de la Pléiade, vol. 1., ed. Raymond Bellour (Paris: Gallimard, 1998), 479.

set in the garden outside an insane asylum, centers on four "madmen" who build alternative worlds: "Often, playing with dice, I suddenly say to myself: 'With this die, I could build a city' and I refuse to stop playing until I have constructed a city."[18] The premise is reminiscent of Kafka's *Description of a Struggle*, where the nameless protagonist causes the landscape to appear at will, but only after the self has been reduced to a site of the shifting phenomena that construct reality. This psychology underwrites the self-effacement discernible in the figures who appear in Michaux as well. "I who have constructed so much in my eyes that I am about to lose my sight!"[19]

Most of the Plume vignettes present situations that either transgress social expectations or defy physical laws. A "peaceable man," Plume takes everything in stride with an equanimity that is incongruous with the occasion—awaking in bed to discover that his house has been stolen during the night, enjoying a meal until the maître d' informs him that the item he is eating is not on the menu, conversing with an eager surgeon who wants to amputate his index finger even though it only aches slightly. The predicaments often recall the short films of Charlie Chaplin, and indeed, in 1924 Michaux had edited a special issue of the Belgian surrealist review, *Le Disque vert*, entirely devoted to the cinematic comic.[20] Among contributions from many avant-gardists—Blaise Cendrars, Jean Cocteau, René Crevel, Max Jacob, Francis Ponge, and Philippe Soupault—was Michaux's own "Our Brother Charlie," which hailed the slapstick genius as the incarnation of the latest aesthetic trends. The volume, incidentally, also included an article by Lucia Joyce, spruced up and prefaced by Valéry Larbaud.

In 1936, while serving as Belgium's representative at the international PEN writers' conference in Buenos Aires, Michaux met Borges, and they apparently discussed their shared fondness for Kafka. So inspired, Michaux delivered two public lectures in Argentina, one on Chaplin, the other on Kafka, who are both portrayed as revolutionaries. In Richard Sieburth's summary: Chaplin is proffered as bestowing "a

---

[18] Henri Michaux, *A Certain Plume* (bilingual edition), tr. Richard Sieburth (New York: New York Review of Books, 2018), 84–5.
[19] Michaux, *A Certain Plume*, 90–1.
[20] On the relationship between Chaplin's persona and Michaux's Plume, see Jean-Claude Mathieu, "Légère lecture de Plume," in *Ruptures sur Henri Michaux*, ed. Roger Dadoun (Paris: Payot, 1976), 101–57, esp. pp. 110–13; and Nathalie Gillain, "Charlot, une source d'inspiration pour Henri Michaux: De la figuration de mouvements à la subversion des genres," *Études françaises* 55 (2019), 95–113.

'new consciousness,' a new 'élan' upon mankind by breaking through its centuries of inertia"; while Kafka is seen as an author who "had cultivated within himself those 'paranormal' states of mind achieved only by ascetics, mystics, magicians, and the mad."[21]

In 1938, Michaux returned to Plume and produced a complete collection that combined the old material with the new: *Plume, précédé de Lointain intérieur*—the latter title variously translated as "Far-off Inside" (Ellmann) and "Faraway Within" (Sieburth). Michaux's battered anti-hero drew further comparisons with Kafka's protagonists and style.[22] As Claude-Edmonde Magny observes: "In Kafka as in Michaux, the same short sentences, without consolation; the same absolute simplicity pushed to banality in the midst of which, however, the unusual is installed from the start."[23] A telling example is the piece entitled "Plume on the Ceiling," where Michaux's anti-hero loses himself in distraction and walks "across the ceiling on his feet, instead of keeping the on the ground."[24] Gregor Samsa, as well, "for mere recreation had formed the habit of crawling crisscross over the walls and ceiling. He especially enjoyed hanging suspended from the ceiling; it was much better than lying on the floor; one could breathe more freely" (CS 115/KGW 1, 126–7). In both texts, the absurdity is posited then explored to its logical conclusions. After a search party manages to carry Plume down from the ceiling, all find themselves ill at ease. "Plume just flicked the dust off his sleeves, too embarrassed to reply" (180–1).

Michaux's nom de plume resembles aspects of Kafka's signature K. in the humorous amenability that takes things as they come without asking embarrassing questions, in the quiet passivity in the face of mistreatment. Having proclaimed himself a land surveyor off the cuff only to discover that the Castle has been expecting one, K. takes everything in stride, just like Michaux's Plume.

---

[21] Richard Sieburth, "Translator's Afterword: A Pen in Search of an Author," in Henri Michaux, *A Certain Plume* (New York: New York Review of Books, 2018), 214.

[22] For a comprehensive comparison of Michaux and Kafka, see Maja Goth, *Franz Kafka et les Lettres françaises* (Paris: Corti, 1956), 65–96; and Richard Ellmann's "Introduction" to his translation, Henri Michaux, *Selected Writings: The Space Within* (New York: New Directions, 1968), viii–ix.

[23] Claude-Edmonde Magny, "L'univers d'Henri Michaux et de Kafka," *La Revue internationale* (October 1946), n. p.

[24] Michaux, *A Certain Plume*, 178–9.

Plume cannot claim that people are overly considerate of him when he travels. There are those who shove him aside without the slightest warning and others who calmly wipe their hands clean on his jacket. These are things he has ended up getting used to. He prefers to travel modestly.

(12–13)

For both authors, as well, humor is but the reverse side of anguish. In a later poem, Michaux seems to furnish a gloss on the confusion suffered by Kafka's protagonists:

> La prison ouvre sur une prison
> Le couloir ouvre un autre couloir
> . . .
> Rien ne débouche nulle part.[25]
>
> The prison opens onto a prison
> The corridor opens another corridor
> . . .
> Nothing leads anywhere.

EXTREMISM

Throughout the 1930s, Kafka was embraced by the Surrealists. Having passed away only months before the First Surrealist Manifesto was published, Kafka had witnessed the devastation of the Great War and the dissolution of the thousand-year-old Habsburg dynasty. Thus, his works would be expected to reflect the same exhaustion the Surrealists felt: The ennui, the despair, the visceral disgust with the bourgeois world, its myopic materialism, and desiccating routines. Kafka's portrayals of narrating animals seemed to tap into the dark side of reality, the underbelly of human consciousness, and convey messages from the magnetic fields.

> Prisoners of drops of water, we are but perpetual animals. We run through the cities without noise and the charming posters do not touch us. What good are these grand fragile enthusiasms, these dried-out leaps of joy? We know nothing more than dead stars;

---

[25] Michaux, *Épreuves, Exorcismes* (Paris: Gallimard, 1949), 66–7.

we look at the faces; and we sigh with pleasure. Our mouth is drier than deserted beaches; our eyes turn aimlessly, without hope.[26]

André Breton and his allies discerned a common fascination with religious-mystical motifs, a proclivity towards the fantastic, and an overall belief that quotidian reality can be irradiated by revolutionary transcendence. Kafka, they surmised, shared in their great Refusal. They were thus attracted to figures which exhibited their sensibilities: Schmar, the somnambulant murderer liberated to sadistic desires in *A Fratricide*, the father in *The Judgment* who radiates with mad insight, the elderly bachelor Blumfeld fatigued by utilitarian society, the Hunter Gracchus, no longer alive yet unable to die, or Josef K. in *A Dream*, who slips into his freshly dug tomb. The Surrealists mined Kafka's texts for passages that confirmed their worldview, texts that depicted the incursion of dreams in reality, eroticism, humor, madness, revolt, and delirious self-surrender.[27] The clairvoyant madman in *Description of a Struggle* might recall Breton's Nadja, while Michel Carrouges relates the torture apparatus of the *Penal Colony* to the design in Marcel Duchamp's *Large Glass*.[28]

Whereas Kafka, under Paulhan's editorship, had been cast as a modern French classic, he was also seen to keep company with a more eccentric lot in search of transgressive experience: Henri Parisot, known primarily for his translations of Lewis Carroll; Jean Carrive, one of the signatories of Breton's first Manifesto; and the Belgian surrealist, Marcel Lecomte, who proposed that *The Metamorphosis* narrates a dream that Gregor Samsa is having while asleep in his bed.[29] Kafka's work appeared in Surrealist magazines, his stories were illustrated by Max Ernst and Mario Prassinos, his unnerving narratives accompanied by Benjamin Péret, Paul Éluard, and Ferdinand Alquié. Like Lautréamont and Rimbaud, Kafka was celebrated as a poet who could shock the populace, instill a healthy anarchism, and combat self-censorship and hypocrisy.

---

[26] André Breton and Philippe Soupault, *Les champs magnétiques* [1920], in Breton, *Œuvres complètes*, vol. 1. Bibliothèque de la Pléiade, ed. Marguerite Bonnet (Paris: Gallimard, 1988), 53.
[27] For a useful comparison of Kafka and the Surrealists, see Goth, *Franz Kafka et les Lettres françaises*, 13–63.
[28] Michel Carrouges, "La Machine-Célibataire selon Kafka et Marcel Duchamp," *Mercure de France* 1066 (June 1952), 262–81.
[29] Marcel Lecomte, *Note sur Kafka et le rêve (La Métamorphose)*, in *Rêve*, ed. André Breton (Paris, 1938).

In the wake of the global financial crisis, Kafka readily accommodated the extremist positions that rose up against the perceived failures of bourgeois democracy and capitalism, positions that Paulhan would come to designate collectively as Terror.[30] In Paulhan's view, if the Great War was a national conflict, the next would be ideological: Nationalism versus internationalism, fascism versus communism, a struggle between the reactionary anti-parliamentarians who viewed the democratic system as compromising, timid, and incompetent and the progressive wing, which railed against capitalist exploitation, greed, and corruption.[31] The pressures of this fervent, troublesome decade motivated Breton's allegiance to Soviet communism, which even seduced Gide: "If the success of the USSR required that I give my life, I would give it immediately,"[32] but likewise inspired the anti-communist, anti-capitalist stance of a young Maurice Blanchot, whose subsequent devotion to the exigencies of Kafka's writing would betray the purism of his dissident years. Like Kafka, whose creative pursuits had been hampered by obligatory work, Blanchot began working on his first novel, *Thomas the Obscure*, in 1932, in the midst of producing daily articles for the *Journal des Débats*, writing through the night, in search of "the other night" reserved for the "space of literature." Given the madness of the day, Blanchot would have to wait until the German invasion of France in May 1940 before he felt ready to submit his manuscript to Paulhan, and only after he had withdrawn from political engagement. Meanwhile, in the mid-30s, anti-German nationalists, once inspired by Charles Maurras—Blanchot, Thierry Maulnier, and Jean-Luc Maxence—launched the journal *L'Insurgé* in January 1937 to denounce Léon Blum's Front Populaire, a government of conciliatory fellow travelers which was also lambasted by extremists like Breton. Right and Left were thus united in their revulsion of the middle ground.

It is while caught in this milieu that Breton published, in 1937, his *Têtes d'orage* ("Storm heads") in the surrealist journal *Minotaure*. Here, he reflects on the work of writers he regards as kindred spirits.[33] The ' list features three French and three German radicals from the eighteenth-century to the present. For the French representatives, Breton begins

---

[30] Jean Paulhan, *Les Fleurs de Tarbes, ou la terreur dans les lettres* [1941], ed. Jean-Claude Zylberstein (Paris: Gallimard, 1990).
[31] Cf. Anna-Louise Milne, *The Extreme In-Between: Jean Paulhan's Place in the Twentieth Century* (London: Routledge, 2006), 11–44.
[32] Entry of April 23, 1932, in André Gide, *Journal*, vol. 1, ed. Éric Marty (Paris: Gallimard, 1996), 1126.
[33] André Breton, *Têtes d'orage*, Minotaure 10 (1937), 9, 17–19.

with Xavier Forneret (1809–84), a leading member of the Bouzingos, a late-romantic bohemian group, which included Théophile Gautier and Nerval.[34] Next, one finds Jean-Pierre Brisset (1837–1919), the notorious *fou littéraire* who developed a theoretical system for learned fools (*morosophy*) and linguistically demonstrated that human beings were descended from frogs; in 1912, Jules Romains staged a mock election that bestowed on Brisset the title of "Prince of Thinkers."[35] To round off the French list, Breton turns to the recently deceased Raymond Roussel (1887–1933), the experimental provocateur who would gain great acclaim among the associates of OuLiPo in the 1960s. As for the Germans, Breton reaches back to the arch-satirist and aphorist Georg-Christoph Lichtenberg (1742–99) and the rather caustic dramatist Christian-Dietrich Grabbe (1801–36), before alighting on Kafka with a discussion complemented by a drawing entitled *Odradek* by Max Ernst. The article was expanded in Breton's *Anthologie de l'humour noir* (*Anthology of Black Humor*), first published in 1940, which amasses an inebriating array of forty-five authors and artists, still mostly French and German, yet also including Jonathan Swift, Thomas de Quincey, and Edgar Allan Poe. Since the publication of the first Surrealist Manifesto in 1924, one had become accustomed to Breton's eclectic lists.

Like Groethuysen, Breton appeals to the universal human significance of Kafka's writings, finding therein "the most important question of all times: where is one going [*où va-t-on*], to what is one subjected [*à quoi est-on soumis*], what is the law?"[36] Although he alludes to Kafka's Prague, Breton insists that the work applies to all mortals from all ages. Accordingly, Breton links Kafka to yet another French romantic, Alphonse Rabbe (1784–1829), the author of *Album d'un pessimiste*, whom he cites:

> God has subjected the world to the action of certain secondary laws that are executed for the accomplishment of a goal that is unknown to us, announcing to us, however, by the powerful voice of moral instinct, the *invisible world of solemn reparations*, where everything will be revealed, explained.
>
> (263; emphasis in text)

---

[34] See Enid Starkie, "Bouzingos and Jeunes-France," in *On Bohemia*, ed. César Graña and Marigay Graña (London: Taylor & Francis, 1990), 364–9.
[35] For a comprehensive account of Brisset's life and work, see Walter Redfern, *All Puns Intended: The Verbal Creation of Jean-Pierre Brisset* (London: Taylor & Francis, 2017).
[36] Breton, *Anthologie de l'humour noir* [1940], 2nd ed. (Paris: Sagittaire 1950), 263.

The optimism, which could be viewed as corroborating Brod's interpretation, portrays Kafka as a creator of a mysterious universe, a surrealist at heart, who understood the power of dreams and their capacity to offer a means of escape from a dead, hyper-rationalized world. Yet, to maintain this interpretation, Breton must be highly selective and pass over those texts in Kafka that are less amenable to surrealist appropriation.

To spare himself the effort, Breton gives the last word to Vialatte, citing the translator's advertisement printed on the inside cover of the 1933 edition of *Le Procès*, yet without attribution. "'It is man,' it has been said, 'who boils in Kafka's cooking pot. He meticulously simmers in the murky broth of anxiety, but humor blows the lid off with a whistle and traces in the air cabalistic formulas in blue letters'" (264). The striking image of universal man stewing in the author's cauldron, the explosive humor born of pent-up anxiety, and the enigmatic inscriptions that form as a result—all rhyme with Breton's aesthetic sensibilities. In occluding his source, Breton endorses Vialatte's will to be the absent translator, while also reconfirming the surrealist precept, that what is most powerfully revealing comes from an unknown source that eludes subjective anchoring and rational censorship, that the origin of knowledge is itself unknowable, not unlike a dream, not unlike a river.

Perhaps closer to Kafka's susceptibilities was Michel Leiris, the ruthless autoptician, whose writing persistently gravitated towards a profound sense of futility, mediocrity, and guilt. An early contributor to *La Révolution surréaliste* and also one of the *Cadavre* dissidents who broke with Breton in 1929, Leiris subsisted in the margins as a master of self-effacement or camouflage. His novel, *Aurora*, written in the late 1920s, portrays a protagonist meandering through a dreamscape that shares a long border with Kafka's terrain, while his autobiographical texts, *L'Âge d'homme* (1939), which was dedicated to Bataille, and the *Règle du jeu* tetralogy (1948–76), as well as his private journals (1922–89), exhibit an eyes-wide-shut compulsion to register and ponder and obsess in ways that are often quite reminiscent of Kafka's diaries and notebooks. Driven by a need for precise observation, both attend to the seepage of dreams into reality and their torturous effects.

> In the afternoon while falling asleep. As though the solid skullcap encircling the insensitive cranium had moved more deeply inwards and left a part of the brain exposed to the free play of light and muscles. To awaken on a cold autumn morning full of yellowish light. To force your way through the half-shut window and while still in front of the panes, before you fall, to hover, arms extended, belly arched, legs curved backwards, like the figures on the bows of ships in old times.
>
> (Kafka, *Diaries*, Nov. 14, 1911; KGW 9, 193/D 117)

The dream carries on in the everyday, the banality. The last image is a kind of leaflet distributed to the workers by a socialist entrepreneur; at the bottom of the paper is drawn a pair of brodequins with buttons, in a style reminiscent of some old shoemakers' signs.

(Leiris, *L'Âge d'homme*)[37]

NON LIQUET

Unlike the preface to *The Trial*, Brod's afterword to *The Castle*, written for the original 1926 edition and included in Vialatte's 1938 translation, offered a comprehensive interpretation which would have a significant impact on the continuing development of Kafka's reception in France. The basic premise, that the two novels should be read in conjunction, is already suggested by the similarity of the protagonists' names, even though, as Brod notes, Kafka began writing the later novel from a first-person perspective and only subsequently replaced the *I* with the third-person *K*.[38] Beyond this shared link, Brod insists on an exact complementarity. Both works grapple with the same "invisible mysterious authority" from distinct angles: While Josef K. tries to flee from the court to which he is summoned, K. actively attempts to penetrate the inner recesses of the Castle, which wards off his efforts (495). In Brod's view, this incomprehensible, inaccessible power is divinity itself, "the *non liquet* above the lives of all," and its different modes of revelation correspond to "the two manifestations of the Deity (in the sense of the Kabbala)—judgment and grace" (496). Whereas Josef K. anticipates a verdict, K. waits for an appointment. Condemnation in the former case is answered by election in the latter. Apart from the allusion to the Kabbala, Brod does not emphasize the connection to the Jewish diaspora—a connection implicit in his Zionism—that both scenarios have to do with being chosen or singled out, either for conviction or for acquittal, as in the fate of the Jewish multitude, the chosen people condemned to wandering.

The religious reading is nonetheless maintained when Brod turns to Søren Kierkegaard, specifically his reflections on the figure of Abraham in *Fear and Trembling*, a book that "Kafka loved very much, read often, and profoundly commented on in many letters" (500). To illustrate,

---

[37] Michel Leiris, *L'Âge d'homme* (Paris: Gallimard, 1939), 207. See Charles Juliet's essay, "La littérature et le thème de la mort chez Kafka et Leiris," originally published in Bataille's journal *Critique* 126 (November 1957).
[38] Brod, "Nachwort," in Kafka, *Das Schloss* (Munich: Kurt Wolff, 1926), 495.

Brod points to the plight of Amalia, the young woman who spurns the lascivious advances of the Castle official Sortini, which he reads as a direct parallel to the predicament that the biblical patriarch confronted when God issued the criminal command to sacrifice his son. The Castle thus assumes the role of God, whose actions clash with and are thoroughly incommensurable with earthly understanding. According to Brod, both Kierkegaard and Kafka sensed this incommensurability, yet while the conflict led the Christian philosopher towards a renunciation of this world, Kafka's hero adheres to the immanent, human realm, "stubbornly and to the point of exhaustion" (501). Despite the inscrutability of the orders that come from on high, despite the perplexity, the false leads, and the rude rebuffs, the would-be land surveyor allows the Castle to define his life. Even the vituperative outbursts confirm K.'s profound reverence for an authority he can never fathom. Every incident in the novel demonstrates the "distance between human comprehension and the divine dispensation of grace" (501). The reading concurs, therefore, with Kierkegaard's musings on the suspension of the ethical.

Within the scope of an afterword, Brod refrains from delving further into the complexities and ambiguities that mark Kafka's long involvement with Kierkegaard.[39] The task would soon be assumed by other commentators who, in having recourse to the published correspondence and notebooks, would derive and cultivate a repertoire of motifs for theorizing Kafka's achievement and its contribution to formulating new conceptions of the literary. For now, in adducing Kierkegaard, Brod's interpretation would have found much resonance. A year before Vialatte's *Castle* appeared, the novelist Daniel-Rops emphasized the affinity to distinguish Kafka's worldview from that of the surrealists and their adopted precursors, Rimbaud and Lautréamont, whom he charged with striving to escape human reality. "With Kafka, nothing of the sort. This soul, dominated by the passion for the absolute, was truly a spiritual son of Kierkegaard, who, even in the midst of the worst anguish, accepts the human condition and draws from its suffering the fundamental element of its greatness."[40]

Kierkegaard had long been in vogue, generally considered to be the father of existentialism as it was being formulated in the work of Martin

---

[39] For a perspicacious reading of Kafka's reception of Kierkegaard, see Paul North, *The Yield: Kafka's Atheological Reformation* (Stanford: Stanford University Press, 2015), 136–46.

[40] Daniel-Rops, "L'univers désesperé de Franz Kafka," *Les Cahiers du Sud* (March 1937), 161–76; here, p. 173.

Heidegger and Karl Jaspers. The political and religious crises that shattered French society invited serious engagement with the Danish philosopher of anguish and the Absurd, an engagement, however, that tended to bypass the specifically Christian, doctrinal aspects and instead focused on metaphysical questions pertaining to the human finitude and moral choice.[41] In 1932, Jean Wahl, soon to be appointed professor of Philosophy at the Sorbonne, published a series of influential papers, including an article on Kierkegaard's concepts of "existence, isolated man, and subjective thought."[42] For Wahl, Kierkegaard was the efficacious antidote to Hegel insofar as his work supplied compelling arguments for rejecting the idealist identification of the rational and the real. This view was corroborated and expanded in 1936 by the French translation of *Kierkegaard and Existential Philosophy*, a book-length study by the Russian refugee Lev Shestov, who magnified the power of paradox by accentuating the finitude, singularity, and evil that could short-circuit reasoning and thus broach alternative paths of thinking and new conceptions of human freedom.[43] Shestov enchanted rogue surrealists like Bataille who were interested in exploring the darker, irrational undercurrents in human cultures, effects attributable to an experience of the sacred and its detachment from ordinary, useful society. In naming both the holy and the accursed, the sacred—that which is *sacer*—relates to the paradoxes of faith which break with conventional logic and ethics in a sacrificial, sacralizing leap. Such Kierkegaardian themes, infused by a good dose of Nietzsche's Dionysianism, inspired Bataille's new journal *Acéphale* and the formation of the Collège de Sociologie, an informal gathering of intellectuals that included Roger Caillois, Leiris, Wahl, Paulhan, Klossowski, the Hegelian interpreter Alexandre Kojève and the experimental artist André Masson—a galvanizing coterie that would also attract thinkers from across the political spectrum: Pierre Drieu la Rochelle, Julien Benda, and Walter Benjamin among others.[44]

What we see taking shape across the first decade of Kafka's French reception is a complex image imbued with multifarious lines of

---

[41] See Margaret Teboul, "La réception de Kierkegaard en France 1930–1960," *Revues des sciences philosophiques et théologiques* 89 (2005), 315–36.
[42] Jean Wahl, "Sur quelques catégories kierkegaardiennes: l'existence, l'homme isolé, la pensée subjective," *Recherches philosophiques* 3 (1933–34). This article would form the basis of Wahl's subsequent study, *Études kierkegaardiennes* (Paris: Aubier, 1938).
[43] See Treboul, "La reception de Kierkegaard," 326.
[44] For a comprehensive account, see Denis Hollier, *The College of Sociology, 1937–1939*, tr. Betsy Wing (Minneapolis: University of Minnesota Press, 1988).

reflection and driven by diverse concerns, from Groethuysen's phenomenological dialogism and Brod's theological exegeses to Breton's assault on inhibition, Wahl's importation of *Existenzphilosophie*, and Bataille's promulgation of the sacred. All contributed to a forceful and persistent undercurrent replete with thematic figures which, in the wake of another world war, would sometimes corroborate and sometimes challenge the interpretations ascribable to the existentialist humanism of Sartre and Camus, as Kafka steadily transmogrified into the Kafkaesque.

IV Contingencies

PREOCCUPATIONS

It was a cloudless morning in Montparnasse, a Friday in late summer, warm and tranquil. As she took her seat at the Brasserie aux Trois Mousquetaires, Simone de Beauvoir found herself in a surprisingly excellent mood. Everything in her life seemed to have settled into place. The morning newspapers had tempered their alarmist tone, even if they failed to express much hope. Beauvoir stared blankly ahead, motionless, as if waiting for something decisive to surface, something that would break the eerie peace, which must have increasingly assumed the air of guilty pleasure. She braced herself like a defendant unaware of the charge, anxious for the jury to return and provide clarification, however dismal. After breakfast, she strolled down the Avenue du Maine and entered Le Dôme Café, just in time for the delivery of the noontime paper, the *Paris-Midi*. The waiter glanced at the headline, stood somberly amid the tables, and announced the news that everyone had been expecting but few wished to believe: "They've declared war on Poland!"[1] The verdict was in.

Sartre wasted no time in fetching his draft papers and his military-issued musette bag, even though the French government had not yet given the mobilization order. When official notification came through later that evening, Beauvoir accompanied him to the designated assembly point at the Place Hébert, near the Porte de la Chapelle. The scene was not what they had anticipated. Although notices to the People of Paris had been posted, the square was completely empty save for two policemen standing nonchalantly beneath the streetlamp. There were no crowds of conscripted men, no bustling, no tearful farewells, only this pair of uniformed men who failed to exhibit the urgency of the moment. Apparently the only person who bothered to show up, Sartre presented the officers his papers and politely requested that he be sent at once to Nancy. According to Beauvoir, "Sartre was playing Monsieur Plume mobilized."[2]

"Come at midnight if you like," one of the policemen replied, "but we can't send a train just for you." Having made no progress, Sartre, like Michaux's peaceable misfit, agreed to come back the next morning,

---

[1] Details are taken from Simone de Beauvoir's account of September 1–2, 1939 in her *Journal de guerre: Septembre 1939–Janvier 1941*, ed. Sylvie le Bon-de Beauvoir (Paris: Gallimard, 1990), 13–16. [Beauvoir, *Wartime Diary*, tr. Anne Deing Cordero (Champaign: University of Illinois Press, 2008), 37–9.]

[2] Beauvoir, *Wartime Diary*, 38 [*Journal de guerre*, 14].

when surely others would have responded to the nation's call of duty. Yet when they returned just before dawn, they discovered that the scene had not changed at all. The same two policemen still stood beneath the streetlamp's anemic glow in the otherwise desolate square. It was as if the guardians of the law had been posted for Sartre, for him and him alone. Beauvoir thus shifts from Michaux to another author: *On dirait un roman de Kafka*, "It looked like a Kafka novel."

Beauvoir and Sartre had been preoccupied with Kafka at least since 1933. "*The Trial* appeared, but created little excitement at the time, the critics showing a marked preference for Hans Fallada; but for us it was one of the finest and best books we had read in a very long while. We perceived at once that it was pointless to reduce it to mere allegory, or search through it for symbolical interpretations."[3] The reminiscence, published in Beauvoir's 1961 autobiography, is telling in at least two respects. First, the jab against professional critics of the day recalls that, although Kafka's novels and stories were currently, circa 1960, lauded as uncontested classics—perhaps as the most important body of work of the twentieth century—it was not immediately the case; that despite a rather small group of afficionados, Kafka would remain relatively unknown until after 1945. The claim that she and Sartre recognized Kafka's greatness early on serves to confirm the astuteness of their aesthetic judgment. As for the second point, the couple is said to have recognized the limitations of reading Kafka's work as allegorical or symbolic. With this claim, Beauvoir's statement becomes defensive, for it counters the view, currently being voiced, that so-called "existentialist" readings reduce Kafka's texts to an allegorical function, that for Sartre and his ilk, Kafka is more an abstract philosopher than a literary artist. In presenting Sartre and herself as anti-allegorists, Beauvoir aims to set the record straight and have an oft-expressed charge dismissed. As Jo Bogaerts has shown, however, the debate is much more complex. Existentialist interpretations may appeal to a common human condition, one that transcends historical-cultural determinations, and they may for this reason decontextualize the work in favor of its universal applicability, but only when literature is seen as a privileged medium for comprehending lived experience irreducible to conceptual understanding.[4]

---

[3] Simone de Beauvoir, *Prime of Life*, tr. Peter Green (New York: Harper and Row, 1976), 150.

[4] Jo Bogaerts, "Against Allegory: A Reappraisal of French Existentialism's Encounter with Franz Kafka," *Journal of the Kafka Society of America* 37 (2015), 27–44.

In comparing Sartre's mobilization in 1939 to a Kafka novel, Beauvoir's journal entry anticipates a major trend of the postwar period—namely, to conflate the existentialist worldview with the "Kafkaesque."[5] This merger of a philosophy and a literary style developed gradually and not without many significant detours, fueled by a network of texts published during the Occupation—essays by Camus, Blanchot, Magny, and, of course, Sartre himself. Kafka thus generated a new attitude towards literature in general, a multifaceted, dynamic, and at times self-contradictory theory that grappled with the role and value of literature in human society.

As Sartre would affirm towards the end of his life, the period of intense engagement with Kafka had coincided with his own personal transformation, an emphatic reversal of his earlier detachment, a move from introverted solitude, infused primarily by Husserlian phenomenology, to a more collective commitment to politically engaged literature and Marxism.

> What made it all explode was that one day in September 1939, I received mobilization papers [. . .]. That's what made the social world enter my head. [. . .] The war truly divided my life in two. [. . .] It is there [. . .] that I passed from my prewar individualism and the idea of the pure individual to socialism. This is the real turning point of my life: before, after.[6]

Kafka was the fulcrum. As his letters at the time attest, Sartre's conversion to the social began with what came to be known as the *drôle de guerre*, the tense face-off between German and French troops, without military engagement, from September 1939 to May 1940, a war that Sartre would consistently characterize as a *guerre à la Kafka*.

NOTHING BUT NOTHING

From the start, a foreboding tone is discernible in Beauvoir's account of those first days in September 1939. She cannot evade the looming sense

---

[5] This conflation has been consistently noted by historians and critics. See, for example: Goth, *Kafka et les Lettres françaises*, 137–8; Walter Sokel, "Kafka und Sartres Existenzphilosophie," *Arcadia* 5 (1970), 262–77; and Jo Bogaerts, "Sartre's 'Guerre Fantôme': A Kafkaesque Subtext in the Postwar Writings," *The Germanic Review* 94 (2019), 57–74.

[6] Sartre, "Autoportrait à soixante-dix ans," in *Situations X: Politique et autobiographie* (Paris: Gallimard, 1976), 133–226; here, pp. 180–1.

that History is about to intrude. The possibility of hope is uttered only to be immediately dismissed. Her repeated references to the emptiness of the cafés correlate to her mental blankness, as if she were pure consciousness, absolute nothingness, entirely void, there only to be filled by something. When the news of Germany's attack comes in, that *something* is at hand; and now it is Sartre who allows himself to be carried away by the moment, behaving like Michaux's Plume.

It is unlikely that Beauvoir is implying some delusional fall into literary pretense, some self-deceiving flight into "bad faith." Sartre is hardly a romantic. He is not inebriated by the opportunity to enter the fray, to die nobly for his country or emerge triumphantly as a war hero. The author of *Nausea*, which appeared a year before with Gallimard, recognized the vanity of such narratives and their false promises of conferring meaning to one's life. Delusional readers, Sartre would say, make the mistake of allowing stories to dictate their behavior. Although it is true that narratives possess meaning, readers all too often fail to understand that they are the ones who give the text its meaning and not vice versa. As Sartre will formulate it: "What [the reader] lacks, is meaning, since it is precisely this meaning, total, that he will give to the book he is reading; the meaning he lacks is obviously the meaning of his life."[7] To play "Mr. Plume mobilized," therefore, is to act freely, without determination, which reveals the absurdity of the situation and the gratuity of existence. It is to affirm Michaux's dream to be "nothing and nothing but nothing" (*rien et rien que rien*).[8]

Michaux's latest collection, *Plume, précédé de Lointain intérieur*, was one of Gallimard's best-selling books of 1938. In retrospect, the mishaps that Plume endures, from the banal to the bizarre, spoke to the era by providing a healthy dose of sardonic humor in the face of events felt to be spinning out of control. Against the backdrop of precarious appeasements and general strikes, Michaux's beloved yet discomfiting character shone some light, however weakly, into the growing fog that benighted the times. Michaux's fidelity to Chaplin's spirit would have been especially attractive to Sartre, who, as an adolescent, would accompany his mother to the cinema to drink in "Charlot." Now, in 1939, Sartre's Plume-like, Chaplinesque performance before the recruiting officers would count as his own take on Michaux's *lointain intérieur*, the "far-off inside" or the "faraway within."

---

[7] Sartre, *Que peut la littérature?* ed. Yves Buin (Paris: L'Herne, 1965), 122.
[8] Henri Michaux, "Clown," from *Peintures* (1939), in *L'espace du dedans, Pages choisies, Poésie* (Paris: Gallimard, 1966), 249.

The motif rhymes with Beauvoir's concluding judgment on the episode: The absurdity of two insouciant gendarmes idling in an empty square while the nation should be readying for war, this inane mobilization without movement.

> It looks like a Kafka novel. One gets the impression that Sartre is making an absolutely individual move [*une démarche absolument individuelle de Sartre*], a move free and gratuitous, yet with a profound inevitability [*fatalité*] that comes from within, from way beyond men.[9]

The striking description of a Kafkaesque *fatalité* as both deeply intimate ("from within") and inaccessibly distant or exotic ("from way beyond men") rehearses Michaux's *lointain intérieur*. It registers the contrast between freedom of action and fatal necessity, between gratuitousness, which denotes a deed that need not be done, and inevitability, which signifies what must take place. While contingency yields freedom by negating determination, fatality imposes necessity by rigorously determining activity. Derived from the verb for speaking or telling (*fatur*), fate is essentially a story, a *histoire* or script that constrains "an absolutely individual move." Something powerful and inescapable casts a gloom over Sartre's free decision, revealing the sentiment that his decision is not in fact free, that the story he finds himself in is one that belongs to a transcendent Other, perhaps to History itself. Beauvoir will insist on this portrayal, for example when she describes that evening to their friend, Jacques-Laurent Bost: "It started to resemble Kafka so much, everything seemed free and gratuitous and at the same time ineluctable."[10]

Beauvoir already conjured the fatalistic course of History in an earlier passage of the diary entry from September 1. After the initial non-event at the assembly point at the Place Hébert, the couple wandered back to their usual haunt, the Café de Flore, then passed before the Church of Saint-Germain-des-Prés, whose tower glowed in the moonlight, with a serenity that felt more provisional than usual.

> At the base of everything, and before one, an ungraspable horror; one can predict nothing, imagine nothing, touch nothing. In any case, it's better not to try. One is entirely barred and strained

---

[9] Beauvoir, *Wartime Diary*, 39 [*Journal de guerre*, 15–16].
[10] Simone de Beauvoir–Jacques-Laurent Bost, *Correspondance croisée (1937–1940)*, ed. Sylvie le Bon-de Beauvoir (Paris: Gallimard, 2004), 433.

inside, strained in order to preserve a void—and an impression of fragility: a single false move would suffice to turn suddenly into intolerable suffering. On the Rue de Rennes, for a moment, I feel like I am melting into little pieces.[11]

Beauvoir's use of the indefinite pronoun (*on ne peut rien prévoir, rien imaginer, rien toucher*, "one can predict nothing, imagine nothing, touch nothing"), while perfectly idiomatic for describing the general situation, supplies foil for the emergence of the personal pronoun at the paragraph's conclusion (*je me sens fondre en petits morceaux*, "I feel I am melting into little pieces"), an assertion of subjective presence at the very moment of its dissolution. It is the iterative perception of nothingness (*rien ... rien ... rien*), against which there can be no struggle. For how can anyone struggle against nothing? It is a nothingness that functions not only as the objectless source of anxiety, but also as that which constitutes the contingency of existence. A nothingness that allows Sartre to make an absolutely individual move, free and gratuitous, yet also powerful enough to counter this freedom, to sweep him off, fatally.

SEASICKNESS ON LAND

The tension between the gratuitous and the ineluctable points directly to Sartre's *Nausea*. Indeed, Beauvoir's description of the encounter in the deserted Place Hébert seems to adapt one particular scene in the novel, when the narrator-protagonist, Antoine Roquentin, chases after an adventure that might bestow meaning on his meaningless existence.

> Something is going to happen: something is waiting for me in the shadow of the Rue Basse-de-Vieille, it is over there, just at the corner of this calm street that my life is going to begin. I see myself advancing with a sense of fatality ... I stop for a moment, I wait, I feel my heart beating; my eyes search the empty square. I see nothing. A fairly strong wind has risen. I am mistaken.[12]

---

[11] Beauvoir, *Wartime Diary*, 39 (tr. modified) [*Journal de guerre*, 15].
[12] Sartre, *Nausea*, tr. Lloyd Alexander (New York: New Directions, 2013), 54–5. [*La Nausée*, in Sartre, *Œuvres romanesques*, Bibliothèque de la Pléiade, ed. Michel Contat and Michel Rybalka (Paris: Gallimard, 1981), 66–7.]

Just as Roquentin pounces on the idea that his life is finally about to begin, that some fatality or destiny is in fact driving him forward, so Sartre himself freely pursues military service, only to discover, like his literary counterpart, nothing but an "empty square." One thinks, for instance, of Kafka's K., how he seeks legitimization from the Castle authorities who evade his inquiries, or Josef K. in *The Trial*, who strives for exoneration for an unknown crime from a high court that is never in session. Roquentin differs from them only in that he reflects on the conflict. He comes to recognize the fiction or non-existence of any narrative that would confer redemptive meaning to one's life. He comes to realize that nothing of value ever happens. In the passage above, the claim that *something is going to happen* is merely a set-up for the ultimate confession: *I am mistaken*.

In *Nausea*, the distinction between existential gratuity and necessity correlates to the difference between real-life and art. As Roquentin asserts:

> One has to choose: Live or tell.... Nothing happens while you live ... There are never any beginnings. Days are tacked on to days without rhyme or reason, an interminable, monotonous addition.... Neither is there any end: one never leaves a woman, a friend, a city in one go.... That's living. But everything changes when you recount a life.
>
> (48–9/39)

In contrast to life, stories exhibit a determined structure, with beginnings and endings driven by a causal logic that makes them meaningful. The nausea that accompanies the experience of nothingness, the recognition of life's absurdity, can therefore be treated by a turn to imagined forms. In bad faith, one wholly identifies with the necessity of art and artifice, one believes that this necessity can be one's own. Hence, the seductive charm of the adventures one foresees divulging to a captive audience, the stories that demonstrate a rationale after the fact, the plots that prove one's life to be meaningful and purposive both to others and to oneself. In *Nausea*, the Autodidact's humanism, Pancôme's self-sufficiency, Doctor Rogé's confidence—all suffer, according to Roquentin, from this delusion. Yet that does not preclude an authentic option, when the turn to art recognizes that the form receives its meaning from consciousness alone, that everything is contingent.

> To exist is simply *to be there*; those who exist let themselves be *encountered*, but you can never *deduce* anything from them. I believe there are people who have understood this. Only they

tried to overcome this contingency by inventing a necessary, causal being. But no necessary being can explain existence: contingency is not a delusion, a probability which can be dissipated; it is the absolute, consequently, the perfect free gift [*gratuité*]. All is gratuitous [*gratuit*], this park, this city and myself.

(155/131)

Sartre's novel derived from the notebook he titled *Factum on Contingency*, the Latin term referring to a common designation among Normaliens for their extended essays. Although this preliminary work dates to 1931, it reflects on a transformative experience from Sartre's adolescence. The epiphany occurred one afternoon as he left the cinema with his mother, when the contingency of life on the streets, including the superfluousness of his own existence, contrasted starkly with the necessity of the events that had unfolded in the film.[13] In the novel, this recognition—in inverted order, from contingency to necessity—can be alleviating or even salutary. The most important example concerns the phonograph recording of the song, *Some of These Days*. When Roquentin listens to it, he is overwhelmed by its exigency. "It seems inevitable. So strong is the necessity of this music: nothing can interrupt it [. . .] it will stop of itself, as if by order." With mechanical drive, the shellac disc rotates in linear time, from beginning to end, analogous to a cinematic reel. "What has just happened is that the Nausea has disappeared" (29/22). As Thomas Flynn remarks: "Liberation from the nauseous experience of the contingency of our temporal existence seems achievable by appeal to the experience of the necessity unfolded in the 'other' temporality of art."[14] At the novel's end, after the famous meditation on the tree root and after his meeting with Anny, Roquentin returns to the recording and flirts with the idea of writing a book, not like his failed project—a historical biography of the Marquis de Rollebon—but rather "something which would not exist which would be above existence. A story, for example something that could never happen, an adventure. It would have to be beautiful and hard as steel and make people ashamed of their existence" (210/178).

The novel's concluding emphasis of shame readily recalls the final chapter of Kafka's *Trial*, when Josef K. freely—peaceably—allows himself to be carted off by his executioners. After the knife pierces his

---

[13] See Thomas Flynn, *Sartre: A Philosophical Biography* (Cambridge: Cambridge University Press, 2014), 15.
[14] Flynn, *Sartre*, 143.

heart, his sight begins to fade. "K. saw the two men leaning cheek to cheek close to his face as they observed the final decision. 'Like a dog!' he said. It seemed as if his shame would live on after him" (KGW 3, 241/T 165). Shame, which here is explicitly connected with being reduced to a non-human animal before the others' gaze, will play a central role in the phenomenological ontology that Sartre expounds in his magnum opus, *Being and Nothingness* (1943). In contrast to determinate, physical substances or "being-in-itself" (*l'être-en-soi*), consciousness is "being-for-itself" (*l'être-pour-soi*), nothing in itself, undetermined and therefore free. Consciousness, however, is transcended by the Other, like "fatality" but more frequently like another's consciousness, which equally cannot be determined. Just as fatality overshadowed Sartre's free and gratuitous move at the Place Hébert, so the Other stands as a menace, threatening to turn one's being into a determined object, transforming a "being-*for*-itself" into a "being-*in*-itself." The resultant shame of being thus reified, of being treated like a dog, consists in the horror of being pre-inscribed by an inaccessible, unknowable, transcendent power. It is at precisely this moment in Sartre's philosophical argument that he turns to Kafka.

> When the other appears [...] he makes an aspect appear within the situation that I did not want, of which I am not the master, and which escapes me as a matter of principle—because it is *for the other*. This is what Gide felicitously named 'the devil's share.' It is the *reverse side* [*l'envers*], unpredictable and yet real. It is to this unpredictability that Kafka applies his descriptive skills in *The Trial* and *The Castle*: in one sense, everything that K. and the land surveyor do belongs to them as their own and, insofar as they act on the world, the results are strictly in conformity with their predictions: they are actions that succeed. But at the same time the *truth* of these actions constantly escapes them; they necessarily have a meaning that is their *true meaning*, and which neither K. nor the land surveyor will ever know. And doubtless Kafka is trying here to capture a divine transcendence; it is for a divinity that human action becomes constituted as truth. But here God is the concept of the Other pushed to its limit. [...] This painful and elusive atmosphere of the *Trial*, this ignorance that is nonetheless lived out as ignorance, this complete opacity that can be sensed only through a complete translucency, is nothing but the description of our being-in-the-midst-of-the-world-for-the-Other.[15]

Sartre's explication dovetails with the general sentiment of the Kafkaesque—awakening to the challenge of undefined or undeterminable charges, vainly searching for decisive knowledge about powers that, in the end, remain frustratingly out of reach. The experience recalls Groethuysen's portrayal of Kafka's other world as one governed by a geometry and a rationality that run "backwards," *à l'envers*. Tellingly, Kafka's novel begins and ends with shame, much as Sartre defines it. Although Kafka neglected to indicate the correct order of the internal chapters of *The Trial*, the placement of the opening and closing chapters—entitled "The Arrest" and "The End"—are beyond dispute. The novel that ends with the shame of being slaughtered "like a dog" begins with Josef K. realizing that he is the object of another's gaze: "from his pillow he saw the old woman who lived opposite him (*ihm gegenüber*) and watched him with a curiosity that was entirely unusual for her" (KGW 3, 9/T 5).

As a man under arrest yet free to carry on with his life, Josef K. becomes obsessed with uncovering the high court that would clarify or determine his guilt. Yet in Sartre's analysis, this desire for definite knowledge—this yearning for *something* substantive regarding his trial—already relegates K. to the shame of being determined. In seeking essential knowledge about his status, he turns his back on the indeterminable nothingness that is his existence. As K.'s Uncle Karl explains: "To have such a trial means to have already lost it" (KGW 3, 101/T 68). All the same, K. expends his energy in search of an answer, passing through endless corridors, racing up countless staircases, until he nearly collapses. "He felt as if he were seasick, as if he were on a ship in a heavy sea." (KGW 3, 84/T 56). The nauseous feeling arises from K.'s realization that he is not the person he thought he was, that he can no longer rely on his usual habits and routines, that his status as a bank professional, with its clearcut role and attendant behavior, are of no use in a process pursued by powers that transcend him. He finds himself adrift, compelled to weather the violent waves that threaten to crash over him and sink his identity. As Roquentin would say, he has no ground to stand on.

Kafka employed the same image of seasickness in *Conversation with the Supplicant*, the oneiric narrative taken from his early *Description of a Struggle*. The narrator is a fat man who recounts how he used to go to church every day secretly to watch a girl with whom he was in love. One day, when the girl failed to appear, he was drawn to a young, emaciated supplicant, who was beating his head on the stone floor, ostensibly enjoying the attention he received. Finding this

---

[15] Sartre, *Being and Nothingness: An Essay in Phenomenological Ontology*, tr. Sarah Richmond (New York: Washington Square Press, 2018), 363.

behavior troubling, the fat man approached the peculiar starveling and interrogated him. Before long, the fundamental problem was discerned:

> Is it not this fever, this seasickness on land, a kind of leprosy? Do you not sense that, with sheer ardor, you can't be content with the true names of things, that you won't get enough, and now in frantic haste, you're just pouring random names over them? Quickly, quickly! But hardly have you run away from them, and you've forgotten their names again. The poplar in the fields, which you called the "Tower of Babel," for you didn't want to know that it was a poplar, it sways again namelessly, and you have to call it "Noah, how he was drunk."
> (KGW 5, 126/CS 33)

According to the fat man, the scrawny man is a social pariah—a kind of leper—and not simply because he makes a disturbing show of his praying. He is an outcast, rather, because of his tendency to speak in overblown metaphors: An ordinary poplar metamorphoses into the Tower of Babel. The supplicant suffers from verbal indirection. As Roquentin understands in contemplating the thick roots of the chestnut tree, the Nausea on firm land emerges from encountering sheer existence in its horrifying nakedness and the incapacity to name it directly.[16] For Kafka's supplicant, it is likewise the mere existence of the poplar tree that drives him to cover it with metaphors: A weak strategy to control existence, to corral it into the confines of one's mind.[17] The fat man can detect the supplicant's problem because he, too, suffers from this infliction. A voyeur who sneaks into a church day after day to watch from the shadows a young girl kneeling in prayer, is a man driven to turn others into objects of his gaze. His diagnosis of the supplicant is part of the same game: *He* invents the metaphors that he ascribes to the supplicant's mind, including the figure of "seasickness on land"; *he* aims to control this bizarre figure through knowledgeable explanations. Yet as Roquentin reminds us, "the world of explanations and reasons is not the world of existence."[18]

---

[16] Sartre, *Nausea*, 127 [*La Nausée*, 150–1].
[17] Cf. Shimon Sandbank, *After Kafka: The Influence of Kafka's Fiction* (Athens: The University of Georgia Press, 1989), 17–18.
[18] Sartre, *Nausea*, 129 [*La Nausée*, 153].

PHANTOM WAR

Even before publication, Sartre's *Nausea* drew comparisons with Kafka's style and sensibility. In a letter to Beauvoir from April 30, 1937, Sartre recounted his visit to the offices of the *NRF* to retrieve what he believed were his rejected manuscripts of the novel and two short stories. He had submitted a version of the novel some years before to no avail and had only the vaguest hope that the revision would meet with success. After giving his name to the receptionist, Sartre waited in the vestibule, where he caught a glimpse of an elegantly attired Jules Romains, the *Unanimiste* whose *L'homme blanc* had appeared alongside Kafka's debut in the *NRF* nearly a decade before. Soon, Sartre was called to go upstairs to see Jean Paulhan, who welcomed him warmly and apologized for the mix-up. Much to Sartre's surprise, both Paulhan and Groethuysen had been impressed by his work and were interested in placing one of the two stories in the *NRF* and the other in *Mesures*. They were especially eager to publish the novel, which at the time was entitled *Melancholia* in homage to Albrecht Dürer's famous engraving. Sartre unabashedly transcribes Paulhan's flattering comment: "Are you familiar with Kafka? Despite the differences, I see no one but Kafka to compare this to in modern literature."[19] Editorial work on the novel proceeded at once with the title now changed, following Gaston Gallimard's personal suggestion, to *La Nausée*.

The book captivated the most discerning minds of the new generation. It was praised as a truly philosophical novel—not merely a novel of ideas but rather one that demonstrated the philosophical potential of the novelistic form—an original work, impelled by astute phenomenological descriptions yet also reminiscent of Kafka. In his brief review for the communist newspaper *Ce Soir*, Sartre's old schoolmate Paul Nizan pronounced the general assessment:

> I would say that Sartre could be a French Kafka by virtue of his gift for expressing the horror of certain intellectual situations, if it weren't that his ideas, unlike those of the author of *The Great Wall of China*, were not completely foreign to moral problems. Kafka always questioned the meaning of life. M. Sartre only questions the fact of existence, which is an order of reality much more

---

[19] Sartre to Beauvoir, April 30, 1937. In *Witness to My Life: The Letters of Jean-Paul Sartre to Simone de Beauvoir, 1926–1939*, tr. Lee Fahnestock and Norman MacAfee (New York: Scribner's, 1992), 93.

immediate than the human and social elaborations of the life that is on this side of life.[20]

The comment touches on a personal dispute. During their years at the lycée, Nizan and Sartre were inseparable yet eventually split over Nizan's involvement with the French Communist Party. Despite repeated efforts, Sartre could not be persuaded to take up the cause of the collective and instead gravitated towards Nietzsche's "solitary man," a figure he first sketched out in his novel, *The Legend of Truth* (1931). Thus, although appreciative of Sartre's philosophical astuteness, Nizan is uncomfortable with the moral ramifications of Roquentin's individualism and detachment, a position that he believes distinguishes *Nausea* from Kafka's work. As noted, it is only over the course of the Occupation when Sartre will reconsider the value of individual freedom vis-à-vis society and perhaps become, at least in Nizan's view, more deserving of the title, *un Kafka français*.

Other critics as well discerned the complementary relationship between Sartre and the Prague author. In the Catholic journal *Esprit*, edited by Emmanuel Mounier, principal spokesman for the anti-capitalist Personalist movement, Armand Robin noted that "Sartre stops where Kafka begins in that he has the goodness or perhaps the indulgence not to compel us to absolute stupidity, like the metamorphosis into vermin."[21] If Robin's Catholic socialism recoiled from Sartre's entrenched individualism and its concomitant view on the absurdity of existence, he was at least grateful that *Nausea* refrained from what he viewed as Kafka's tasteless leap into the fantastic, which here is read as the literalization of the bestiality implicit in "stupidity" (*bêtise*). In contrast, for a twenty-four-year-old Albert Camus, who was more sympathetic to the plight of the modern individual and more amenable to the idea that life is utterly void of meaning, Sartre and Kafka belonged together insofar they courageously gave voice to a shattering truth. From Algiers, Camus wrote: "Sartre's relationship to an author like Kafka is clear, *La Nausée* being less a novel than a relentless monologue in which "a man judges his life and is judged by it."[22] With further

---

[20] Paul Nizan, "La Nausée, un roman de Jean-Paul Sartre" (May 16, 1938), in Nizan, *Pour une nouvelle culture*, ed. Susan Suleiman (Paris: Grasset, 1971), 285–6.
[21] Armand Robin, Review of *La Nausée*, *Esprit*, no. 70 (July 1938), 574–5; cited in Sartre, *Œuvres romanesques*, 1705.
[22] Albert Camus, Review of *La Nausée*, *Alger républicain* (October 20, 1938), reprinted in Camus, *Essais*, Bibliothèque de la Pléiade (Paris: Gallimard, 1965), 1417–19.

laudatory reviews appearing throughout the summer of 1938—by Marcel Arland, Jean Cassou, Edmond Jaloux, and André Thérive, as well as a satirical, rather ambivalent piece by Blanchot in the journal *Aux Écoutes*[23]—Sartre, at the age of thirty-one, finally achieved his long-held aspiration to be a literary writer. His novel would be compared not only to Kafka, but also to Rabelais, Dostoevsky, and Nietzsche, Flaubert, Joyce, Proust, and Céline. With a modern masterpiece to his credit, Sartre would no longer be obliged to teach.

Which is not to say the fatality of history could be held at bay. By the autumn of that year, the Munich Agreement condoned German expansionism in the name of appeasement, which encouraged Prime Minister Édouard Daladier to break with the Communists and thereby dissolve the Front Populaire. While Sartre busied himself with critical essays on contemporary authors for the *NRF*, the gears of war had already started to turn. When asked, Sartre tended to be dismissive, even after Hitler and Stalin signed their ominous pact of non-aggression in late August 1939. To the very last moment, the solitary novelist refused to believe anything grave would develop. "Have confidence," he wrote to Louise Védrine on August 31. "It is impossible that Hitler would even think of starting a war with the state of mind of the German people. It's a bluff. We may go as far as general mobilization, but it's worth remembering this sentence ... mobilization is not war."[24] The very next day he raced back home to retrieve his musette bag.

Perhaps it was Sartre's disbelief in the possibility of protracted hostilities that allowed him to enter the fray with Plume-like aplomb. In the weeks leading up to the outbreak of war, Sartre had been reading Kafka almost incessantly, having proposed to Paulhan his intention to write an essay on the Prague author for the left-wing journal *Les Volontaires*. Sartre saw no reason why mobilization should interrupt his agenda. On the stalled journey eastward to the region of Lorraine, not far from his mother's family home, he simply bided his time: "I slept a bit, finished *The Trial*, read *The Penal Colony* and three or four newspapers that were lying around. And then I began to wait. At some station or other, I realized I was going to wait like this right to the end of the war."[25]

Soon after his arrival to Essey-lès-Nancy, Sartre was one of four men selected for meteorological testing and observation, skills he had

---

[23] For a broad collection of excerpts, see Sartre, *Œuvres romanesques*, 1701–11.
[24] In *Lettres au Castor et à quelques autres, 1926–1939*, ed. Simone de Beauvoir (Paris: Gallimard, 1983), 271. [*Witness to My Life*, 225 (tr. modified).]
[25] Jean-Paul Sartre, *Lettres au Castor*, 274. [*Witness to My Life*, 228.]

learned during his military service a decade before. The small unit would spend the next nine months moving across Alsace and Lorraine, launching balloons then tracking their flights for an infantry that was perpetually held on standby. "It is always vacation [*la villégiature*]," he wrote to Beauvoir, "read a bit of *The Castle*—which, finally, I like a lot— worked a bit on my novel."[26] The absurdity of the phony war correlated well with the persistent ambiguities and perplexities of Kafka's fiction. "The phantom war," Sartre called it. "A war *à la Kafka*. I can't feel it, it's running away from me. The communiqués do not mention our losses. I did not see any wounded."[27] Instead, he was mired in useless activity and boredom. As he reported to Paulhan: "Since my mobilization I have often thought about Kafka; he would have liked this war; it would have been a good subject for him. He would have shown a man, named Gregoire K., stubbornly looking for war everywhere, and yet never finding it. A suspended war, like some of the sentences in *The Trial*."[28]

A phantom war, one that appeared yet remained intangible, an improbable apparition—it rhymed with Kafka's writings insofar as it was transcendent, known only by its effects. Like the high court or the executive office of the Castle, the war lay perpetually out of reach, always on the horizon, which receded with every step taken towards it.[29] Since confrontation was impossible, the decisions required for authentic engagement were equally unachievable. When he was not writing, Sartre reverted to flippancy, entertaining mainly himself with urbane wit. He came to see himself as K., busying himself in the village to no purpose while the Castle loomed in the distance, doling out orders as if he truly were the appointed land-surveyor. "My acolytes are more and more like Kafka's Assistants: I spare them no rebuff, out of a moral pedantry. And they come right back, exactly like the Assistants, silent, laughing mischievous children [*rieurs et gamins*]."[30]

Sartre was hardly alone in regarding Kafka's fiction as resembling the current situation: "the relationship between Kafka's texts, the expectations of French readers and the historical period of the great

---

[26] Sartre, *Lettres au Castor*, 285. He is referring to the novel that would become *The Age of Reason*.
[27] Jean-Paul Sartre, *Les Mots et autres écrits autobiographiques*, ed. Jean François Louette, Gilles Philippe, and Juliette Simont (Paris: Gallimard, 2010), 157. See Bogaerts, "Sartre's 'Guerre Fantôme,' 57–74.
[28] Sartre to Jean Paulhan, December 13, 1939, cited in Annie Cohen-Solal, *Jean-Paul Sartre: A Life*, tr. Anna Cancogni (New York: New Press, 2005), 249.
[29] Cf. Laurent Dubreuil, *L'état critique de la littérature* (Paris: Hermann, 2009), 112; and Bogaerts, "Sartre's Guerre Fantôme," 65.
[30] Sartre to Beauvoir, October 13, 1939. *Lettres au Castor*, 348. [*Witness to my Life*, 289.]

totalitarianisms most likely constitutes one of the most exceptional intersections between a work and the period in which it was read."[31] Kafka's capacity to address the era, however, was not restricted to comments on the farcical absurdity of prolonged inaction. When Paul Nizan again evoked the Czech-German-Jewish writer, he underscored the urgency to engage with the existential dread that effectively coursed through the work. In a letter to his wife Henriette, Nizan explained:

> The General Staff is concerned with the 'morale' of the army, by which they mean the healthy "distractions" of course, but they don't suspect that they ought to be concerned with the "metaphysics" of the army, and that the smallest peasant feels his troubles with emptiness, mystery, and time in the same way as Kafka. There are no remedies and there will be no soldier's mess room that will hold against the feeling of annihilation.[32]

Four months later, on May 23, 1940, Nizan would be killed in combat during the Siege of Calais.

As for Sartre, who at the time was stationed in Morsbronn-les-Bains in Alsace, the German offensive on May 10 forced his company into retreat, roughly 140 kilometers south to Padoux. On May 29, Sartre described for Beauvoir how a comrade suggested that Hitler was the Beast of the Apocalypse, to which Sartre wove a tale set after the Second Coming of Christ, where contrary to Scripture, the world would be populated exclusively by the Unrighteous. "This sudden emptying of the Righteous charmed me. I imagined it the style of Kafka [*à la Kafka*] and would almost want to write a fantastic novella about it."[33] Weeks later, Sartre and his company were taken prisoners by German troops. As his biographer writes: "Suddenly, everything speeds up and the war begins to exist. Suddenly, Sartre has to wake up."[34]

HOMO ABSURDUS

Albert Camus first read Kafka's *Trial* in Vialatte's translation in 1938, around the time he came across Sartre's *Nausea*—a coincidence

---

[31] Pierre-Frédéric Charpentier, *La Drôle de guerre des intellectuels français* (Panazol: Lavauzelle, 2008), 40.
[32] January 9, 1940; cited in Charpentier, *La Drôle de guerre*, 34.
[33] Sartre, *Lettres au Castor*, vol. 2, 255.
[34] Cohen-Solal, *Jean-Paul Sartre*, 146.

underscored in Camus's review of *Nausea* printed in the *Alger républicain* on October 20 of that year.[35] The anti-Fascist newspaper had been launched only twelve days before under the editorship of Pascal Pia, who recruited Camus to oversee the literary section. The new position allowed Camus to resign from the Algiers Institute of Meteorology. (Sartre was not the only existentialist who knew how to launch weather balloons.) The looser schedule gave Camus more time to devote to his own literary projects: A collection of four meditative essays entitled *Noces* (*Nuptials*), the theatrical piece *Caligula*, and the manuscript that would develop into the novel *L'Étranger* (*The Stranger*), which above all exhibited indebtedness to Kafka and hence to Sartre.

In September 1939, having been diagnosed with tuberculosis a decade before, Camus was disqualified for military service. Nonetheless, in the early spring of the following year, through the efforts of Pascal Pia, he accepted a position in the offices of the popular daily newspaper, *Paris-Soir*, and moved to Paris in March, in the midst of the *drôle de guerre*. Isolated in his dreary apartment in Montmartre, far from the sunshine of the Algerian coast, he portrayed the French capital as a "terrible devourer of men."[36] He soon began work on his *Myth of Sisyphus*, which he would dedicate to Pia—an extended essay on the Absurd, on mortal existence confronted by a world indifferent to human suffering—as well as continue writing *The Stranger*, which he completed in May, just as the German army commenced its Western Campaign on France. It was again Pia who stepped in, sending Camus's manuscript to André Malraux, who offered several suggestions for revision before recommending it to Paulhan and Raymond Queneau at Gallimard. The essayist and philosopher, Jean Grenier, Camus's former advisor at the University of Algiers and also a good friend of Paulhan, was concerned that the novel too closely resembled Kafka's writing and suggested that Camus moderate the Prague author's influence.

Meanwhile, soon after Paris fell on June 14, Gaston Gallimard negotiated a deal with the Nazi authorities, who would allow him to maintain his publishing house provided he collaborated with German propaganda efforts. Gallimard thus appointed Pierre Drieu la Rochelle, an outspoken supporter of Hitler, to replace Paulhan as the official director of the *NRF*. The devil's bargain would at least make it possible to bring *The Stranger* to print in June 1942, followed by *The Myth of*

---

[35] On first reading Kafka, see Camus's letter to Liselotte Dieckmann, December 3, 1951, reprinted in James Jones, "Camus on Kafka and Melville: An Unpublished Letter," *The French Review* 71 (1998), 645–50. For further biographical detail, see Edward Hughes, *Albert Camus* (London: Reaktion, 2015), 56–8.
[36] Cited in Hughes, *Albert Camus*, 66.

Sisyphus six months afterward. By this time, Camus was residing in the south, still working for *Paris-Soir* at its new location in Clermont-Ferrand under Marshal Pétain's collaborationist government at Vichy. Sartre, who was released from the German camp in April of the following year, resumed his teaching position at the Lycée Pasteur in Neuilly, just outside Paris, and moved back into his old apartment in the Hotel Mistral in Montparnasse. As Roquentin would say, everything had changed, nothing had changed.

As with Sartre's *Nausea*, critics praised Camus's *Stranger* as an accomplished and original work while also noting its strong affinity to Kafka's presentation of the Absurd.[37] In a review essay published in *Les Cahiers du Sud*, a journal based in Marseilles, Sartre commented on Camus's acute insights into the consciousness of the "absurd man," his recognition of the divorce "between man's longing for the eternal and the *finite* character of his existence, between the 'concern' that is his very essence and the futility of his efforts."[38] Although the theme of absurdity was not new—Sartre traces it from Pascal to Kierkegaard, from Dostoevsky to Heidegger—what Camus contributes is the idea of revolt, particularly in the *Sisyphus* book. "There is a passion of the absurd. *Homo absurdus* will not commit suicide, he wants to live, without abdicating any of his certainties, without tomorrows, without hope, without illusions, but without resignation either. *Homo absurdus* affirms himself in revolt" (154). As for Kafka, however, Sartre must make a stand:

> "It's Kafka written by Hemingway," someone has suggested. I must admit that I don't see Kafka in [*The Stranger*]. M. Camus's views are wholly down-to-earth. Kafka is the novelist of impossible transcendence. For him, the universe is bristling with signs we do not understand. There is something behind the scenery. For M. Camus by contrast, the human tragedy is the absence of any transcendence.
>
> (167)

To illustrate further the distance between Kafka's "impossible transcendence" and Camus's immanence, Sartre cites a passage from *The Stranger* and provides a brief commentary:

---

[37] See Mary Ann Frese Witt, "Camus et Kafka," *La Revue des lettres modernes* 264 (1971), 71–86. For a comprehensive analysis, see Phillip Rhein, *The Urge to Live: A Comparative Study of Franz Kafka's Der Prozess and Albert Camus's L'Étranger* (Chapel Hill: The University of North Carolina Press, 1964).

[38] Sartre, "Explication de L'Étranger," *Les Cahiers du sud* 30 (February 1943): "*The Outsider* Explained," in Sartre, *Critical Essays (Situations I)*, tr. Chris Turner (London: Seagull, 2017), 148–84; here, p. 150.

I woke up with the stars shining on my face. Sounds of the countryside were wafting in. The night air was cooling my temples with the smell of earth and salt. The wondrous peace of this sleeping summer flooded into me.

The person who wrote these lines is as far as can be from the *Angst* of a Kafka. He is thoroughly calm amid the chaos. The stubborn blindness of nature irritates him certainly, but it also reassures him. [. . .] *homo absurdus* is a humanist, he knows only the blessings of this world.

(168)

A subtext informs Sartre's views here. In *Nausea*, Roquentin had ridiculed the Autodidact for his "humanism," which he uses as an occasion to vilify humanists in general: "He is generally a widower with a fine eye always clouded with tears: he weeps at anniversaries. He also loves cats, dogs, and all the higher mammals. The Communist writer has been loving men since the second Five-Year Plan."[39] Roquentin's individualism, which is always but a hair's breadth away from solipsism, is especially allergic to this brand of bourgeois humanism. We recall that Nizan, in his review of *Nausea*, highlighted Sartre's distance from moral problems, which distinguished him from the author of *The Trial*. Now, in a subtle reversal, Sartre applies the same distinction while reassigning the roles, with Kafka now delegated to an inaccessible trans-mundane sphere and Camus as the man filled with moral concern. The shift is consistent with Sartre's self-styled conversion during this period: "I renounced my individualistic, anti-humanist way of life. I learned the value of solidarity."[40] It is likely that news of Nizan's death during the Siege of Calais contributed to this transformation. Did Sartre feel obliged to appoint Kafka to the side of transcendence along with his Roquentin in order to carve out an immanent place for him and Camus to share?

Sartre's explication of *The Stranger* set the terms for the first wave of the novel's reception as a meditation on universal human questions, and in doing so endorsed precisely the kind of decontextualization that also characterized Kafka's initial reception in France. However, whereas the general absence of cultural and national markers in Kafka's fiction facilitated a universalizing reading, the same cannot be applied as easily to Camus's novel. It is arguably less bothersome to detach Kafka

---

[39] Sartre, *Nausea*, 116–17 [*La Nausée*, 138].
[40] In Beauvoir, *Prime of Life*, 433.

from Prague in the final years of the Habsburg Empire because the specific qualities of the city and its political environment are only vaguely discernible in the work. It is a much different affair when we deal with a narrative set in Algiers which vividly and painfully reflects on colonial tensions and ethnic prejudices, centering on a European settler who fatally shoots an Arab adversary. Quite strikingly yet also quite typically—one is tempted to say *absurdly*—Sartre's essay is altogether "deaf" (*surdus*) to this core aspect of the novel. What is perhaps more surprising, however, is that Camus himself, a *pied-noir* who took the Algerian problem very much to heart, appeared to endorse the existentialist's abstractive, universal interpretation of his enormously popular novel.

It would only be around 1960 when critics and scholars would begin to focus on the colonialist implications of *The Stranger* now that the Algerian War of Independence had reached a breaking point. In his critical study, *Les Français d'Algérie* (1961), Pierre Nora regarded Camus's Meursault as a concrete representative of the narrow complacency that he ascribed to the French Algerian mentality and hardly a paradigm of human consciousness thrown into an indifferent universe. In the wake of Nora's publication, the French-Algerian Jacques Derrida wrote a personal letter to the author, his former comrade at the Lycée Louis-le-Grand in Paris, to congratulate him on reversing Sartre's de-historicizing reading of 1943 and resituating *The Stranger* within its full cultural context.[41] As for Camus, his public equivocations on the Algerian War, including an oblique remark made during his acceptance speech for the Nobel Prize in 1957, tended to alienate him from the rising generation on the Left.

The move to re-contextualize *The Stranger* circa 1960 almost perfectly coincided with similar efforts to bring Kafka back to earth, to see his work as grounded in his experience as a German-speaking, Jewish, tubercular man surrounded by the Czech nationalist fervor for independence. By 1960, existentialism had seen its day while Algeria struggled for its own independence. The insurrection against the French government in Algiers, known as the Week of Barricades, was a watershed moment, beginning on January 24 of that year, three weeks after Camus, at the age of forty-six, died in a car accident, with his publisher Michel Gallimard at the wheel.

---

[41] See Hughes, *Albert Camus*, 71–3.

IMPOSSIBLE HOPE

Let us return to 1943. While working on his play, *The Misunderstanding*, in addition to making preliminary sketches for what would be his second novel, *The Plague*, Camus placed his essay, "Hope and the Absurd in the Work of Franz Kafka," in the satirical, semi-clandestine journal *L'Arbalète* ("The Crossbow"), edited by Marc Barbezat in Lyon, where it circulated just below the radar of the Vichy authorities. Camus had originally planned to include the Kafka piece as a chapter in *The Myth of Sisyphus* yet was prudently advised to remove it. In his account of the book's genesis, Louis Faucon explains: "One can think that the authorities, on whom a visa and papers depended, would not have allowed the publication of a piece that praises a Czech-Jewish writer whose ambiguous evocations of a world crushed by arbitrariness and terror lent themselves to current applications."[42] It would only be after the war that Camus would restore the essay back to its initial setting, now as an appendix to a new edition of the *Sisyphus* volume.

Camus's piece opens by stating an obligation: "The whole art of Kafka consists in forcing [*d'obliger*] the reader to reread."[43] The compulsion stems from the open-ended, symbolic nature of Kafka's stories and novels, the many difficulties of which require considering alternative approaches and perspectives. A symbol, Camus explains, does not allow for straightforward decipherment, but rather consists in an inexhaustible movement that transcends the author's designs, making the writer "say in reality more than he is aware of expressing" (124/169). In Ancient Greek culture, a *symbolon* was usually a piece of terra cotta broken in half and allotted to two parties, the unique contours of each piece serving as proof of identity when the two reunited. The reader of *The Trial* or *The Castle*, Camus suggests, is left with only one piece and searches in vain for the missing shard. The fragmentary quality of the work, therefore, is not circumstantial—it has nothing to do with Kafka's failure to bring the novels to completion—rather, its fragmentariness is inherent, there by design.

Although in Kafka the symbolic is lodged "in the general" (*dans le général*) it consistently exhibits a quality of "naturalness" (*le naturel*, 125/170). Here, naturalness does not denote what appears natural to the reader but rather what the characters in the fiction take to be natural, regardless of how strange things may appear to us. The paradoxical

---

[42] Albert Camus, *Essais II*, Bibliothèque de la Pléiade, ed. Roger Quilliot and Louis Faucon (Paris: Gallimard, 1967), 1415. See also Vincent Grégoire, "Camus l'écrivain naissant face à la censure allemande," *Symposium* 63 (2009), 36–50.
[43] Camus, *Myth of Sisyphus*, 124 [169].

effect is that the more fantastic the adventures appear, the more evident their naturalness comes across. What Camus finds particularly striking in Kafka is "the divergence we feel between the strangeness of a man's life and the simplicity with which that man accepts it" (125/171). Through this divergence, Kafka's work confronts us; *we* are the ones who are astonished by his characters' lack of astonishment. Even though it is Kafka who speaks, "we are the ones he confesses" (126/171). The divergence makes the work "absurd."

The Absurd is a consequence of the fiction's symbolic presentation of two distinct spheres, two planes of reality that can never match. If *The Castle* is "a theology in action," it is only because it recounts "the individual adventure of a soul in quest of its grace" (126/171)—in search of grace yet without ever finding it. The fragments never connect, neither for the protagonists nor for us. Camus provides various designations of the two contrasting realities that remain forever apart: "the natural and the extraordinary, the individual and the universal, the tragic and the everyday, the absurd and the logical" (126/172). One comprehends the meaning of Kafka's work not by resolving these contradictions but rather by maintaining them, even strengthening them. The allusions to grace and the diremption of reality into two discrete spheres clearly reach back to the essays included in Vialatte's 1933 translation of *The Trial*: Brod's saintly hero, who sets off on a spiritual quest, and Groethuysen's daydreamer-adventurer, who transits between two orders of human experience, serve as the basis for Camus's explication.

In Camus's view, the two conflicting planes—perpetually separate for Groethuysen, reconcilable for Brod—are engaged in the movement he accords to the symbolic. "Kafka expresses tragedy by the everyday and the absurd by the logical" (127/173)—that is, the Absurd is formulated in logically consistent terms. For an illustrative example, Camus conjures the image of a man fishing in his bathtub: When asked if the fish are biting today, the man replies, "Of course not, you fool, since this is a bathtub" (129/175). The Absurd, therefore, consists not in an absence of logic but rather in an excess of logic. From a moral perspective, it means acting in the world despite "knowing that nothing will come of it" (129/175). Precisely for this reason, the Absurd does not preclude hope. There is hope, Camus stresses, albeit "in a 'strange form'" (*sous une forme singulière*, 130/176). Whereas *The Trial* poses the problem, *The Castle* provides treatment—a *treatment*, not a cure: "It merely brings the malady back into normal life. It helps to accept it." One learns to cherish a hopeless hope; and so, Camus proposes: "Let us think of Kierkegaard" (130/176).

Camus essentially follows Brod in taking the Amalia episode in *The Castle* as a parallel to Kierkegaard's account of Abraham. Upon witnessing the injustice against Amalia and her family, K. aims "to recapture God through what negates him, to recognize him, not according to our categories of goodness and beauty, but behind the empty and hideous aspects of his indifference, of his injustice, and of his hatred" (179/133). K.'s final attempt for redemption thus amounts to a "deification of the absurd"—he must forsake "morality, logic, and intellectual truths in order to enter, endowed solely with his mad hope, the desert of divine grace" (133/179). This hope is mad, and yet it is still hope. For Camus the lesson is vitally urgent: One must follow the absurd logic that leads from the utter hopelessness of *The Trial* to the hopeless hope of *The Castle*. With Kierkegaard, Camus characterizes the passage from one pole to the next as a "leap" and cites from Kierkegaard's *Purity of Hope*, a non-pseudonymous work which is arguably the philosopher's most sincere confession of faith: "Earthly hope must be killed; only then can one be saved by true hope," which Camus revises as, "One has to have written *The Trial* to undertake *The Castle*" (134/180). The sentiment is a variation on Brod's proposal to read the two novels as a complementary pair and corroborates Kierkegaard's discussion of the religious state, a state that can only be achieved through a despair profound enough that one withdraws from the temporal world. Yet, whereas Brod distinguished Kierkegaard's renunciation from Kafka's commitment to immanence, Camus aligns the two authors as philosophers who recognized that hope endures in those who do not passively resign but rather act in the world from a position of despair. According to Camus, herein lies the true "universality" of Kafka's work, a universality that is not abstract but rather concretely human, one that expresses the pathos that every human experiences. This pathos derives from the universal contradictions in life—the injustices, the irrationalism, the agonizing frustration of acting in a meaningless world— contradictions that, in the end, give us reason to believe and revolt. Kafka's work is an inspiration, cognate with the religious insofar as it presents the lucid nobility of human struggle, which presses on despite the paradoxes and futility of the human condition, despite the utter lack of transcendence. Kafka, like Kierkegaard and Shestov, embraces "the God that consumes" him (135/181).

An alternative interpretation of Kafka's relation to Kierkegaard is found in an essay by Jean Wahl, also published in *L'Arbalète*, three months after Camus's piece appeared. Here, Wahl analyzes Kafka's aphorisms on *Fear and Trembling* in a series of glosses, which maintains an intellectual piety towards the cited passages while pressing Kafka's text towards a multiplication of meanings and ramifications—a dizzying play of reflections as one reads Kafka reading Kierkegaard reading the Bible. What comes to the fore is what Kafka calls "the intellectual poverty [*geistige Armut*] of Abraham" (KGW 6, 220), the vacuity of consciousness and the lack of understanding that enable him to carry out God's horrifying command. Wahl underscores Kafka's fascination with the portrayal of a man who is obliged to communicate a paradox that he fails to grasp. "The incommunicability of the paradox perhaps exists, but does not express itself as such, for Abraham himself does not understand it" (KGW 6, 219). For Wahl, while Kierkegaard presumes to comprehend the paradox and therefore authorizes himself to communicate its general import, Kafka insists that whatever is understood and communicated is no longer a paradox; it renders the paradox "impossible."[44] In Wahl's assessment, Kafka presents the possibility of paradox by upholding its incommunicability and letting it "express itself as such." In the subsequent note, Kafka refers to this incommunicability as "equivocation," which calls for a redefinition of "the general" (*das Allgemeine*), not as the "repose" that results in communication, but rather as the constant vacillation between communication and its failure, between the general and the singular (*das Einzelne*, KGW 6, 219). Thus, whereas Kierkegaard contrasts this singular, incommunicable event with the communicable repose of the general, Kafka gathers these moments into a movement in which the singular resists absorption into the general just as the general is undercut by the singular. "For Kafka the general"—no less than the singular—"becomes an unattainable ideal and a mysterious driving force" (Wahl, 280). Although there is hope that the two spheres will be reconciled, it is a "senseless hope"—not Camus's heroic hope out of cognizant despair, but rather the kind of inane hope expressed by the ape-protagonist in the *Report to the Academy*, a narrator Wahl provocatively describes as "a disciple of Shestov in the body of Maldoror" (Wahl, 289). In any event, as we shall see, the hopelessly vibrating to-and-fro between communicability and incommunicability will constitute a core theorem in Maurice Blanchot's prolonged investigation of Kafka's literary space.

OBJECTIVE STYLE

In November 1942, a month before *The Myth of Sisyphus* appeared without the Kafka essay, Claude-Edmonde Magny published her essay, "Kafka, or Objective Writing of the Absurd."[45] Magny is the *nom de*

---

[44] Wahl, "Kafka et Kierkegaard," which would be reprinted in his *Esquisse pour une histoire de l'existentialisme* (Paris: Éditions du club Maintenant, 1947). ["Kafka and Kierkegaard," in *The Kafka Problem*, ed. Flores, 277–90; here, p. 278–9.]
[45] "Kafka ou l'écriture objective de l'absurde," originally published in *Les Cahiers du Sud* and later reprinted in Magny, *Les Sandales d'Empédocle*, 173–200.

plume of Edmonde Vinel, a prolific intellectual who attended the École Normale Supérieure and taught philosophy at the Lycée in Rennes up to the Occupation. At that point, she began writing literary reviews, now under her protective pseudonym, for Mounier's *Esprit* before the review was shut down by the Nazi regime.

Magny's reading of Kafka overlaps with Camus's essay in significant ways. She, too, starts off with Brod's reading, which discerns a quasi-religious, Kierkegaardian mood, interpreting *The Castle* as a novel about fear and trembling in a world that fails to provide any satisfactory answers; yet whereas Brod takes the plot as a sincere search for grace that never arrives, Magny senses a trick, a "sleight of hand" (*escamotage*, 173). In reducing the novel to an abstract scheme with a single plan, Brod's interpretation contradicts the very aim of the plot he outlines: He essentially claims that the novel *means* the failure of meaning. He rationalizes its irrationalism. Here, Magny comes closer to Wahl's conclusions. Deceived by a sophistic paradox—that the answer lies in the absence of answers—the reader neglects what is truly fascinating about Kafka's work, namely, "the objective, ordinary aspect, down to the banality of the events recounted, whose quotidian character contrasts with the essential absurdity" (173–4). Like Camus, Magny underscores the discrepancy in Kafka's approach between the strangeness of the world he depicts and its ordinary naturalness, a discrepancy that has an experiential effect on the reader. What this effect entails is that the reader cannot be detached from the work and exercise the kind of subjective cognition that would reveal a definitive answer; rather, the reader is drawn in, forced to confront the meaninglessness of Kafka's reality, which is the reader's reality, and realize there is no exit. We do not watch K. from a comfortable distance, we *are* K. Camus would concur: While Kafka does all the talking, he doesn't confess himself, rather "we are the ones he confesses."

In confessing us, Kafka forgoes subjective self-expression. Magny refers to Brod's assertion that Kafka began *The Castle* in the first-person narration and eventually switched to the third person, which converted the project to an "objective style" (174). As Magny demonstrates, the narratives show no traces of a narrator's subjective determination. There is no "puppeteer." The stories, she insists, do not even appear to have been written by a human consciousness. In this regard, the text is not "literary," but more like a "meteorite" that has fallen from the sky (174). Unlike the subjectively driven work of Proust, the author is nowhere discernible in Kafka's writing. He does not use his plots and characters to communicate his thoughts or express his feelings. Instead, his authorial task is limited to letting the story manifest itself and unfold in accordance with its inherent law. Kafka does not "instrumentalize" the text; rather, the text instrumentalizes him and therefore us (175).

Magny presents Kafka as an anti-idealist who senses the limits of the rational subject, the shortcomings of a *cogito* that poses as a quasi-divine origin which creates and orders a meaningful world, as a *causa efficiens* that envisions a project and sees it through to the end. Kafka's purely objective style consists in the absence of the subject, an absence that results in a scandalously absurd world, reminiscent of the reality described by Sartre's Roquentin, one that is motivated neither by reason nor cause.

> The world, for Kafka, is essentially a scandal, something that is not rational; consequently, only a fantastic tale can express its essence. To make a philosophy of it (even if this philosophy admits in its bosom the scandal and the paradox, as that of Kierkegaard), it would still make it too rational, and consequently distort it. Only the gratuity of the pure event, the *contingit*, can manifest the essential absurdity of things.
>
> (175–6)

Kafka's protagonists may be overburdened with guilt, but there is never any discernible *cause* for this guilt. Moreover, their actions are already judged, they are already convicted. Thus, in *The Metamorphosis*, there is no justifiable cause for Gregor's transformation: It simply occurs, scandalously (177n1).

Like Wahl, Magny distinguishes Kafka from Kierkegaard, albeit along a different track. In her view, the scandal resembles the Christian doctrine of "original sin," further intensified by an existentialist insistence on responsibility. There is no rational measure that could codify the relationship between Man and God. The divine will remains as inscrutable as the inner sanctum of the Castle is inaccessible. In providing no answers and no consolation, Kafka's work is profoundly unsettling (178–9). Instead, Kafka presents us with nightmarish scenes, not dissimilar to the depictions in Lewis Carroll or the Surrealists, scenes that interrogate or shatter preconceived notions of reality. Kafka's objective style, its implicit critique of subjective intentions and conceptualization, is the necessary corollary to an absurd reality, one that is irredeemably untethered, mercilessly set adrift. No amount of willpower can overcome this scandal. Magny again turns to *The Metamorphosis* for illustration: Gregor *intends* to speak to his mother and then to the bank executive who checks in on him, but Gregor's voice emits nothing but incomprehensible squeaking (192). He is confined to isolation, like Sartre's solitary man, reduced to an insect. Interpersonal communication breaks down. The shards each of us holds never match, never coincide perfectly into one symbolic whole. Writing at the height of the Nazi Occupation, Magny concludes:

Everywhere, all around us are the dark things that one sees, that one would see, if one had the strength to keep one's eyes wide open to look at them in the face. But that is almost intolerable; and so, one gives up, or closes one's eyes, and everything falls back into obscurity. Perhaps it is better that way.

(200)

V Judgments

UPSIDE DOWN, RIGHT SIDE UP

Although they precede his critical engagement with the writer, Maurice Blanchot's first two novels of the Occupation have been regarded as evoking Kafka's style and sensibility. In *Thomas the Obscure* (1941), which Blanchot will considerably abridge for a 1950 edition, the reader encounters a protagonist in perpetual metamorphosis, who plunges into an intensely felt environment at constant risk of suffocation or self-abolition. Here, however, the Kafkaesque traits of intensity, disorientation, and ambiguity are rather vague and subtle, perhaps owing more to Blanchot's early engagement with Husserlian phenomenology, which he shared not only with his dear friend Emmanuel Levinas but also, through the Brentano School, with Kafka himself. One could just as well ascribe the narrative approach to Nerval or Lautréamont, to Mallarmé or Giraudoux. With Blanchot's second novel, *Aminadab* (1942), the resemblances are much clearer: Thomas arrives in a village as a stranger, he is beckoned to enter a house by a woman whom he will never see again, and instead drifts from room to room amid tenants who guide him elliptically or sometimes speechlessly from one dead end to another until the novel fades out with the calm assurance of perplexity: "Who are you?" Thomas asks in the novel's final sentence. "It was as if this question would allow him to bring everything into the clear."[1]

For Sartre, Blanchot's indebtedness to Kafka is irrefutable, to the point of outright imitation. Blanchot's claim not to have read the Prague author when he wrote his novel cannot dissuade Sartre from seeing in *Aminadab* "the same meticulous, urbane style, the same nightmarish civility, the same weird, starchy ceremoniousness, the same vain quests—vain since they lead to nothing; the same exhaustive, stagnant reasoning; and the same sterile initiations—sterile because they are not initiations into anything."[2] Sartre's essay does not restrict itself to a review of Blanchot's novel. First published in 1943 in the *Cahiers du Sud* under Vichy watch, months after his magnum opus, *Being and Nothingness* appeared, Sartre's article takes the opportunity to set the proliferating Kafka legacy straight by comparing *Aminadab* to Camus's

---

[1] Maurice Blanchot, *Aminadab*, tr. Jeff Fort (Lincoln: University of Nebraska Press, 2002), 199.
[2] Sartre, "Aminadab: Or the Fantastic Considered as a Language" [1943], in *Critical Essays*, tr. Chris Turner (London: Seagull Books, 2017), 187. ["'Aminadab': ou du fantastique considéré comme un langage," in *Situations I: Essais critiques* (Paris: Gallimard, 1947), 114].

Stranger against the foil of Kafka's work, all in an attempt to define existentialist absurdity. What precisely is the Absurd? And to what extent and in what manner is it discernible in Kafka, Camus, and Blanchot? These questions, Sartre proposes, can only be addressed when one first distinguishes the *Absurd* from the *Fantastic*. In addition, Sartre posits what he believes to be the fundamental criterion of literary criticism, that a writer's style and narrative technique ought to reflect the writer's metaphysical views. Blanchot's style may be superficially similar to Kafka's, yet do the two authors share the same metaphysics?

According to Sartre, absurdity stems from a complete lack of transcendence, which can only mean that Kafka's fiction is not absurd at all. In Kafka there is transcendence, there is a higher meaning, despite the fact that this meaning can never be reached or recovered. On this basis, rather than discuss Kafka in terms of the Absurd, it is more correct to relate his work to *la littérature fantastique*, including its most recent surrealist variants. In the Fantastic, transcendent meaning persists; though inaccessible, it is still capable of impinging on everyday reality in the form of dreams or madness. With the Absurd, in contrast, there is no meaning beyond existence; all transcendence is but a construction, articulated out of fear or bad faith.

Kafka's work belongs to the tradition of the Fantastic, even if it has little to do with the imaginative flights of fancy that one finds, for example, in Hoffmann or Charles Nodier. In these early iterations, fantasy fuels the imagination to escape the human condition, while in Kafka, the Fantastic compels us to maintain the contingencies of human existence. What all fantastic literature holds in common, however, is a commitment to depicting "a world upside down" (*un monde à l'envers*). Although uncited, Groethuysen's reading is operative here. Fantastic literature is directly opposed to literature of the Absurd, which portrays "a world right side up" (*un monde à l'endroit*, 194/118–19). The distinction is most discernible in the different relationships between means and ends. In the world right side up, things are utensils, available for human use and serving human purposes; while in the world upside down, there are only means without any specific ends, or conversely, specific goals without the means for achieving them. In fantastic literature, a door opens onto a bricked wall, or one views the upper level of a café but there is no stairway leading up to it. According to Sartre, this topsy-turvy world is precisely what one finds in Kafka's fantastic scenarios. The Castle is there but one can never penetrate its secrets.

The state of affairs is much different in Camus's *Stranger*, for it describes the right-side-up world of the Absurd. Here, the ends are not inaccessible, they are utterly absent. Hence, human being is confined to a life of senseless routine and Sisyphean labor. The same holds for Blanchot who, according to Sartre, also does not believe in transcendence.

The problem with *Aminadab* is that, despite Blanchot's absurdist-existentialist metaphysics—that the world is evacuated of meaning—he adopts Kafka's fantastic-surrealist style. In Sartre's assessment, Blanchot's novels are situated in a world right side up, which he confusingly portrays as a world upside down. "The system of signs he has chosen doesn't entirely correspond to the thought he expresses" (212/129). Blanchot's novels are confusing, insofar as they appear to draw on Kafka's repertoire to depict a world that conflicts with it.

Sartre hereby detects a political effect that alludes to Blanchot's youthful endorsement of the ultra-right, nationalist vision of Charles Maurras. For Maurras and his retinue, the image of a glorious France persisted as transcendent ideal, one that had been rendered inaccessible by capitalist corruption and communistic internationalism alike. Somewhat tendentiously, Sartre's own burgeoning adherence to Marxism is brought to bear on his judgment: "Seen against a transcendence tinged with Maurrassianism, the fantastic looks like something that has been tacked on" (213/130). In this way, Sartre implicitly questions the sincerity of Blanchot's retreat into a neutral literary space presumably divorced from political partisanship. Blanchot may have renounced all ideology, yet his fiction, which mismatches style and worldview, can be regarded as a sign of Blanchot's inauthenticity, that what he says may not be what he means.[3]

For many contemporary readers, Sartre's criticism was seen as harshly ad hominem. The separation of a writer's style and metaphysics is in itself questionable but becomes worrisome when it is deployed to score a political point. In a letter to Georges Bataille—one of Blanchot's close friends—Michel Leiris complained about the inappropriateness of the review and said he conveyed his misgivings to Sartre face-to-face.[4] Bataille, who had cited from Blanchot's works in *Inner Experience*, also published in 1943, spoke out in support of *Aminadab*, having recently claimed that "agreement with oneself is perhaps a kind of death."[5] Soon, in the postwar period, Leiris, Bataille, and Blanchot would collectively proffer a reading that would aim to redeem Kafka from the existentialist monopoly.

---

[3] See Laurent Dubreuil, "Histoires d'une hantise: Kafka, Sartre," in *Sillage de Kafka*, ed. Philippe Zard (Paris: Éditions Le Manuscrit, 2007), 213–18.

[4] Leiris to Bataille, July 6, 1943; cited in Christophe Bident, *Maurice Blanchot: A Critical Biography*, tr. John McKeane (New York: Fordham University Press, 2019), 516n.4.

[5] In Marcel Arland, "Chronique des romans," *NRF* 335 (January 1, 1942), 94; cited in Bident, *Maurice Blanchot*, 165.

From the perspective of 1943, it was clear that Sartre had a score to settle. It was, after all, Blanchot who instigated the trouble back in 1938 in his review of *Nausea* for the satirical journal *Aux Écoutes*. As Anna Boschetti points out, Sartre's review of *Aminadab* mimics the structure of Blanchot's review of *Nausea*: Where Blanchot charges Sartre with borrowing mythical elements that belie the text's commitment to immanence, Sartre accuses Blanchot of appropriating fantastic elements that contradict his metaphysics; where Blanchot decries Sartre's overdependence on Heidegger, Sartre denounces Blanchot's reliance on Kafka. What added fuel to Sartre's fire was an article that Blanchot wrote for the *Journal des Débats* (May 14, 1941), where he flatly dismissed *Nausea* as a prime example of how disappointing the French novel had become.[6] The question, who represents the true Kafka legacy, thus became a deciding factor in determining the shape and direction of contemporary French literature and thought.

DISENGAGEMENT

Although Sartre, born 1905, and Blanchot, born 1907, shared much in terms of personal upbringing, cultural milieu, and philosophical orientation, the general trajectory of each man's development comprises a nearly perfect inversion of the other. Sartre's shift from an isolated position in thought and literature to political engagement on the Left transposes Blanchot's withdrawal from activism on the Right to the solitude of literary space. Both turning points occurred over the timespan that stretches from late 1937 through the phony war into the Occupation; and both involved a direct encounter with the work of Kafka. One could say that Kafka was the pivot where the two critics met before traveling in opposite directions, with Sartre heading towards an understanding of literature as engaged in the world and Blanchot towards the view that literature is the "refusal to take part in the world."[7] Kafka is the point of convergence that defines their divergence.[8]

---

[6] Anna Boschetti, *Sartre et 'Les Temps Modernes': Une entreprise intellectuelle* (Paris: Minuit 1985), 18–19, and 53. See Bident's overview of the debate in *Maurice Blanchot*, 516n.4.

[7] Blanchot, "Literature and the Right to Death," in *The Work of Fire*, tr. Charlotte Mandell (Stanford: Stanford University Press, 1995), 315 [in Blanchot, *De Kafka à Kafka* (Paris: Gallimard, 1981), 11–61].

[8] This point is stressed by Aukje van Rooden, "Kafka Shared Between Blanchot and Sartre," *Arcadia* 55 (2020), 239–59.

On October 1, 1945, Gallimard published the premier issue of Sartre's new periodical, which sported a Chaplinesque title: *Les Temps Modernes*. Sartre and his editorial committee— Raymond Aron, Simone de Beauvoir, Maurice Merleau-Ponty, Albert Ollivier, and, with some hesitation, Jean Paulhan—envisioned a journal for the new generation, one that would chart the progress of French letters and debates now that the nation had emerged from the darkest night. It would attend to the most urgent questions, pursuing lines of thought wherever thinking led, without retreating into facile, partisan dogmatism, to promote a refreshed alliance between philosophy, literary writers, and politics: *La littérature engagée*. Accordingly, the first number contained a brief editorial, unsigned yet clearly written by Sartre, and printed on the last page, which addressed the thorny topic of the on-going purges regarding those who had collaborated with the Nazi and Vichy governments. The editorial is titled "À la Kafka," intended sardonically to decry the arbitrariness and vagueness of official decisions in charging and trying suspects and sentencing the convicted. The moral-philosophical themes of guilt, responsibility, and grace which had steered earlier reflections on Kafka were now gravely concrete.

The fraught context is self-evident. Since the summer of 1945, the French public had been grappling with the severity of the current state of affairs. Sartre's old student from Le Havre, Jacques-Laurent Bost, was now working as a correspondent in Dachau, writing pieces for *Combat* that described in horrific detail the reality of the gas chambers and the crematoria. The eighty-nine-year-old Marshal Pétain stood trial in August and was expeditiously sentenced to death, until two days later, when President de Gaulle personally commuted the sentence to life imprisonment. Weeks after the first issue of *Les Temps Modernes* appeared, Pierre Laval, twice Prime Minister of France (1931–2 and 1935–6), then Head of the Vichy government from 1942, would be executed by firing squad, while the Allies' International Military Tribunal were preparing indictments against Nazi leaders and organizations for the trials at Nuremberg. Yet, while the severe sentencing of political leaders generally found consensus among the Parisian intelligentsia, the culpability of writers, filmmakers, and critics, as well as their publishers and producers, was met with troubled ambivalence. After all, writers of unquestioned patriotism published under the Occupation, including Sartre who, moreover, on more than one occasion, was scrutinized by the hardline communist branch of the Resistance for his affiliation with Heidegger. But what about those who were more outspoken in their support of the fascists? The fate of Robert Brasillach, novelist, critic, and editor of the fascist periodical *Je suis partout*, had been an especially prominent example. Tried in Paris as a collaborator in January 1945 by a judge who had served under the

Vichy government, his death sentence sparked protest, culminating in a petition circulated by François Mauriac, and signed by the nation's leading literary figures—Paul Valéry, Paul Claudel, Collette, Jean Cocteau, Jean Anouilh, and Albert Camus among many others. Although repulsed by Brasillach, the signatories called for commuting the sentence. Sartre refused to sign, debates proliferated in the press, but de Gaulle rejected the pleas for leniency and sent Brasillach to his execution on February 6, 1945.

The case of the film director Henri-Georges Clouzot was even more complicated. During the war, Clouzot had been in charge of the script department at Continental Films, a French company owned and operated by the Nazi occupation regime, yet surprisingly capable of maintaining artistic independence. His most important wartime film was *Le Corbeau* (1943), set in a provincial French town that is torn apart by an informant, "le Corbeau" or "the Raven," who sends anonymous letters to the local authorities denouncing misdemeanors committed by purportedly upstanding members of the community. Despite the film's clear potential for being viewed as an allegory of the Vichy climate, after the Liberation, Resistance-fueled critics vilified the director's complicity with the Nazi regime as a former executive at Continental. In a civic court working with the Comité de libération du cinéma français, Clouzot was convicted as a collaborator, banned from filmmaking for life, prohibited from any film set or location, and even forbidden to use a camera.[9]

Sartre's editorial "À la Kafka" protests the double standards in dealing with creative artists: Some receive harsh sentences, while others, apparently by means of clever bribery, get off with a slap on the wrist. Who, Sartre asks, are the judges? Sartre reports that the decree was issued under order by the "Commission d'Organisation de l'Industrie Cinématographique" and highlights the identifying initials—"Take the initials and you find C.O.I.C."—to emphasize that this body is in fact the Comité d'Organisation de l'Industrie Cinématographique, the very committee formed in 1940 by the Vichy government and overseen by Pétain's Ministry of Information. Is Sartre being serious? Is it necessary to abbreviate *Commission* to discern its link to *Comité*? At any rate, Sartre draws the obvious conclusion: "Thus, the collaborators will have been judged by collaborators.... But the most curious thing is that you will not find the judges. We say to them:

---

[9] See Christopher Lloyd, *Henri-Georges Clouzot* (Manchester: Manchester University Press, 2007), 25–6.

'Who condemned Clouzet [sic]?'"[10] The name is misspelled. Of course, one might well write it off as a simple typographical error, were it not for the fact that Sartre has just underscored, quite ludicrously, the importance of letters. What Sartre is doing, I would suggest, is performing à la Kafka, staging a Chaplinesque comedy, perhaps to ridicule the carelessness of the purges or maybe to evoke K.'s awkward confusion in *The Castle* between one official named Sortini and another named Sordini. For Sartre, the Clouzot or Clouzet affair—the secret court, the nameless, corruptible judges, the open-ended sentencing, the dodgy system where no one is willing to take responsibility—is Kafkaesque in this sense. "Only in Kafka's universe does one find such absurd [*saugrenues*] decisions."

As Sartre sees it, the present situation resembles a scene from fantastic literature. The infiltration of collaborators in post-Liberation offices, the wavering, ad hoc opinions of those in power, the double standards, the utter lack of clarity and consistency—it is all part of a world upside down, just like the phony war, the *guerre à la Kafka*. One knows there is a court with real judges, yet it all remains inaccessible, just as in 1939 one knew France was at war with Germany, without military engagement ever taking place. Once one realizes the existentialist truth that there is no transcendent meaning, that all values are merely constructs, then the Kafkaesque can only be something tacked on to reality, something detached from the work itself. It would be more advisable to let inauthenticity and inanity goad the human subject into action, to expose the contradictions and the hypocrisy, and thereby intervene in the world. Accordingly, soon after his editorial was published, Sartre—perhaps mindful of his former reluctance over the Brasillach affair—gathered letters of support for Clouzot and managed to have his life sentence commuted to two years. The proceedings *à la Kafka* inspired him to effect change in real life.

Blanchot questions the validity of reducing Kafka to the Kafkaesque and does so precisely by examining the tension between literary work and life. His first essay devoted to the Prague author, "Reading Kafka" ("La lecture de Kafka"), published one month later in the November 1945 issue of *L'Arche*, begins by noting the common impulse to look for evidence from Kafka's life to resolve ambiguities in the texts, to appeal to extra-literary information to make sense of the literary. The *Diaries* are a typical source in this regard. Yet, rather than provide a general "theory" that would explicate the work, Kafka's entries come across as uniquely literary, embedded in fiction; any diary passage thus fails to

---

[10] "À la Kafka," *Les Temps Modernes* 1:1 (October 1, 1945), 191.

"arrive at the point of what it is supposed to be explaining; and more important, it does not succeed in soaring over it."[11] According to Blanchot, everything Kafka has written wavers between two poles, "solitude and the law," "silence and everyday speech" (3/65). The distinction implicitly elaborates on the polarity that Wahl derived from Kafka's reading of Kierkegaard, between the general and the singular. On the one hand, there are narratives that are unique and therefore incommunicable or "silent," while on the other hand, there are those that attempt to convey an overarching, transcendent, informative theory. Still, for Blanchot, solitude—Kafka's solitude—is not absolute since it communicates this solitude, it relates the unrelatable or communicates the incommunicable.

With rapid strokes, Blanchot rattles off an inventory of existentialist interpretations which comprise the basis for the so-called Kafkaesque— "the absurd, contingency, the will to make a place for oneself in the world, the impossibility of keeping oneself there, the desire for God, the absence of god, despair, anguish" (5/67)—theoretical accounts that contradict each other and cannot be reconciled. Still, for Blanchot, the issue is not merely a conflict of interpretations but rather the fact that each explication, each communicative law, is posited only through its singular disavowal. "Transcendence is exactly this affirmation that can assert itself only by negation. It exists as a result of being denied; it is present because *it is not there*" (7/69; my emphasis). Whereas the *law* proffers something that can be represented and communicated, *solitude* guards the secret that there is nothing there. Blanchot elaborates on this affirmative negation by contrasting it with death. Death stabilizes, it fixes meaning once and for all. In contrast, the *movement* of Kafka's writings forestalls death, as in the figure of *The Hunter Gracchus* who no longer lives yet cannot die. "Death," Blanchot writes, "ends our life, but it does not end our possibility of dying" (8/71). The indeterminacy of living corresponds to the text's interminability.

Towards the end of his essay, Blanchot seems to allude to a detail from Sartre's editorial "À la Kafka"—specifically, that filmmakers convicted of collaboration must wait for a sentencing which may or may not be overturned, reduced, or lengthened, what Sartre calls "torture through hope."[12] Blanchot recognizes the same in Kafka, albeit solely on the basis of literary praxis: The narratives "torture hope ... not because hope is condemned but because it does not succeed in being condemned" (10/73). The writing never finds repose, neither in

---

[11] Blanchot, "Reading Kafka," in *The Work of Fire*, 3. [*De Kafka à Kafka*, 64.]
[12] Sartre, "À la Kafka," 191.

the full light nor in the utter darkness of theoretical understanding. Rather, it persists in a twilight zone of dying without death. Writing is an *arrêt de mort*, simultaneously a "death sentence" and a "cessation of death." The ambivalence results from literature's linguistic constitution, a language that only tenuously refers to a world that is distinct from it. The oscillation in Kafka's texts, between solitude and law, casts literature as a site of undecidability, and it is this point that makes Sartre's committed action impossible. Literature fails to provide the basis for action in the world, just as, conversely, the world fails to supply the grounds for perfect understanding of the text. Instead of viewing literature as an opportunity for engagement, Blanchot sees it as cause for engaged disengagement, a praxis that never escapes the literary.

Although equally a nominalist, Sartre still believes in practical action. In *What is Literature?* (1947), he reiterates one of the central theses from *Being and Nothingness*, that "human reality" (*la realité humaine*, Sartre's translation of Heidegger's *Dasein*) is not only "condemned to be free" but also obliged to act freely in the world, to change the world. Literature, according to Sartre, is specifically designed for engagement. The premise responds to Gide's quip regarding Sartre's manifesto, which appeared at the front of the inaugural 1945 issue of *Les Temps Modernes*: "I truly hope," Gide snidely remarked, "that, after literature [Sartre] will also 'commit' painting and music."[13] Now, two years later, Sartre formulates his rebuttal:

> No, we do not want to "engage" painting, sculpture, and music "too," or at least not in the same way. . . . it is one thing to work with color and sound, and another to express oneself by means of words. Notes, colors, and forms are not signs. They refer to nothing exterior to themselves.[14]

It is this connection between language and the world that undergirds literature's engagement as well as its free capacity to move beyond the given reality of lived situations; hence, the power of Kafka's imagination:

> The work of Kafka is a free and unitary reaction to the Judeo-Christian world of Central Europe. His novels are a synthetic act

---

[13] Gide in *Terre des hommes* (Nov. 3, 1945); cited in Cohen-Solal, *Jean-Paul Sartre*, 257–8.
[14] Sartre, *What is Literature?*, tr. Bernard Frechtman (New York: Philosophical Library, 1949), 7–8. *Qu'est-ce que la littérature?* was originally published in *Les Temps Modernes*, Feb. to July 1947 (Paris: Gallimard, 1948), 13–14.

of going beyond [*dépassement*] his situation as a man, as a Jew, as a Czech, as a recalcitrant fiancé, as a tubercular, etc., as were also his handshake, his smile, and that gaze which Max Brod so admired. Under the analysis of the critic, they break down into problems; but the critic is wrong; they must be read *in movement*.

(296/293; emphasis in text)

In focusing solely on themes, the critic merely provides an inventory for the Kafkaesque without hitting upon the core of the texts' significance.

As for Kafka, everything has been said: that he wanted to paint a picture of bureaucracy, the progress of disease, the condition of the Jews in eastern Europe, the quest for inaccessible transcendence, and the world of grace when grace is lacking. This is all true. Let me say that he wanted to describe the human condition. But what we were particularly sensitive to was that this trial was perpetually in session, which ends abruptly and evilly, whose judges are unknown and out of reach, in the vain efforts of the accused to know the leaders of the prosecution, in this absurd present which the characters live with great earnestness and whose keys are elsewhere, we recognize History and ourselves in History.

(227/227)

Having engaged in his world, Kafka engages ours and exposes its absurdity. Blanchot would agree that the power of Kafka's texts lies in its movement, yet he would reject the reduction of literary language to its referential function. In Blanchot's view, the movement in Kafka's text is one that vacillates between the general and the singular, all within fiction, rather than a movement from fiction to the real world. In "Literature and the Right to Death," published in Bataille's *Critique* (January 1948), Blanchot grants literature's capacity to transform History but only on the basis of its utter divorce from History. What Sartre identifies as literature's *dépassement*, its ability to go beyond one's given situation, Blanchot sees as a pure refusal of the world. "If [literature] is not really in the world, working to make the world, this is because its lack of being (of intelligible reality) causes it to refer to an existence that is still inhuman."[15] Literature is not merely nothing, not because it is something but rather because literature's substance consists

---

[15] Blanchot, "Literature and the Right to Death," 339 ["La littérature et le droit à la mort," 55]. Cf. van Rooden, "Kafka Shared Between Blanchot and Sartre," 246.

in being nothing. History recognizes literature's paradoxical existence, its substantive nothingness, and therefore spurns it. The engagement is broken off.

"Literature and the Right to Death" (1948) picks up the argument of "Reading Kafka" (1945), which is presumably why Blanchot reprinted it at the head of his 1981 collection *De Kafka à Kafka*, as if this article should be read as programmatic. Just as, in the earlier essay, Blanchot described Kafka's writing as oscillating between the poles of incommunicative solitude and communicable law, he now identifies two "slopes": *Meaningful prose*, which negates reality in order to know it, control it, and communicate it; and *literature*, which attends to that which evades this knowledge—what Bataille would call *non-savoir* ("non-knowledge")—a writing that gives itself over to what is free, unknown, and silent. Literature "knows it is the movement through which whatever disappears keeps appearing" (329/43). Caught between these two slopes, literature turns ordinary language into ambiguity. The writer posits by negating and negates by positing, affirms by renouncing, and denies by asserting. In this regard, Blanchot draws on Hegel and Alexandre Kojève's reading of Hegel to bring Kafka into proximity with Mallarmé: Writing confirms the writer's existence by abolishing it. "Why," Blanchot asks, "would a man like Kafka decide that if he had to fall short of his destiny, being a writer was the only way to fall short of it truthfully?" (341/56). Kafka's writing consists in this ambiguous wavering between the success of communication and its failure, where the former slope spells a stabilizing, determinant death, and the latter the interminable impossibility of death.

> Kafka inherited this idea from the Cabala and Eastern traditions. A man enters the night, but the end in awakening, and there he is, an insect. Or else the man dies, but he is actually alive; he goes from city to city, carried along by rivers, recognized by some people, helped by no one, the mistake made by old death snickering at his bedside; his is a strange condition, he has forgotten to die. But another man thinks he is alive, when the fact is, he has forgotten his death, and yet another, knowing he is dead, struggles in vain to die; death is over there, the great unattainable castle, and life was over there, the native land he left in answer to a false summons; now there is nothing to do but struggle, to work at dying completely, but if you struggle, you are still alive; and everything that brings the goal closer also makes the goal inaccessible.
>
> (338/53)

While for Sartre Kafka is an author who communicates literature's ability to step beyond (*dépasser*) the status quo—for Blanchot Kafka will always be simply an author for whom every affirmation is also a negation. Blanchot will use the ambiguity of the term *pas*, which denotes both the noun "step" and the adverbial "not," to encapsulate the dynamic that relishes in and recasts literature as a *pas-au-delà*, a "step beyond" and "no beyond."

This double movement will inform most of Blanchot's critical essays devoted to Kafka up until "The Very Last Word," which was published, provocatively, in the May 1, 1968 issue of the *NRF*—one day before the administration shut down the University of Paris. Here, Blanchot again calls attention to the struggle in Kafka between "writing" and "what is other than it" (*l'autre qu'elle*)—how this "other than . . . belongs to writing insofar as writing cannot belong to itself."[16] Kafka's work thus demonstrates the substantive nothingness of theory, which Blanchot will emphasize in the aftermath of the protests:

> Theory obviously does not consist of the elaboration of a program or platform, but, on the contrary, and outside of any programmatic project, and even of all project, of maintaining a refusal that affirms, of releasing [*dégager*] or maintaining an affirmation that does not adapt itself [*ne s'arrange pas*], but which upsets and upsets itself [*qui dérange et se dérange*], in contact with disarrangement [*le désarrangement*] or disarray [*le désarroi*], or even with the non-structurable.[17]

For Blanchot, engagement with Kafka is always also a disengagement.

INCENDIARIES

On May 31, 1946, the official periodical of the French Communist Party (PCF), *Action*, printed a provocation signed by the paper's literary editor, Pierre Fauchery: *Faut-il brûler Kafka?* ("Should Kafka be

---

[16] Blanchot, "The Very Last Word," in *Friendship*, tr. Elizabeth Rottenberg (Stanford: Stanford University Press, 1997), 272 ["Le tout dernier mot," in *De Kafka à Kafka*, 229.]

[17] Blanchot, "Affirmer la rupture," first published as part of "Tracts affiches bulletins" in *Comité* (Oct. 1968), reprinted in Blanchot, *Écrits politiques: Guerre d'Algérie, Mai 68, etc.* (Paris: Lignes, 2003), 105; cited and translated in Allan Stoekl, "Blanchot: Death, Language, Community and Politics," *Parallax* 12 (2006), 40–52; here, p. 50.

burned?"). Fauchery admits that the question, which he claims came from an anonymous friend, is shocking yet is, upon reflection, "quite reasonable" provided one admits that:

> 1, society has the right to take defensive measures against a writer if it judges that his activity endangers its essential interests; 2, that Kafka's work expresses, in a contagious way, a certain state of social decomposition, and that by describing manifestly morbid states of consciousness, it risks awakening or confirming them in the reader.[18]

The article rides on the crest of the communists' broad legitimacy in the immediate postwar period. From the first days after the Liberation of Paris, the party had styled itself, not without some justification, as having led the resistance against fascism. A large swath of the population placed faith in Maurice Thorez, leader of the PCF and recently appointed to serve as de Gaulle's Deputy Prime Minister, that the Fourth Republic would thrive with a non-Bolshevist, civilized revision of communism. Many intellectuals endorsed an emphatically humanist interpretation of Marx as the most viable option for achieving social equity, while staving off American imperialism and fascist recidivism.[19] The Zhdanovist tone of Fauchery's query into the value of Kafka's work, however, goes one step further towards full-fledged Stalinism—precisely the kind of zealotry that will alienate Western Marxists by 1947. His hypothesis is that if Kafka's work triggers anguish, despair, and pessimism, then it militates against the ideals of Soviet-sponsored social realism, which calls for optimistic literature and the promotion of morally conservative, proletariat values. Insofar as posterity rests in the hands of readers, Fauchery asks, rather cagily, whether it would not be advisable to eliminate this unwholesome example of *la littérature noire* for the sake of a better future? He closes by inviting writers to submit their opinions for publication.

It is not clear what occasioned the solicitation, though it is likely that Sartre's extraordinary success and public influence played a key role. The conflict between Sartre and the communists was long-standing. Already during the Occupation, the far-left branch of the Comité National des Écrivains had difficulties with Sartre who, although sympathetic to the Marxist cause, rejected deterministic materialism as much as abstract

---

[18] Pierre Fauchery, "Faut-il brûler Kafka?" in *Action* 90 (May 31, 1946), 12.
[19] See Tony Judt, *Past Imperfect: French Intellecutals, 1944–1956* (Berkeley: University of California Press, 1992), 159–61.

idealism. For the philosopher of being and nothingness, any attempt to control literature would rob culture of the freedom that served as its very basis. He lamented how the Soviet Union's commitment to revolution reverted to the most conservative means; how the communists, no less than the capitalists, turned the free individual into an object, a cog in the machine. From the party's postwar perspective, Sartre's Marxism was dangerously heretical, with existentialism, along with its favored literary artist, Franz Kafka, now being viewed as a potent rival, one that the communists regarded with suspicion and envy.

Fauchery's bid might be dismissed as a typical example of ideological overreach were it not for the fact that it attracted a significant list of writers, which demonstrates Kafka's position in this fraught environment. At least in theory. Out of the dozens of replies, few even mention Kafka, choosing instead to defend every author's right to publish freely. The first response by Julien Benda sets the tone by merely rehearsing the argument he presented in *Trahison des clercs* (1927), that a pure, apolitical precinct should be preserved for all writers.[20] More surprising is the next piece by Jean Paulhan, who likewise neglects to name the author whose French career he directly launched. Instead, he denounces Fauchery's question as presuming that readers are "imbeciles," incapable of judging for themselves: "The reader is generally a clever guy who doesn't let himself be imposed upon, who reacts against optimism on command, with the hope towards a pessimism a little too black." While Michel Leiris does refer to Kafka, he does so only in passing: Communists who want to burn Kafka would resemble the devotees of Hitler. The perpetually introspective Leiris takes the occasion, rather, to define authentic writing as a means for discovering oneself and encouraging others to know themselves better; all external imperatives that aim to steer self-examination are therefore fruitless. Implicitly, Leiris regards Kafka as one of those honest writers who contribute to emancipation, "since what paralyses us at all times is the incapacity—through lack of intelligence or through cowardice—to look our condition in the face." Overall, the initial remarks attend to the more urgent issue, that literature should not be controlled, censored, or self-censored. François Mauriac will follow suit in a subsequent number (June 28): "All literature that is not 'black' falsifies life." The same holds for Maurice Merleau-Ponty (July 12): "I do not believe that one can make a society, nor a politics, nor, for that matter, an art, by means of 'imperatives.'" If these writers do not bother to discuss Kafka specifically, it is because his literary value is beyond dispute.

---

[20] *Action* 93 (June 14, 1946), n.p. Subsequent references to *Action* are marked by publication date.

Some replies, however, do deal with Kafka directly. For his contribution (June 21), Francis Ponge offers a dialogue between a speaker who represents Fauchery's position and one who clearly stands in for himself. Ponge is an interesting case. In addition to having worked in the 1920s as an assistant at Gallimard under Paulhan—who mentored his early poetry and published his acclaimed collection of prose poems, *Le parti pris des choses* (1942), in the series *Métamorphoses*—Ponge currently served as the artistic director of *Action*. Before he addresses the issue of Fauchery's proposal, Ponge identifies a more fundamental "imperative," the one that makes someone a writer, namely the command "to plug the hole that is constantly digging into your side." While Ponge admits that his poetry adopts a different approach, so-called *black literature* is one that describes the unique hole that drives the writer to write. As for Kafka, he fell into his hole, "for lack of having known how to plug it," to the point where his work reveals the abysses that gape inside each and every one of us. The Fauchery voice asserts that common man would not realize he suffered any existential lack unless a writer like Kafka revealed it. But ignorance, Ponge counters, does not mean the gap is not there. One can try, if one likes, to banish all disturbing literature from one's life; perhaps Kafka's ashes would be sufficient to fill the inner hole; but in the end the belief that burning this work would solve the problem is nothing more than fragile optimism. When asked what he would therefore recommend, Ponge replies "nothing"—he is too busy. "Busy with what?" his interlocutor inquires. "Everything that's needed to burn me one day."

As a poet, Ponge questions the reliability of words and therefore yields to "the committed position of things" (*le parti pris des choses*). His sensibility places him in some proximity with Blanchot, who, in reviewing the 1942 collection, contrasted his approach to the one discernible in the work of Michaux: "What is a tree?" Blanchot asks. "One can lend it a divine nature like Ronsard, or with strange customs like Henri Michaux. Francis Ponge contents himself with entirely rigorous observations which reveal little by little his manner of being."[21] Whereas for Sartre, Kafka summons us to engage in the world by pointing to holes in the society's logic, for Ponge, the encounter with Kafka compels a search inward by exposing the gaps in one's own being. Ponge would resign from *Action* and withdraw his membership from the PCF the following year.

---

21 Blanchot's review appeared in the *Journal des Débats* (July 15, 1942); cited in Jérôme Roger, "Ponge, lecteur de Michaux: un différend sans merci," *Litttérature* 115 (1999), 70–86; here, p. 70.

Mental holes into which one falls but which can never be filled, affirmations that are always also negations—the paradoxical, post-*Symboliste*, quasi-vatic style that Blanchot was developing in his essays on Kafka was not to everyone's taste. It was a style congruent with the philosophical reflections of his friend Emmanuel Levinas and lightly echoed in Ponge's response, one that troubled more conventional intellectuals bent on morally sound clarity. For such writers, the dominant existentialist reading of Kafka as a poet of anguish and absurdity was equally troubling. Hence, the brief essay by the novelist Jean-Marie Dunoyer, which also appeared in the June 21 number of *Action* opposite Ponge's dialogue: "Should Kafka be burned? It is tempting when one considers the appalling amount of nonsense that is currently being spouted about him." Dunoyer admits that Kafka was for him the most relevant author to read when he served as soldier during the phony war of 1939–40. "I got into *The Castle* like butter. We were living a bad dream, and Kafka is a bad dream being lived." But now, after what the nation has been through, "the time of passivity is over ... it must be said, Kafka is out of date." As a moralist, Dunoyer proclaims, Kafka ought to be condemned if only because of the various readings his texts have generated:

> The irrationality of Kafka and of all "black literature" is infinitely dangerous ... because it fatally gives birth to philosophies that resurrect old errors. It is much more serious to return to obscurantism than to drive certain stupid brains to anarchy or despair.

If he had to choose, Dunoyer would prefer existential nihilism, its "anarchy or despair," over what he views as the dogmatic mystifications of a Blanchot. Still, would it not be better, he asks, to move on? In any event, he admits that it would not be prudent to burn Kafka: books that are banned only become more powerful among the population. Instead, one should face these demonic texts directly and "exorcise" them.

Roger Caillois, a founding member of Bataille's Collège de Sociologie, similarly alludes to demonism in his contribution (July 12). Having spent the war in exile in Argentina, Caillois returned to Paris, disenchanted by the heavy-handed rationalism of the PCF. Hence, his ironic reply to Fauchery's prompt:

> I think it would be appropriate to burn Kafka ... For the works of this author are among the most discouraging that exist, due to their depiction of a mechanical and absurd world, where nothing has sense nor reason nor effort. Moreover, it is to be feared that evil minds will one day claim (wrongly, but the damage will be done) that Kafka, in the mysterious judges of the *Trial*, in the

Judgments 131

invisible officials of the *Castle*, with their unexpected, irrevocable, incomprehensible but indisputable and, to say the least, transcendent decisions, did not describe anything other than the Communist party.

(July 12)

In the end, not one of the twenty-nine responses recommended burning Kafka, a fact that Fauchery had to acknowledge in his final summarization, entitled "From Kafka to Spinoza," printed in the August 7 issue. No French writer, Fauchrery concedes, would be comfortable dragging any author to the pyre. But what about Kafka specifically? Fauchery does not conceal his opinions:

> To evoke this tortured and masochistic little Jew, meticulous builder of a world without windows, while around me the real world offers so many, and so fulfilling, and so urgent reasons to abandon black literature and all literature; to speak about Kafka in July 1946 whereas reading him can be at best a mortification intended to hurl us afterwards more avidly into the joys of the summer (a guilty, complicated pursuit, and not at all recommendable to one who does not have too many vacations to count and savor the profusion of these joys): what vanity!

Admittedly not a "Kafkaphile," Fauchery denounces Caillois for his slanderous jibe against the Party, singling him out as holding a view that no rational person would endorse. "Kafka's world, the world of absurd decisions, the world of hopeless servitude—it's easy to recognize: It's the capitalist world." As for Fauchery's own slandering, his reference to Kafka as "this little Jew" (*ce petit juif*) appears to be intended, at least within the context of the present article, less as an antisemitic slur and more as another instigation, another call to action. In his estimation, the fate of the Jews depends on a choice: Either accept the humiliation, injustices, and catastrophes suffered under the Nazis and prophesied by Kafka or stand up in revolt against the fascists who continue to be fueled by global capitalism, just as Spinoza revolted for "freedom of thought against intolerance." For Fauchery, Spinoza represents the stronger Jewish spirit, in contrast to Kafka who knows only how "to brood over his abjection." Accordingly, Fauchery discerns two basic positions:

> Those who honor Kafka for having heralded a "human condition" without remedy and think that all authentic consciousness is condemned to bruise itself on the opaque walls of the dungeon where he has walled us in. And those who have already, in their

hearts, agreed to *burn Kafka*: that is, to refuse the world that makes Kafka possible—the world of the humiliated Jew—the world of humiliated man.

The argument ironizes Sartre's philosophy of contingency, freedom, and authenticity, which Fauchery finds perilously inconsistent. "There is some contradiction in affirming too schematically that the writer at the same time 'cannot escape' the game of historical conditions and that he is responsible for his own choice." Indeed, Sartre's presence can be felt throughout this concluding essay, for example when Fauchery disingenuously claims to fear that he will be mocked by "the esthetes of Saint-Germain-des-Prés," or when he portrays *la littérature engagée* as worthless if it champions the individual over the collective.

Sartre did not deign to honor Fauchery with a reply. Instead, on May 31, 1947, one year after *Action* announced its inquiry, Sartre gave a public lecture to a packed audience in the Salle d'Iéna in Paris—"Kafka, a Jewish Writer." Having recently written his *Réflexions sur la question juive* ("Reflections on the Jewish Question," 1946, published in English as *Anti-Semite and Jew*), Sartre had been invited by the French League for a Free Palestine to elaborate on the theme of antisemitism. To this end, he chose to speak on Kafka, which would also provide him with the opportunity to correct the view that Kafka's works and existentialism promoted pessimism and regression.[22] Sartre appears to have focused on Kafka's psychological difficulties with his oppressive father, who represents the Kierkegaardian realm of the ethical—that is, the realm of law, purpose, and meaning. Not dissimilar to Blanchot's distinction between "law" and "solitude," Sartre's terms define the movement of Kafka's literary practice, one that simultaneously depicts his tyrannized situation and the means for emancipation, yet only by remaining adolescent, only by being the failed son, incapable of belonging to the world of the father.

Sartre would pursue these points in his essay on "The Situation of the Writer in 1947," which he appended to the book version of *What is Literature?* Here, he does not refrain from asserting that the Communist Party is organized in such a way that it invariably distrusts free-thinking intellectuals. Following Caillois, he states that, in facing the Stalinists,

---

[22] Although no typescript of Sartre's lecture was preserved, we have a contemporaneous review by Françoise Derins, published in *Le Nef*: Derins, "A Lecture by Jean-Paul Sartre," tr. Denis Hollier and Rosalind Krauss, *October* 87 (1999), 24–6. Sartre's preparatory notes have also been published in the third volume of *Situations* (Paris: Gallimard, 2013). See Jo Bogaerts' review of this volume in *The Germanic Review* 90 (2015), 145–9.

the independent writer will always have to endure "a long trial, similar to the one Kafka has described for us, in which the judges are unknown and the dossiers secret, where the only definitive sentences are condemnations. It is not up to his invisible accusers to give proof of his crime . . . it is for him to prove his innocence."[23]

THE CHILD

To open his reflections on Kafka, first published in 1950 in *Critique*, the journal he founded with Blanchot, Georges Bataille rekindles the debate.[24]

> *Should Kafka be burnt?* . . . Even before it had been formulated, the inquiry had received an answer which the editors omitted to publish—Kafka's own answer. For he lived, or at any rate died, titillated [*chatouillé*] by the desire to burn his books.
> (127/109)

Titillated or aroused, yet without ever entirely gratifying the desire. As Brod argued, if Kafka seriously wanted his work burned, he should have entrusted his work to anyone other than the one person he knew would never carry through with the wish. The failure to accomplish a wish, falling short of gratifying a desire, is key. Throughout his essay, Bataille contrasts the purposive life characterized by rational adults with the useless life of irrational children. Kafka's writing is childish—playful, not serious—insofar as it accomplishes nothing. Whether or not his books are burned, they "have already been annihilated [*anéantis*]" (127/109), already consigned to nothingness, *le néant*. Viewed from the utilitarian perspective of the communists, who are committed to action that would change the world and achieve something, Kafka's literature can only be black.

What interests Bataille above all in Kafka is that his childishness reveals the essential nature of human being, the mere fact of being alive—a reading that relates back to Bataille's former concerns of the Collège de Sociologie and marks his decisive distance from Sartre. In Sartre's view, literature stages a communication between free and

---

[23] Sartre, *What is Literature?*, 259 [*Qu'est-ce que la littérature?* 256].
[24] Bataille, "Franz Kafka devant la critique communiste," *Critique* 41 (Oct. 1950), 22–36, revised in *Literature and Evil* [1957], tr. Alistair Hamilton (London: Calder & Boyars, 1973) [*La littérature et le mal* (Paris: Gallimard, 1957)]. Citations are from these editions.

equal adults, who together work towards the historical realization of a just society. Bataille, in contrast, sees literature as transgressive, as serving no social purpose, as an end in itself.[25] Having a goal subordinates present life to a future goal. This world of action is what the father symbolized for Kafka, the son who tortured himself with the realization that, being what he was, he could never accomplish anything, not despite but precisely because he *wished* to achieve something. The wish is the source of Kafka's profound sense of guilt, for it is a desire to transgress the law of the father—a transgression that can only occur under the father's watch. As a useless writer, he knew he was banished, yet, rather than wanting to escape, he wished to stay within the paternal sphere that banned him, as a child, as an exile. "He wanted to remain within the puerility of a dream" (132/114). This guilt distinguishes Kafka's work from escapism, and also marks its sovereign freedom. Kafka's triumph was to have never won.

> If he wins, the man who once rejected constraint becomes, for himself as well as for others, like those whom he once fought against and who constrained him. Puerility, sovereign, uncalculating caprice, cannot survive their victory. Sovereignty can only exist on the condition that it should never assume power, which is action, the primacy of the future over the present moment, the primacy of the promised land.
>
> (134/116)

A central issue across Bataille's career, *sovereignty* cannot be grasped, calculated, or known. In serving no meaning, it is radically meaningless and therefore absolutely free. As he writes elsewhere, "What is *sovereign* does not *serve*."[26] Sovereignty opposes goal-oriented action, opposes historical progress, or history itself: "Sovereignty . . . cannot be given as the goal of history. I even maintain the contrary: that if history has some goal, sovereignty cannot be that goal, and further, that sovereignty could not have anything to do with that goal."[27] Hence, Bataille's conclusion in the Kafka essay:

---

[25] See Edward Greenwood, "Literature: Freedom or Evil? The Debate between Sartre and Bataille," *Sartre Studies International* 4 (1998), 17–29.
[26] Bataille, "Hegel, la mort et le sacrifice" [1955], cited and translated in Bataille, *Essential Writings*, ed. Michael Richardson (London: Sage, 1998), 189.
[27] Bataille, *Sovereignty* [1953], cited in Michel Surya, *Georges Bataille: An Intellectual Biography*, tr. Krzysztof Fijalkowski and Michael Richardson (London: Verso, 2002), 440.

If the adult gives a major sense to childishness, if he writes with the feeling that he is touching sovereign value, he has no place in Communist society. In a world from which bourgeois individualism is banished, the inexplicable, puerile humor of the adult Kafka cannot be defended. Communism is basically the complete negation, the contrary of what Kafka signifies.

(141/124)

And so, Kafka was tickled by the desire to see his work go up in flames. Bataille's approach to Kafka is indebted to Blanchot, who places two essays on Kafka at the head of his 1949 collection, *La Part de feu* (*The Work of Fire*). Here, Blanchot explores the ramifications of a non-vehicular conception of language, a language unbound from referential function or subjective control, a childishly sovereign language, one might say, which eludes purpose-driven, efficacious activity. For Blanchot, Kafka's writing demonstrates how literary language can be neither stabilized subjectively from within nor grounded referentially from without. This impossible stabilization is how Blanchot reads Kafka's famous confession to Felice Bauer: "I have no literary interest, but rather am made of literature. I am nothing else and cannot be anything else" (Aug. 14, 1913; BF 244/LF 304). The statement is crucial for Blanchot's theory, for it implies that Kafka did not see himself as an author who believed he could steer language according to his own subjective-expressive or referential ends. He had no "literary interest" in this way. On the contrary, he was literature: Constituted by it and driven by it.[28] In a subsequent essay, Blanchot calls this "the exigency of the work"—a "demand" but also an "expulsion," a "driving out" (*exigere*)—the imperative that the work imposes on the writer, as opposed to any intention the writer might impose on the work. Through this exigency, writing drives the writer out of himself, and drives language itself from every grounding source or origin.[29]

For Blanchot, Kafka's focus falls on writing (*écriture*) rather than on the aesthetically finished work (*œuvre*). If the work is the aim or goal of writing, then writing must ultimately be abandoned, even though no work can ever be accomplished without writing. One recalls the concluding sentence of *The Judgment*: "At this moment an *unending* stream of traffic was just going over the bridge" (KGW 1, 52/CS 88; my

---

[28] Blanchot, "Kafka and Literature," in *The Work of Fire*, 12–14. ["Kafka et la littérature" (1949), in *De Kafka à Kafka*, 75–6.]
[29] Blanchot, "Kafka and the Work's Demand," in *The Space of Literature*, tr. Ann Smock (Lincoln: University of Nebraska Press, 1989), 57–83. ["Kafka et l'exigence de l'œuvre" (1958), in *De Kafka à Kafka*, 94–131.]

emphasis). Kafka confessed to Brod that, in writing this last sentence, he thought of "a violent ejaculation."[30] Hence, Bataille's reading: "the phrase expresses the sovereignty of joy, the supreme lapse of being into the nothing."[31] With Blanchot, one could say that writing "ends" with this "unending," a writing that sovereignly refuses to serve any end. The infinitude of writing destroys the finitude of the work. Writing is *unworking—désœuvrement*, "idleness," "inactivity." Kafka stopped writing when he had to go to work.

Consistently, Blanchot returns to the relation between life and work as a tension entirely articulated by writing. He cites a note that Kafka wrote: "I could never understand that it was possible, for almost anyone who wanted to write, to objectify pain while in pain." The comment is reminiscent of Brentano's psychological method, which distinguishes observable effects from mental states. Blanchot stresses the implications for literature: Writing does not express subjective pain nor even refer to it, but rather objectifies it in the materiality of language. Lived pain is the non-verbal horizon towards which literature strives; and like every horizon, this lived pain is never reachable, it remains impossible; and it is this impossibility that drives writing, endlessly.[32] Blanchot thus concurs with Magny, who located Kafka's literary style in the shift from the first person to the third person, from *ich* to *er*. Georg Bendemann of *The Judgment* is the verbally constituted figure that is detached from the subjective, living Kafka. On this basis, Blanchot concludes that the more Kafka's literary figures move away from him, the closer the writer becomes present as writing itself. The greater the distance between author and character, the more they are mutually implicated in the text. Stanley Corngold calls it a survival in writing: "The dwindling empirical personality produces, through writing, another self, its deep self—it reproduces itself, becoming the self it was."[33] The gap that separates the living writer and the written character, the impossibility of their coincidence, lies at the core of the literary endeavor, like the hole that Ponge says can never be filled. This gap renders impossible the politically engaged literature that Sartre endorses. As Blanchot remarks: "Presently we will observe that when literature tries to forget its gratuitous character by committing itself seriously to political or social action, this engagement turns out to be yet one more disengagement."[34]

---

[30] Brod, *Franz Kafka: A Biography*, tr. Humphreys Roberts (New York: Schocken, 1960), 129.
[31] Bataille, *Literature and Evil*, 137 [120].
[32] "Kafka and Literature," 20 [85].
[33] Stanley Corngold, *Lambent Traces: Franz Kafka* (Princeton: Princeton University Press, 2006), 98.
[34] "Kafka and Literature," 25–6 [92].

THE AUTHOR IN THEATER

In their stage production of *The Trial*, which premiered on October 10, 1947 at the Théâtre Marigny, André Gide and Jean-Louis Barrault brought Kafka's work before a broader audience. The play, which was running when Gide received the Nobel Prize, catapulted Kafka to the center of the nation's attention and would have substantial influence on the burgeoning Theater of the Absurd. Eugène Ionesco, who was associated with Barrault's company, acknowledges the debt in his essay on Kafka, "In the Arms of the City" (1957). Here, Ionesco defines the Absurd as "that which is devoid of purpose ... Cut off from his religious, metaphysical, and transcendental roots, man is lost; all his actions become senseless, absurd, useless."[35] Gide and Barrault stage this absurdity by having the drama pertain to the political and social milieu defined by the Occupation and the Purges. The frustration of being in thrall to arbitrary power—the miscommunication, the misconstruals, the utter sense of futility—predominates every scene.

In order to make *The Trial* relevant for the audience, the playwright and director were compelled to compromise. Particularly striking is the way the play implicates the public right from the very opening, namely, in the silent gesture of Frau Grubach who, in a stark departure from Kafka's novel, is seen eavesdropping outside Joseph K.'s bedroom door: *"Madame Grubach's furtive appearance lets it be understood that she has been listening at the door."*[36] The position of the spectator or voyeur is thus replicated. Here and throughout the performance, the audience looks on as the actors look on. Yevgenya Strakovsky provides a succinct description:

> Gide highlights the public nature of K.'s ordeal by repeatedly drawing attention to passive, curious, but ultimately indifferent observers. Throughout the play, bank workers, pedestrians, and nameless citizens witness K.'s struggle against the Law, sometimes observing, sometimes helping the authorities. K.'s trial is not an absurd nightmare, but the interplay between lawmakers and citizens who choose to allow and even facilitate oppression from a safe distance.[37]

---

[35] Eugène Ionesco, "Dans les armes de la ville," *Cahiers de la Compagnie Madeleine Renaud—Jean-Louis Barrault* (October 20, 1957); cited in Martin Esslin, *The Theatre of the Absurd* [1961] (New York: Vintage, 2004), 23.
[36] André Gide and Jean-Louis Barrault, *Le Procès* (Paris: Gallimard, 1947), 41.
[37] Yevgenya Stratovsky, "Agency and Political Engagement in Gide and Barrault's Post-war Theatrical Adaptation of Kafka's *The Trial*," *Comparative Literature and Culture* 20:3 (2017), 3: http://docs.lib.purdue.edu/clcweb/vol19/iss3/6, last accessed on June 15, 2022.

The adaptation thus offers a clear picture of shared guilt and responsibility that would resonate with the existentialist interpretation of Kafka. The climactic scene of K. standing before the court, which Gide moves close to the play's end, culminates with exposing the insidious mechanics of the proceedings. As the bearded court assistants approach the defendant, they lift up their collars and "*reveal* [laissent paraître] *the same badge* [insigne] *which is very apparent: a large observing eye*" (198). Just as, in the opening scene, Madame Grubach "lets it be understood" (*laisse comprendre*) that she has been listening in, so the guards "let" the telltale badge "appear." Even if K.'s crime is never disclosed, an intelligible sign—a "very apparent *insigne*"—is provided to make sense of what is happening. K. addresses the men accordingly:

> Ah, as far as I can see, you are all part of this band of sellouts and slaves. All in cahoots, gathered here to watch me, spy on me, circumvent me. If you were applauding just now, it was in the hope of tripping up an innocent. No need! I won't give you that pleasure.
> (198–9)

The mild qualification—"as far as I can see"—does little to lessen the effect: Everything comes into focus. Everyone is guilty beyond a reasonable doubt—everyone, that is, except K.

In the novel, things are not as straightforward. K. notices the examining judge has just nodded to a man in the courtroom, which he takes to be "a secret sign": "I do not know whether the sign is meant to produce booing or applause, but by exposing this before it can take effect, I quite deliberately forgo the opportunity of learning what the sign means" (KGW 3, 54/T 36). The novel is in fact replete with signs. Clues abound, yet without ever appearing to integrate into a single, cogent plot. The more information we receive, the less we seem to understand. As Magny stressed, Kafka's thoroughly objective style strays from the contextualization that is necessary to discern meaning.[38] The reader cannot decide on conviction or acquittal because the legal code is inaccessible or non-existent, which is precisely K.'s predicament. As one of the arresting officers, Willem, points out: "Look, he admits he doesn't know the law and at the same time claims he's innocent" (KGW 3, 15/T 9). Ambiguity, along with K.'s vain efforts to understand, haunts the novel, which thereby contrasts with the relative clarity of Gide and Barrault's *mise-en-scène*. For them, K. is the innocent victim of a corrupt system that must be changed. While ambivalence does persist insofar as the spectators might want to flatter themselves and identify with the

---

[38] Magny, "Kafka ou l'écriture objective de l'absurde," 173–4.

protagonist only to recognize that they number among the "sellouts and slaves," K.'s guiltlessness is indisputable, a fact that is communicated through evident signs. *Le Procès* turns out to be hardly a trial at all: In persecuting and executing an innocent man, it is more a play about social injustice.

While most contemporary reviewers lauded the play's dramatic effectiveness, some noted the price paid for such communicability: "Whatever scruples Messrs. Gide and Barrault may have made in respecting Kafka's intentions, their play unquestionably lacks what makes the best part of the novel: the fever, the anguish, the quivering of mystery."[39] In attending to Blanchot's slope of purposive, law-bound speech, the playwrights neglect the slope that Bataille would characterize as the transgressively sacred.

To be sure, the medial specificity of the theater, especially in the traditional sense, requires a certain level of explicitness in presentation. Without the resources of a narrator, omniscient or focalized, a play must convey motivation and judgments through dialogue and soliloquy. Yet, the extent of Gide-Barrault's adaptation goes well beyond these formal principles. Following the courtroom exchange, K. finds himself in the cathedral scene, the penultimate episode in Brod's edition of the novel. The dramatization is noteworthy in many respects. To begin, it entirely elides the pivotal parable, "Before the Law," and instead has the chaplain cite from the Book of Lamentations, where the prophet refers to God's wrath: "He has walled me in so I cannot escape" (Lam. 3:7). Not only does Kafka altogether refrain from biblical quotations but also instills much ambivalence in the discussion that ensues. The adaptation, in contrast, is unequivocal: The chaplain immediately identifies his visitor as Joseph K., the accused (204–5). Moreover, the priest pronounces a clear judgment: "You must say to yourself: I am hunted, I am chosen" (211), while in Kafka, the conclusion concludes nothing:

> "One doesn't have to take everything as the truth, one just has to accept it as necessary.' 'A depressing opinion," said K. "It means that the world is founded on untruth." K. said this as his final comment [*abschließend*], but it was not his final verdict [*Endurteil*]."
> (KGW 3, 233/T 159)

---

[39] Review printed in *Opéra* (Oct. 15, 1947); cited in Ira Kuhn, "The Metamorphosis of *The Trial*," *Symposium* 26 (1972), 226–41; here, p. 227. Kuhn's essay provides further examples of the simplifications and rationalizations at work in Gide's text.

With this, K. insists on leaving—"Certainly, I have to go. I am senior accountant at a bank, people are waiting for me" (KGW 3, 234/T 159)— and the chaplain lets him go. In the play, however, the roles are perfectly reversed, with the priest adopting a distinctly Jansenist tone:

> Chaplain: In the silence, the voice of the one who cannot speak resounds. The blind man sees. The deaf hear. All solitude is populated. The darkness shines and that which prostrates you magnifies you. (*The lamp held by K. turns off.*) For now, I must leave you. My minister summons me elsewhere; and you yourself are expected.
>
> K. (*as in a cry for help*): Don't leave me. How would I find my way back in the dark? (211)

The chief inspector appears alongside the executioners, and K. continues to protest: "It's not so much for me . . . It's a matter of principles" (214). He has refused to acknowledge the chaplain's sentence: "You must say to yourself: I am hunted [*traqué*]." Again, the difference from the novel is acute. Here, no principle is discovered, no guiding criterion. K. renounces resistance and surrenders to his fate, perhaps out of exhaustion, perhaps out of self-condemnation. As the chaplain advised, he accepts his situation as necessary (*notwendig*), whether or not it is truthful: "It's been left to me to tell myself everything that is needful [*das Notwendige*]" (KGW 3, 239/T 163). Either persuaded by Barrault's dramaturgical expertise or by his own change of heart, Gide appears to read the novel much differently than he did during the Occupation. On August 28, 1940, he recorded a less certain reaction in his journal:

> I read Kafka's *Trial* with even greater admiration if that's possible . . . As clever as Groethuysen's preface may be, it is barely satisfying . . . [Kafka's] book escapes all rational explanation. I can't say what I admire more: the naturalistic 'transcription' of a universe that is fantastic yet one which the meticulous accuracy of the depictions brings before our eyes, or the boldness of the swerves towards the strange. There is much to learn here. The anguish that this book breathes is, at moments, almost intolerable. For how can one not constantly say to oneself: this creature being hunted [*traqué*], is me.[40]

In the postwar adaptation, K. fails to say what Gide told himself seven years earlier.

---

[40] Entry dated Aug. 28, 1940; cited in Hans Siepe, "André Gide et Franz Kafka," *Bulletin des Amis d'André Gide* 25: 114–15 (April–July 1997), 283–98; here, p. 283.

VI Labyrinths

SIGNS OF CHANGE

In 1960, long in the habit of abstaining from judgment, Roland Barthes, despite his personal sympathies, refused to sign the Manifesto of the 121 in support of the Algerians' right to independence, yet he did not refrain from writing.

> We are coming out of a moment, that of committed literature [*la littérature engagée*]. The end of the Sartrean novel, the imperturbable indigence of the socialist novel, the defects of political theater, all that, like a receding wave, reveals a singular and singularly resistant object: literature.[1]

The simile portrays literature as a sandy, grainy surface, flooded over by surges of non-literary intentions. Yet, no sooner had literature appeared in the ebbing of politicized initiatives when another "contrary" wave crashed in: "the wave of declared disengagement [*dégagement*]: revival of the love story, hostility to 'ideas,' cult of fine writing, refusal to be concerned with the world's significations." And so, history seems to proceed in an endless cycle of tidal impositions that wash over the shoreline and conceal the essence of literature that lies beneath the waters.

> Is our literature, therefore, forever condemned to this exhausting to-and-fro between political realism and art-for-art's-sake, between a morality of engagement and an aesthetic purism, between compromise and asepsis? Must it always be poor (if it is nothing other than itself) or embarrassed (if it is something other than itself)? Can it not have a proper place [*une place juste*] in this world? To this question, today, a precise answer: Marthe Robert's Kafka.
>
> (133)

Barthes is referring to Robert's recently published study, *Kafka*, which derives from a decade and a half of involvement with the Prague author, beginning with her *Introduction à la lecture de Kafka* (1946). Trained as a Germanist both at the Sorbonne and the University of Frankfurt, with a

---

[1] Roland Barthes, "Kafka's Answer," in *Critical Essays*, tr. Richard Howard (Evanston: Northwestern University Press, 1972), 133–7; here, p. 133. ["La réponse de Kafka" [1960], in Barthes, *Œuvres complètes*, ed. Eric Marty (Paris: Seuil, 1993), 1, 395–9.]

strong focus on modern literature and Freudian psychoanalysis, her readings of Kafka consistently drew from the autobiographical material transmitted through the diaries, notebooks, and correspondence, not in order to discover the decisive key to the literary works but rather to re-inscribe them within the contexts of the author's life and world. Robert was especially leery of the universalizing abstractions proffered in philosophical interpretations, which she regarded as neglecting the verbal, cultural, and historical specificity of the literature itself. In her 1961 essay on "Kafka in France," she suggests that the trend began with Groethuysen's preface to Vialatte's *Trial*, a preface, she notes, that he wrote "without saying a word about the author's life, without furnishing the slightest information about his times, his milieu, his relationships with the literature of his day."[2] After the surrealists recruited the work for their revolution, the existentialists would soon take over. Although Brod's 1936 biography provided much-needed background, in the end, Robert states, he endorses an allegorical method that would redeem his friend from being regarded as a merely provincial specimen tied to his Bohemian roots and instead proclaim him as a modern classic. However well-intentioned, Brod's enterprise turns the work into a symbolic cipher to which he holds the authorized key (249–50). In terms of theory, however brilliantly accomplished their interpretations may be, Brod and the majority of French interpreters reduce Kafka's texts to a repertoire of *themes* rather than study it as a corpus of *writing*, as *écriture*.

> To grasp this technique, to discover the unity of perspective that it scrupulously maintains amid the distractions of the imagination and which, in spite of the unusualness of the events, guarantees the epic beauty of Kafka's narrative, to adapt the fundamental principle of unity to the current situation of the novelist and the novel, this would be a less spectacular task, but how much more difficult than the appropriation of a few procedures that have already fallen into the public domain. A difficult task, but possible, and from this point of view, one can say that the history of Kafka in France is only just beginning.
>
> (254–5)

Barthes had already devoted himself to this difficult task when he read Robert's *Kafka*. The critic nourished by Saussure would have recognized

---

[2] Marthe Robert, "Kafka en France," *Mercure de France* 342 (May–Aug. 1961), 241–55; here, p. 243.

her call "to discover the unity of perspective" as a bid to grasp the verbal system that produces meaning through the differential relationships between the signs themselves as opposed to treating each word as referring to some extra-verbal sense. If Kafka is viewed as providing the solution to the current impasse between politicized literature and aesthetic purism—between engagement or disengagement—it is not because Kafka furnishes any argument that would legitimize one position over the other, nor is it because his work contains any *theme* that might reconcile both parties, but rather because of his *technique*. Kafka's writing appears to be a privileged site for examining not *what* literature means but rather *how* it creates meaning. As Barthes emphasizes, the pursuit of themes leads nowhere: "Both realistic and subjective, Kafka's oeuvre lends itself to everyone but answers no one."[3] As the history of Kafka's influence in France demonstrates, the texts supply a surplus of themes that can be appropriated by the most contradictory positions. It is as if the thematic excess short-circuits any attempt to identify a single definitive theme that might grant victory to one side and spell defeat for the other. For Barthes, now that the match of themes has ended in a draw, one can begin to focus on how the game is played.

What Barthes learns from Robert's study is that Kafka's texts are particularly well suited for responding to the present crisis, between purist and committed conceptions of literature, between a literary position that is either embarrassed or impoverished, either coerced to addressing matters beyond itself as justification or limited to speaking about nothing but itself as inanity. Barthes' neutral position is no position at all; it chooses *neither* side—it neither engages literature in political partisanship nor disengages it. Despite appearances, neutrality does not covertly adopt the purist view, for to claim that literature subsists in a sacred precinct far above the fray is to assert a decisive position on what literature means. Saying *yes* to any side entails steering literature towards a determined goal, including the autotelism of *l'art pour l'art*. Self-directed writing is as goal-oriented as writing with a political aim. Both approaches regard literature as a means. Aestheticism may embrace the intransitive, non-referential aspects of literature but does so by appropriating it as an identifying badge. "The literary act," Barthes writes, "is without cause and without goal precisely because it is devoid of sanction: it proposes itself to the world without any praxis establishing it or justifying it: it is an absolutely intransitive act, it

---

[3] Barthes, "Kafka's Answer," 134.

modifies nothing, nothing reassures it" (135). *Absolutely intransitive*—which distinguishes the literary act from the dogma of intransitivity to which the purist subscribes. Whereas committed literature embroils writing in the non-literary world of the forum, disengaged literature transports writing far away from reality. Neither option responds to the question that Kafka answers—namely, the question: How can literature, in its vanity, have a just or justifiable place—*une place juste*—in this world?

Again, the answer that Kafka gives is clearly expressed by Robert: "The being of literature is nothing but its technique" (135). More specifically, Kafka's technique does not consist in a set of decipherable symbols, where decipherment would ultimately dispense with the text, nor does it consist in a complete absence of symbols, where reading would withdraw entirely from the world. Rather, his technique operates through a web of indispensable allusions and thereby remains in the world. "Allusion, which is a pure technique of signification, actually engages the world, since it expresses the relation of a singular man and a common language." Robert explains:

> The images in *The Trial*, *The Castle*, *The Metamorphosis*, etc., are therefore not symbols at all; according to Kafka himself, they are allusions to a world whose meaning they cannot state, but which they can make known by exploring its multiple possible meanings. As a result, it is sufficient to avoid interpreting them to understand them, because their function is linked precisely to their multiplicity, to the way in which they respond to each other, associate with each other, chain one story to the next, linking each part of the work to the whole and the whole to the slightest fragment.[4]

Unlike symbols, allusions do not designate some meaning outside language but rather form a system in language which produces meaning that communicates with and in the world. An internal coherence obtains as words and motifs are gathered together, as the links between them are discerned. For example, Robert traces the lines that connect Josef K., who dies "like a dog" in *The Trial*, to the convict in the *Penal Colony* who behaves like a dog, to the canine narrator of the *Investigations of a Dog* and the fasting performer in *The Hunger Artist*, with each text inserting the motif into further trajectories and with the particular value and

---

[4] Robert, *Kafka* (Paris: Gallimard, 1960), 118. On this passage, see Rony Klein, "Une rencontre autour de Kafka, Walter Benjamin, et Roland Barthes," *Études Germaniques* 283 (2016), 405–5; here, p. 418.

function of each instance contributing to the meaning of the whole.[5] Although Robert does not cite Saussure or Lévi-Strauss, Barthes would not hesitate to view this "whole" (*ensemble*) as constituting a closed structure comprised of differential signs, a structure that articulates meaning in the world of signs.

A world, *yes, but* not an extralinguistic world. Barthes underscores Robert's claim that "Kafka's relations to the world are governed by a perpetual *yes, but* . . ."

> One can fairly say as much of all our modern literature (and it is in this that Kafka has truly created it), since it identifies, in an inimitable fashion, the realistic world (yes to the world) and the ethical project (but . . .). The trajectory that separates the *yes* from the *but* is the whole uncertainty of signs, and it is because signs are uncertain that there is literature.
>
> (136)

The coordination of assertion and qualification could be viewed as a variant on the classic distinction between the *is* and the *ought*. Yet, what interests Barthes is the technical consequence of this articulation, the way it concerns the *how* of writing rather than the *what*. Barthes's focus on technique thus couples Robert's Kafka with Blanchot's reading, which likewise turns on the writerly (*scriptible*) collocation of affirmation and refusal, the positing and negating of the world in writing, a writing that opens onto the world by having the world open up through writing.

The affirmative construction and interrogative deconstruction that would characterize the *nouvelle critique* for the next two decades received a major impetus from these reflections on Kafka circa 1960. Barthes's seminal essays from 1963—"Qu'est-ce que la critique?", "Les deux critiques", and "L'activité structuraliste"—elaborate the premises that Robert formulates in her *Kafka* and maintains in her 1963 study, *L'ancien et le nouveau: de Don Quichotte à Franz Kafka*, which in turn motivates Blanchot's "The Wooden Bridge (repetition, the neutral)" published the following year. Here, Blanchot rehearses Robert's argument, that Kafka's work encompasses the critical act. Just as literary critique affirms the work under study while interrogating it, so does *The Castle* create a world while providing its own commentary. This internal questioning motivates all critique, triggering a proliferation that can only become increasingly obscure. As Blanchot writes: "The

---

[5] See Robert, *Kafka*, 119–20.

more a work comments upon itself, the more it calls for commentary; the more it carries on relations of 'reflection' (of redoubling) with its center, the more this duality renders it enigmatic."[6] Commentary is the challenging repetition, which calls upon previous writing. Hence, for Blanchot, Kafka's "Surveyor does not survey imaginary and still virgin countries but the immense space of literature; he thus cannot keep from imitating—and thereby reflecting—all the heroes who have proceeded him into this space" (391/191). Quite explicitly, Blanchot is not proposing a new interpretation of *The Castle*. Rather—like Robert, like Barthes—he shows *how* Kafka's narrative proceeds: How, within the story itself, K. wanders from one explanation to the next, from one interpretation to the other, affirming and interrogating each. Kafka has thus anticipated and already undermined the vast industry of interpretation devoted to understanding his novel.

> *The Castle* does not consist of a series of events or peripeteia that are more or less linked, but of an ever-expanding sequence of exegetic versions that finally only bear upon the very possibility of exegesis itself—the possibility of writing (and of interpreting) *The Castle*.
>
> (393–4)

What Blanchot and Barthes find especially fruitful in Robert's technical approach, is its *neutrality*—a practice that, in her formulation, "registers all the facts, and also all the judgments that precede and follow the— the thoughts, the dreams, and all of this with a neutrality and passivity that the individual feels strangely as a weight and as an injustice" (cited on p. 396/200). This neutrality frees critique from dogma and abstraction by returning literature to life and life to literature. The Neither-Nor thus converts into a Both-And: Real and unreal, engaged and disengaged, just and inane, a work that affirms and a life that questions. For all three non-judgmental critics everything Kafka wrote is *autobiography*—a life and a self expressly written, like the world we inhabit, an ensemble of allusions that continue to produce more allusions until the end. "It's because is not finished that literature is possible."[7] For Barthes, structuralism provided the tools necessary for understanding how meaning is produced in our cultures, yet it was through his encounter

---

[6] Blanchot, "The Wooden Bridge (repetition, the neutral)" in *Infinite Conversation*, tr. Susan Hanson (Minneapolis: University of Minnesota Press, 1993), 391 ["Le pont de bois (la répétition, le neutre)"], in *De Kafka à Kafka*, 190).

[7] Barthes, "Kafka's Answer," 137.

with Robert's *Kafka* that he discovered the method's weak point, namely that the structuralist analysis of language is always conducted in language. Kafka's answer, circa 1960, furnished the crucial question that would drive the next phase of theory.

As for Kafka's work, Barthes was highly consistent. In 1979, he received and read Robert's new study, *As Lonely as Franz Kafka*, which presents a "psychological biography" by tracing "the technical measures that Kafka took to transpose the anomalies of his situation into the very texture of his work—separating the real man from the writer."[8] Barthes' oblique response, "Délibération" (1979), was published in *Tel Quel* months before his untimely death on February 25, 1980. His "deliberation," which, like all deliberations, is conducted with presumed neutrality, reaches back to his seminal discovery nearly two decades before—the challenged affirmation (*yes, but* . . .) that articulates the doubled mode of the realistic and ethical project that he, via Robert, attributed to Kafka's writing.

> Kafka—whose Diary is perhaps the only one that can be read without any irritation—wonderfully expresses this double postulation of literature, Justness [*Justesse*] and Inanity: (. . .) I examined the wishes that I formed for life. The one that turned out to be the most important or the most endearing was the desire to acquire a way of looking at life (and, relatedly, to be able to convince others of this in writing), whereby life would retain its heavy movement of falling and rising, *yes, but* would be recognized at the same time, and with no less clarity, for a nothing, a dream, a state of floating.[9]

Barthes reports that he considered keeping a journal after reading Kafka's diaries, which were translated into French by Robert, and which had long served as the primary source for her commentaries. Brod appears to have been the person who persuaded his friend to start a diary as a free, private place to register thoughts and sketches, which may or may not be developed into literature for the public. In Barthes's view, keeping a diary would be an *inane* act of solitude, were it not for the possibility of ultimately finding a *just* place in the world. "Like the pervert (one says), subjected to the *yes, but*, I know that my text is vain

---

[8] Marthe Robert, *As Lonely as Franz Kafka* [1979], tr. Ralph Mannheim (New York: Schocken 1982), 162.
[9] Barthes, "Délibération" in *Œuvres complètes*, 4, 681; cited with commentary in Emmanuel Bouju, "Après quoi rien à dire: Délibération et réponse de Kafka," *Carnets* 6 (2016), 1–8; here, p. 6 (emphasis added).

(and in the same movement) I cannot tear myself from the belief that it exists."[10]

THE NEW NEW

Most literary scholars would agree that 1960 marks a watershed moment when existentialist-humanist readings of Kafka yielded to the kind of poststructuralist analyses that Barthes would popularize.[11] The premises, vocabulary, and approach that Barthes and kindred spirits developed—mostly publishing in *Tel Quel*, which Philippe Sollers founded in 1960—would be taken up by critics across Europe and especially in North America, after the fabled conference on "The Language of Criticism and the Sciences of Man," organized by Richard Macksey and Eugenio Donato at Johns Hopkins in October 1966.[12] The early work of Stanley Corngold, Henry Sussman and many others clearly demonstrates the fruitfulness and insightfulness of this critical turn. What is less often acknowledged is that Marthe Robert's unique attentiveness to Kafka's allusive technique provided the "answer" to the gridlock caused by Sartre's program. In this regard, one could say, with only slight exaggeration, that Kafka furnished the way out of the problem he inspired.

Less a spokesman for the anguish, frustration, and suffering that mark the human condition, Kafka became a model, explicitly or implicitly, but certainly not exclusively, for new writerly techniques—not only the *nouveaux romans* of Alain Robbe-Grillet, Nathalie Sarraute, Marguerite Duras, Claude Simon, and others, but also the generative experiments conducted by members of the OuLiPo: Georges Perec, Italo Calvino, and Jacques Roubaud, to name the most well-known. In the preface to his 1963 collection, *For a New Novel*, Robbe-Grillet picks up on a legacy that persistently embarrassed existentialist and Marxist readers:

> From Flaubert to Kafka, a line of descent is drawn, an ancestry that suggests a progeny. The passion to describe, which animates them both, is certainly the same passion we discern in the new novel today. Beyond the naturalism of Flaubert and the

---

[10] Barthes, "Délibération," 678; cited in Bouju, "Après quoi rien à dire," 3.
[11] For an overview, see Dorrit Cohn, "Trends in Literary Criticism: Some Structuralist Approaches to Kafka," *The German Quarterly* 51 (1978), 182–8.
[12] See Cusset, *French Theory*, 28–32.

metaphysical oneiroticism of Kafka appear the first elements of a realistic style of an unknown genre, which is now coming to light.[13]

When one restricts reading to the level of themes, sensibilities, and style, it is difficult to reconcile Kafka's work with that of the author he called his spiritual father. As Charles Bernheimer summarizes the problem: "Kafka's style is related to a vision of the world that distorts reality in response to private obsessions, dreams, guilt feelings" while "Flaubert's style has traditionally been thought of as objective, ironic, distanced, famously the result of hard work with a recalcitrant linguistic medium."[14] Yet, when one attends to "psychopoetic structures," as Bernheimer does in a *nouvelle critique* mode, one uncovers the technique that the Prague author shared with Sartre's family idiot. In one sense, Robbe-Grillet is but another example of the effect of writers creating their own precursors, an effect that Borges famously attributed to Kafka.[15] Yet, in another regard, what Kafka's writing now came to solicit was a revolution in how literature could be read—a rejection of the allegorical decipherments that flooded the postwar scene. "Perhaps Kafka's staircases lead *elsewhere*," Robbe-Grillet concedes, "but they are *there*, and we look at them, step by step, following the detail of the banisters and the risers."[16]

That is not to say that Marxist approaches fell to the wayside. On the contrary, the new generation continued to approach Kafka with the methods and terms supplied by Adorno and the Frankfurt School, to approach the novels and stories as a "cryptogram of capitalism's highly polished, glittering last phase, which [Kafka] excludes in order to define it all the more precisely in its negative."[17] One needed only to trade existentialism in for the new and improved dialectical materialism that was being imported *outre Rhin*. With the structuralist reduction of the Subject to a mere grammatical function, ideological critique was positioned to question the self-serving power that manufactures and maintains values. In the wake of the death of the author, the reader was

---

[13] Alain Robbe-Grillet, *For a New Novel* [1963], tr. Richard Howard (New York: Grove, 1965), 18.
[14] Charles Bernheimer, *Flaubert and Kafka: Studies in Psychopoetic Structure* (New Haven: Yale University Press, 1982), ix–x.
[15] Jorge Luis Borges, "Kafka and His Precursors" [1951], in *Selected Non-Fictions*, tr. Eliot Weinberger (New York: Penguin, 1999), 363–5.
[16] Robbe-Grillet, *For a New Novel*, 165. See Dorrit Cohn, "Castles and Anti-Castles, or Kafka and Robbe-Grillet," *Novel* 5 (1971), 19–31.
[17] Theodor Adorno, "Notes on Kafka," 245.

emboldened to interrogate not only the individualism and consumerism ascribed to the United States but also the oppression and state control displayed across the Soviet bloc.

The move hinges on challenging representation, understood as the deployment of language to communicate a subject's thoughts and intentions. For critics of ideology and patriarchal systems, representational thinking upholds institutions of power by presuming a central authority as the source of meaning. Dethroning the Subject, including the classic conception of the Author, is the first step in liquidating the institutions that promulgate tyrannical oppression and injustice. Marthe Robert's focus on the technical allusions in Kafka's writing endorses this move away from representations or themes and the deciphering interpretations they invariably encourage. Instead of submitting to a "major author" who masterfully steers language towards clearly communicated positions, the reader is invited to traffic in the text, remaining on the staircase like an Odradek, and tracing, step by step, the lines of flight from one landing to the next, much to the chagrin of the purpose-driven Father.

RHIZOMES

"The three worst themes in many interpretations of Kafka are the transcendence of the law, the interiority of guilt, the subjectivity of enunciation. They are connected to all the stupidities that have been written about allegory, metaphor, and symbolism in Kafka."[18] Gilles Deleuze and Félix Guattari share Robert's allergy to representation as well as her call to attend to the chain of allusions that comprise the writing system known as Franz Kafka, a system which has now been upgraded to a machine that produces effects in the world. By affecting readers, as opposed to informing them intellectually, the text seems to reshape, reform, and redirect how reality and life may be approached. Hardly a major author, Deleuze and Guattari propose, Kafka is a minor writer who operates within a major tradition, one who burrows beneath the ground of tradition and thereby weakens the edifices built upon it. Every reader is invited to enter the burrow in any way and follow the textual pathways to wherever they may lead. The itineraries will always be *unpredictable*, passageways that are neither predictive nor predicable but rather put the reader perpetually on trial without final sentencing, without definitive categorization (< *katēgorein*, "to accuse"—in Latin,

---

[18] Gilles Deleuze and Félix Guattari, *Kafka: Toward a Minor Literature*, tr. Dana Polan (Minneapolis: University of Minnesota Press, 1986), 45. [*Kafka: Pour une littérature mineure* (Paris: Éditions de Minuit, 1975), 82–3.]

praedicare, "to charge with an explicit crime"). Allegoresis is accusatory in this sense, as interpreting the case to "speak otherwise" (*allēgorein*), a move to subordinate the text to a law that transcends it, to make the writing say something it does not say. The indictment can only be dodged through allusive and elusive lines of flight. In tracing these lines of flight and nothing more, Deleuze and Guattari defer any judgment that might be pronounced on the basis of legal interpretations.

Beginning with their *Anti-Oedipus* (1972), Deleuze and Guattari teamed up to chart the theoretical waters that flooded the shores across the 1960s and peaked during the uprisings of May 1968. They met at the new, "experimental" University of Vincennes, which was founded in 1969 in response to the call for educational reforms. Michel Foucault chaired the philosophy faculty that included Jean-François Lyotard, Alain Badiou, Gilles Deleuze, and Félix Guattari. Although committed to the Marxist cause, Deleuze and Guattari engaged in a playful methodology that served to criticize all manners of systematic-representational-interpretive thinking. Here, it is useful to recall the sense of *experimentum* as "proof or trial," as that which puts theories to the test and measures laws against "experience." Accordingly, Deleuze and Guattari leave no theory or law unscathed. All propositions are subject to a trial by fire—existentialist humanism, thematic criticism, structuralism, semiotics, and above all conventional psychoanalysis—trials, however, that are never resolved by a final judgment.

Deleuze and Guattari do not dispute the validity of psychoanalytic method per se but rather the institutionalization of its models, specifically, the universal applicability of Freud's Oedipal Complex. The issue with Oedipal theory is that it not only characterizes individuals and society as neurotic or paranoiac, but that it also upholds the familial triangle of father-mother-child as a universal determinant. In their view, the Oedipal triangle maintains the legitimacy of the bourgeois-capitalist system that Marxism aims to overturn. Liberating individuals and society from the constraints of this system require a departure from *neurosis* and a turn to *schizophrenia*, which appears to evade the Oedipal scheme altogether. By tracking the unsystematic, disorganized flows and processes of the "schizo," Deleuze and Guattari attempt to discern the unforeseeable lines of flight that escape reactionary systems of meaning. In their conception, systematic paradigms amount to a territorialization, one that organizes the textual lines into powerful coherence grounded in a central authority, a centripetal movement that clearly alludes to imperialist agenda for order and control. In contrast, schizo lines of flight are centrifugal, performing a deterritorialization, an unleashing of "nomadic" intensity. A shift in accent is all that is required to see how the *nómos* or "posited law" can become a *nomós*, the open field for pasturage, for wandering, for the *nomadic*. To be sure, deterritorialization almost invariably inspires refreshed efforts to reterritorialize, yet the main difference remains in force: Whereas territorialization distributes authoritative power through hierarchical, vertically ordered systems of codes, deterritorialization proceeds along energized lines that are non-hierarchical, horizontal—an open network or *rhizome* without any privileged center or a sole guarantor of meaning.[19]

Deleuze and Guattari's 1975 study on Kafka deploys these terms of "schizoanalysis." By insisting on the multiplicity of entry points, the method is a political strategy, one that prevents "the introduction of the enemy," which is to say, the great Signifier or master key, and thus baffles "those attempts to interpret a work that is actually only open to *experimentation*" (3/7; my emphasis). The apparently arbitrary starting point that they select is a detail from *The Castle*: The portrait of the Castle Warden, which K. discovers on the wall of the Bridge Inn. In the novel, the picture is described as "a dark portrait in a dark frame [*ein dunkles Porträt in einem dunklen Rahmen*]"—"the sitter's head was bent so low on his chest that one could hardly see his eyes" (KGW 4, 15/C 10). K. asks if the picture is a portrait of Count Westwest, which turns out to be a false interpretation. Yet, Deleuze and Guattari are not interested in K.'s misreading. Instead, they recall other instances of bent heads in Kafka. Rather than serve as a detail to be interpreted, the image of the bent head marks an entry point that connects to other instances in other contexts, where the form of content (the bent head) and the form of expression (the portrait) sometimes appear together and sometimes split apart. As in a machinic valve system, the bent-head blocks or neutralizes desire (a territorialization) as opposed to the straightened head that transmits energy and sound (a deterritorialization, 4–5/8–9). It would be wrong, however, to regard this distinction simply as a binary relation that one generally finds in conventional structuralist analyses; for the pairs of terms fail to stabilize into a straightforward code. The opposition only obtains in the realm of the images' *content* (bent/straightened), while in the realm of *expression*, "sound is not opposed to the portrait" (6/12–13). Sound, the analysis continues, is a form of expression that tends to abolish all forms, all stabilizations. To illustrate, they refer to the example of the mouse Josephine, whose performances instigate and frustrate the search for form and thereby meaning: Is she singing or merely piping? Kafka's text does not provide

---

[19] Deleuze and Guattari, *Anti-Oedipus*, vol. 1 of *Capitalism and Schizophrenia*, tr. Robert Hurley, Mark Seem, and Helen R. Lane (Minneapolis: University of Minnesota Press, 1983) [*L'anti-Œdipe: Capitalisme et schizophrénie* (Paris: Minuit, 1972).]

a definitive answer. The text, rather, is a machine that facilitates the ramification of intensities, a flow of details which evades conclusive interpretation. The evasion is demonstrated in the study's subsequent chapter, where the bent-head motif is shown to undergo a deterritorialization itself, which consequently leads to new connections and fresh assemblages. The illustration here is the paternal portrait Kafka provides in *Letter to the Father*, which is obviously a central text in any Freudian reading. In Deleuze-Guattari's view, however, the portrait manifests a "schizo-logic" that magnifies the father's image to the point of absurdity. The image of the father becomes a vast terrain—an open *nomós* or field—of multiple, uncontrollable connections which lead in all directions, a "molecular agitation" rather than a "molar stabilization" (10/18–19). Whereas for the paranoiac, every text, every surface can be taken as a clue to some hidden meaning or concealed conspiracy, the schizo nomad traverses the textual planes, moving from place to place without ever happening upon the inner sanctum where all might be finally revealed. The paranoiac seeks out the complete, transcendent law and assembles the barrage of confusing events into an ultimate, coherent plot, while the schizo dismantles these assemblages on an immanent plane untethered by any power above or below (59/108).

Deleuze and Guattari's conception of "minor literature" has given rise to an utterly misconstrued belief that Kafka wrote in German dialect and that his work therefore anticipates creative enterprises of the subaltern under colonial regimes.[20] Yet it is still worth considering their concept on its own terms. They derive the term mainly from Kafka's diary entry of December 25, 1911, where he reflects on the "liveliness" (*Lebhaftigkeit*) of the Yiddish Theater performances headed by the Warsaw actor Jizchak Löwy (KGW 9, 243–5/D 148–51). What matters for Deleuze and Guattari is the cardinal distinction that reaches back to Barthes' contrast between the classic and modern author, between the writer who implements language as a vehicle for signification and representation and the one who turns a major language into an energetic force of connectivity. If the major author deals in themes, the minor author traffics in allusions. A major literature rests on *what* is uttered (content, the *énoncé*), while minor literature is charged with the conditions of the utterance (expression, the *énonciation*). Consequently, minor literature does not address an ordered, molar *population* but rather a discontinuous, disorderly, molecular *multitude*. For example, in the

---

[20] On this point, see especially Stanley Corngold, "Kafka and the Dialect of Minor Literature," *College Literature* 21 (1994), 89–101.

Josephine story, the individuated "master" artist ultimately blends into the collective layout or assemblage (*agencement*), a heroine to be forgotten or remembered as the one forgotten. In this way, minor literature "no longer designates specific literatures but the revolutionary conditions for every literature within the heart of what is called great (or established) literature" (18/32–3).

Regardless of how the concept has been deployed by subsequent theorists, minor literature reconfigures writing as a process that is perpetually in a state of becoming, one that challenges or deterritorializes established patterns of meaning and thereby marks out a path for escape until sense is reasserted through a reterritorialization. In Kafka's work, "becoming-animal" often emerges as an escape route out of oppressive systems where one is invariably judged. As Bataille underscored, Kafka exhibits a childlike desire to avoid the fixed world of adulthood, the sphere of the father, where mature humans are not animals. In becoming an insect, Gregor Samsa breaks out of the various triangles that aim to domesticate him: The family triangle, the bureaucratic triangle, and even the financial triangle composed of the three lodgers are disrupted by Gregor's presence. Yet, this presence turns out to be too weak to be sustained. In the end, the Oedipal triangle reconfirms its power; Gregor passes away and "the family happily closes in on itself" (15/27–8).

The reterritorializations reaffirm the law, which is often thematized in Kafka's novels and stories. What these texts expose, however, is that the law is in fact empty.

> The famous passages in *The Trial* (as well as in *The Penal Colony* and *The Great Wall of China*) present the law as pure and empty form without content, the object of which remains unknowable: thus, the law can be expressed only through a sentence, and the sentence can be learned only through a punishment. No one knows the law's interior.
>
> (43/79)

As Blanchot repeatedly stressed, the secret of the law is that there is no law. Likewise, for Deleuze and Guattari, the law is nothing but an enunciation, no more than an expression of power, issued from a source that is not transcendent but rather immanent: "it is always in the office next door, or behind the door, on to infinity" (45/82). Hardly a pronouncement on behalf of hidden transcendence, the law is merely the statement itself: "the enunciation that constructs the law in the name of an immanent power of the one who enounces it" (45/82). Moreover, the law is constituted and disseminated by writing. One might have presumed that the law precedes writing, when in fact writing comes before the law.

Whatever efficacy one may grant the conceptual repertoire of Deleuze and Guattari's *Kafka*, it is clear that their book marks a high point of the new reflections on the author that began in 1960 in the wake of existentialist readings. Rather than promulgate an Everyman at the mercy of transcendence and burdened by dread, anxiety, and futility, Kafka proffers an affective writing machine that converts everything into assemblages and dismantles them, a process that comedically reverses the portrait of the tragic artist and may even inspire joy and laughter. The attentiveness to the expressive conditions of minor literature emphasizes the joyful flights that escape imposed forms and thereby recall Nietzsche's "joyful science," the *gai savoir* that flows from Provençal poetry to Rabelais: A poetic wisdom, a creative memory, erotically charged and unencumbered by definitive and debilitating knowledge. For Deleuze and Guattari, the machine's secret is that there is no law, only immanent desire. "*Where one believed there was the law, there is in fact desire and desire alone*" (49/90; emphasis in text). When Josef K. returns to the now empty courtroom and inspects the magistrate's desk, what he finds is not a set of law books but rather pornography.

PRIMAL SCENES

The critical and creative work of Hélène Cixous has persistently been driven by a curiosity about the origin of writing, which invariably poses questions regarding the origin of law. As a French writer of Jewish descent, born and raised in colonial Algeria, Cixous not only felt the effects of social marginalization but also suffered the confusion of having once been placed outside the law, when in 1941, at the age of four, she and her family lost their French citizenship under the anti-Jewish laws of the Vichy government. These fraught origins were something she shared with Jacques Derrida, seven years her senior, whom she first met in Paris in 1963, and might possibly explain their fascination with the exilic, nomadic figure of James Joyce, as well as their participation in the *Tel Quel* group. Both developed a keen instinct for investigating origins and the enigmas of primal scenes, for detecting fissures and temporal effects that would unsettle the purportedly ahistorical nature of synchronic structures. Where Derrida enlists Husserl's phenomenology and Heidegger's fundamental ontology to insist on the priority of writing—a priority that is already constituted by self-difference and self-deferral—Cixous exhibits a penchant for discovering how writing might evade established laws and lead to new modes of thinking and living. For her, the question concerning the origin of writing is a woman's question, a *question-femme*, one that motivates what she comes to call *écriture féminine*.

To explore the ramifications of this question, to submit it to experimental trial, Cixous founded—or *originated*—the Center for Women's Studies in 1969 at the University of Vincennes. First coined in *La Venue à l'écriture* ("Coming to Writing," 1977), the term *écriture féminine* is a theoretically rich concept that addresses issues of embodied difference and limit experiences. Hardly a category of essential characteristics, *écriture féminine* is performative, an act that one does, a process of becoming, which interrupts masculine forms and patriarchal conventions of subjectivity. Insofar as such conventions are *convenient*, in the multiple and related senses of that which is easy, efficacious, agreeable, and appropriate, where everyone and everything appears "to come together" (*con-venire*), then the "coming to writing" introduces something radically *inconvenient*, a writing that is discomfiting, recalcitrant, incapable of fitting in and therefore the advent of the new, the incalculable, the unforeseeable: The *be-coming* of writing (*devenir-écriture*) as opposed to a writing that is simply "becoming" or *convenable*. As Cixous famously expresses it in her essay "The Laugh of the Medusa" (1975), "writing is precisely the very possibility of change."[21]

In a lecture for her 1980-1 seminar at Vincennes, Cixous turned to Kafka's parable *Vor dem Gesetz* (*Before the Law*), which she discussed in relation to three other authors: Clarice Lispector, James Joyce, and Maurice Blanchot—a comparative enterprise that traces motifs of origin and the law, their textual appearance, function, and power. Similar to Robert's psychological-biographical approach, Cixous proceeds by registering discrete textual details that comprise a complex mosaic of meanings grounded in the textual figuration of each author. Yet, whereas Robert collates the allusions to chart the significances in Kafka's corpus, Cixous is interested in producing a constellation among multiple writers so as to grasp what is at stake in writing itself. Cixous's practice thus further contrasts with earlier existentialist readings: Sartre and Camus read Kafka to incite responsibility, while Cixous investigates Kafka to stimulate intertextual responsiveness.

What links all four writers together is the "primal scene," a conception that Freud first developed in his analysis of the "Wolf Man" in the 1918 essay "From the History of an Infantile Neurosis." Here, the primal scene refers to a child witnessing or fantasizing his parents copulating, a scene that arouses both fear and sexual desire, which further relates to the child's own moment of conception—that is, to a time when the child did not yet exist and therefore to the time when the individual will no longer exist. The primal scene, therefore, exceeds the

---

[21] Hélène Cixous, "The Laugh of the Medusa" [1975], tr. Keith Cohen and Paula Cohen *Signs* 1 (1976), 875–93; here, p. 879.

subject and is thus difficult to capture or convey. Although Cixous does not cite from this work explicitly, Freud's interpretation is operative throughout.[22] Specifically for Cixous, the primal scene is the origin of writing, a writing that proceeds from the unrepresentable and is inscribed in some way by death.

As she states explicitly from the outset, Cixous is not particularly concerned with writing, which "is something already finished, something that follows the drive to write," but rather with "the origin of the gesture of writing," how writing becomes writing.[23] Of the four selected authors, Lispector's *Near to the Wild Heart* (*Perto do coração selvagem*) is closest to the initial drive to write. The novel was Lispector's first, written in 1937 when she was seventeen and published six years afterward. The book therefore counts as her "firstborn," a work that is indeed "near or close" (*perto*) to something "wild" and impassioned: "One has to have a touch of something savage, uncultured, in order to let it happen" (1). In contrast to any purely intellectual pursuit, this writing responds to a bodily need or imperative, even if, as Cixous points out, the title is a quotation from Joyce's own novel of coming to culture, *Portrait of the Artist as a Young Man*. Lispector's unmastered text bears witness to the raw life that authors like Flaubert and his progeny Joyce and Kafka struggled to craft into literature. Young Lispector had the audacity to publish the primitive barbarity that her male counterparts saw fit to destroy. Like Flaubert, Kafka wanted everything that he did not authorize for publication to be burned; Joyce consigned the novel's first draft, *Stephen Hero*, to the flames before his sister retrieved the manuscript. Again, to focus on the birth itself, to ask where the writing originates and what the writer is looking for are "women's questions," determined by the body. Raising and following these questions are more important than finding the answer (2–3).

Cixous begins with Joyce's *Portrait*, which she reads as the birth of the writer *before* he writes. The opening episode is "embryonic," containing the germ cells of the entire book. Rather ambivalently, the first pages gather maternal and paternal images—the "moocow" and the father's gaze through his glasses—which set up an Oedipal scene, culminating with a threat: His mother affirms, "O, Stephen will apologise," to which "Dante," his auntie, replies, "O, if not, the eagles

---

[22] For an extensive discussion of Cixous's essay and its indebtedness to Freud's theory, see Stefan Polatinsky and Anthea Buys, "Facing the Void: Primal Scenes in Maurice Blanchot and Hélène Cixous," *Arcadia* 46 (2011), 15–26.

[23] Hélène Cixous, "Writing and the Law: Blanchot, Joyce, Kafka, and Lispector," in *Readings: The Poetics of Blanchot, Joyce, Kafka, Kleist, Lispector, and Tsvetayeva*, tr. Verena Andermatt Conley (Minneapolis: University of Minnesota Press, 1991), 1–27; here, p. 1.

will come and pull out his eyes." Cixous calls attention to how the child hides in the womblike space beneath the table and converts the fear of symbolic castration into an auditory pleasure, which furnishes a line of escape: "*Apologise, Pull out his eyes.*" As in Deleuze and Guattari, sound deterritorializes; it unblocks the system. The pleasure of language's phonic dimension is the primal scene that sets the young man on the path to becoming a young artist, a way to evade the domesticating law by means of silence, exile, and cunning.

Lispector exhibits the same phonic obsession, yet one that more closely merges living and writing. "Clarice . . . did not write the portrait of the artist; she wrote the portrait of the subject in formation, a feminine subject that reveals at the same time all the traits of the artist" (8). In *Near to the Wild Heart*, the primal scene is a theft: Joana's aunt catches her stealing a book, yet the girl does not feel guilty. She stole because she wanted to steal. Whereas Joyce evokes the menacing law so that Stephen can transgress it, Lispector portrays Joana as a child untouched by the law. She implicitly understands that the law poses no threat to her because she already embodies the lack. Sexual difference is crucial for Cixous, yet it fails to allow for a convenient binarism that upholds conventional laws. Instead, she deploys difference to chart variations in the relationship between writing and the law. Where Joyce's artist says no to prohibition, Lispector's artist is altogether indifferent to any law that she does not give to herself. With Kafka, the case is more complicated: He says yes to the agreeable law of marriage in order to say no to marriage for the sake of writing. In Cixous's view, the birth of the writer in Kafka takes place in the vacillation between engagement and disengagement (12–13). The indecision, however, is not synonymous with Lispector's indifference, because Kafka's drama is wholly incorporeal. It is in this regard that Cixous begins her reading of *Before the Law*: "it is not the *body* that prevents the man from the country from going through the door, but the *word*"—a *logos*, and therefore "not a real being" (14).

In Kafka, the law is unreal and yet still imposed. Moreover, it never manifests itself as itself, but rather is consigned to a forbidden place. In terms of the body, the man from the country can enter the law whenever he wishes, but he respects the word of law and stays outside the gate. Although he remains forever outside the law, his desire to enter and his respectfulness already inscribe him within the law: He obeys the law by not transgressing (15). Indeed, if did enter the law he would be an outlaw. For Cixous, this paradox correlates to the self-division already mentioned in regard to Kafka's vacillation in an out of marital commitment. To underscore and complicate the point further, she cites a diary entry that Kafka wrote on November 6, 1913: "Whence the sudden confidence? If it would only remain! If I could go in and out of every door in this way, a passably erect person. Only I don't know whether I want that" (KGW 10, 201/D 236). The desire to enter through every door broaches a new question: Does the man in fact want what he wants? Being from the country, he is closer to raw nature than the doorkeeper; he is closer to the wild heart, which lies at the origin of the gesture of writing. For Cixous, *Before the Law* is Kafka's primal scene, one that conceives a writing that is entirely unique.

In Cixous's reading, the face-off between the man and the guardian is reminiscent of the predicament that Moses confronted when he was prohibited from entering the Promised Land. Curiously, she does not quote Kafka's remarks, which compare Frédéric Moreau's futile infatuation for Madame Arnoux to Moses' failure to reach Canaan.[24] Still, she makes the same point in a more Freudian key: The Promised Land is forbidden, yet it is not a forbidding place; on the contrary, it stimulates desire, just like the Oedipal predicament, which is fueled by the desire to penetrate the forbidden body of the mother (16). "The law is the divided desire inside him" (18). Yet why must this law be protected? Cixous proposes that the man from the country does not enter the law because there is no law, because there is nothing hiding within. The law "defends its own secret, which is that it does not exist" (18)—or it exists only as a word, an internalized moral law, like Freud's super-ego. And if the law is already within one's psyche, how can one physically enter it? The law is the threat of lack, which gives birth to writing. Unlike Lispector, whose writing is engendered by an embodiment of lack, both Joyce and Kafka come to writing as symbolic compensation, which imagines the law and thereby guards its absence. In Kafka's legend, every opening of the door is also a closing, every "step" (*pas*) that writing takes towards the law is also the law's "annulment" (*pas*, 19). The terminology immediately evokes Cixous's fourth author: Maurice Blanchot.

Her reading focuses on two closely related italicized passages from Blanchot's *L'Écriture du désastre* (*The Writing of Disaster*, 1980); both appear to relate to the same childhood experience and both are headed by the same parenthetical question: "(A primal scene?)". That there is not one but rather two "primal scenes" already challenges the very notion of primacy, which might account for Blanchot's question mark: An origin or subject already divided in and from itself. Cixous does not conceal the fact that Blanchot is very close to Kafka; she calls him "Kafka's phantom and vampire," a theorist who "preys upon [Kafka]

---

[24] See Ritchie Robertson, "Style," in *Franz Kafka in Context*, Carolin Duttlinger, ed. (Cambridge: Cambridge University Press, 2018), 84.

incessantly," a writer who "pushed the Kafkaesque dilemma toward an algebraic formulation" (19).

Blanchot's first primal scene opens with an act of gazing:

> (A primal scene?) *You who live later, close to a heart that beats no more, suppose, suppose this: the child—is he seven years old, or eight perhaps?—standing by the window, drawing the curtain and, through the pane, looking. What he sees: the garden, the wintry trees, the wall of a house. Though he sees, no doubt in a child's way, his play space, he grows weary and slowly looks up toward the ordinary sky, with clouds, grey light—pallid daylight without depth.*[25]

The addressee is already posthumous, living afterward, "close to a heart" like Lispector, like Joyce, and, Cixous adds, like the reader, for here we are at the "heart" of Blanchot's book (20). She does not hesitate to identify the heart that beats no longer as that of the dead, Oedipal mother, without considering her as the antecedent of Eurydice, a central figure in Blanchot's oeuvre, the feminine other whose death inaugurates masculine song. At least here, Cixous appears unconcerned by the implications that Luce Irigaray will soon articulate, that the decentering of the male subject almost invariably depends on the absent feminine object of seduction.[26] In the Orphic paradigm, no less than in the Oedipal frame, a death initiates writing, which thereby characterizes the writer as posthumous. Instead, Cixous focuses on the child peering through the glass, which is both a transparent medium and an obstruction, an opening and a closing, like the gate to Kafka's law, while also underscoring the resemblance to Joyce's child, Stephen Dedalus, who views his father's visage through the glass of his spectacles.

In regarding the sky, Blanchot discovers a horrifying secret:

> *What happens then: the sky, the same sky, suddenly open, absolutely black and absolutely empty, revealing (as though the pane had broken) such an absence that all has since always and forevermore been lost therein—so lost that therein is affirmed and dissolved the vertiginous knowledge that nothing is what there is, and first of all nothing beyond. The unexpected aspect of this scene (its interminable feature) is the feeling*

---

[25] Maurice Blanchot, *The Writing of Disaster* [1980], tr. Ann Smock (Lincoln: University of Nebraska Press, 1995), 72. [*L'Écriture du désastre* (Paris: Gallimard, 1980), 117.

[26] Luce Irigaray, *Speculum of the Other Woman*, tr. Gillian C. Gill (Ithaca: Cornell University Press, 1985). On this point, see Lynn Huffer, "Blanchot's Mother," *Yale French Studies* 93 (1998), 175–95, esp. p. 178.

of happiness that straightaway submerges the child, the ravaging joy to which he can bear witness only by tears, an endless flood of tears. He is thought to suffer a childish sorrow; attempts are made to console him. He says nothing. He will live henceforth in the secret. He will weep no more.[27]

Blanchot's *poème en prose* therefore depicts the "disaster" of a sky emptied of stars (*dés-astre*), "that nothing is what there is." It is as if the windowpane had broken, which would allow an immediate experience of this nothingness, an event that arouses great happiness that can only be expressed by "an endless flood of tears." Here, Cixous broaches Freud's theory of the primal scene explicitly. Yet whereas in Freud, masculinity is born of the fear of and resistance to castration, and whereas neurosis amounts to the petrification portrayed in the Medusa myth, Blanchot speaks of a flood, which Cixous reads as "a resistance to castration put in place by a kind of femininity" (20–1). Like Kierkegaard's Abraham, she writes, what must be said cannot be said, the primal scene cannot be transmitted, which results in two masculine options: Remain true to the unique experience and therefore silent, or resort to "easy symbolization" (21). The alternatives rehearse the two poles that Blanchot consistently discerned in Kafka's work: The incommunicable solitude and the communicable law. Accordingly, Cixous alerts us to the fact that the child "looks" (*re-garde*), a look that both respects and guards the nothingness that happens. On this basis, she takes Blanchot's scene as a commentary on *Before the Law* (21–2). The subsequent desiccation—the child "will weep no more"—is the writing that guards and respects the "secret of the law," the secret "that there is no secret" (25).

The moral law that Kafka's man from the country internalizes is and is not analogous to the moral law which Kant tellingly addresses in the *Critique of Practical Reason* when he speaks of "the starry sky above his head and the moral law in his heart" (23). For Blanchot as for Kafka, the sky is starless. And for Lispector as well. Yet Lispector's indifference to the law, Cixous argues, the retained savagery of her young heart, stems from her embodied difference and produces a writing that evades symbolic logic. Lispector "de-hierarchizes" the conventional institutions that steer masculine literature and thereby founds a new law, "the law of the living" (26). Kafka's *Before the Law* stages the primal scene that initiates the process: The man from the country comes to civilization with the feminine desire of curiosity; like Lispector's Joana he wants to peer behind the curtain, he wants to see the nothing that is there, until he passes away.

---

[27] Blanchot, *The Writing of Disaster*, 72 [117].

DERRIDA'S PHARMACY

The story has become legendary. On December 26, 1981, Jacques Derrida traveled to Prague to hold a clandestine seminar before the Jan Hus Educational Foundation, a dissident organization of professors and students who protested the "normalization" policies that aimed to align Czechoslovakia more closely with the Soviet program. As an executive officer of the association's branch in France, Derrida had agreed to meet the group in the Czech capital, despite the risks. On this particular occasion, as on every other trip, Derrida was cautious to shield the anonymity of his colleagues. The day after his talk, Derrida headed to the airport, where he was accosted by a large man who suddenly appeared from behind a curtain by the baggage control desk. When Derrida's bag was inspected, the officer retrieved four brown packets and immediately placed Derrida under arrest for drug trafficking. Pleas of innocence, that the packets were clearly planted, were futile. While waiting for trial, his assigned lawyer whispered to him, jokingly: "You must have the impression of living in a Kafka story . . . Don't take things too tragically; consider it a literary experience."[28] Through the efforts of the French State Department, Derrida was released. He traveled by train back to Paris, arriving at the Gare de l'Est on January 2.

As it so happened, Derrida had already begun writing a lecture on Kafka's *Before the Law* for a colloquium at Cerisy-la-Salle on the "Faculty of Judgment," organized by Jean-François Lyotard. Now the question was how to process this frightening event, a kind of primal scene in that the drugs found in the baggage were not in fact there. How to convey the feeling that struck Josef K., a realization further confirmed by the judge in Prague, who characterized Derrida's innocent plea as something that the guilty always say? Was it a personal story or, as the lawyer suggested, a "literary experience"? What is the institutional law that determines literariness? What criteria could be applied to distinguish the two? Who decides, who judges? The questions came to organize Derrida's lecture on Kafka, which he first presented at the Royal Philosophical Society in London in 1982.

For the title of the lecture, Derrida chose "Before the Law," which already blurs the distinction between text and commentary, while illustrating Blanchot's remark that commentary is always also a repetition.[29] Particular focus falls on the concept of *prejudice*: a judgment

---

[28] Details are taken from Benoît Peeters, *Derrida: A Biography*, tr. Andrew Brown (Cambridge: Polity, 2013), 332–41.

[29] Jacques Derrida, "Before the Law," in *Acts of Literature*, tr. Derek Attridge (New York: Routledge, 1991), 181–220.

made beforehand, a rush to close the case. Prejudice comes before the law and further defines the chaplain's accusation in the parable's contextualization in *The Trial*, that Josef K. is too quick to interpret the legend's meaning. Likewise, in the story itself, the man from the country arrives with many prejudgments about the law: That the law indeed exists, that it is generally accessible, and that it is universally applicable. The parable, of course, overturns every one of these *praejudicia*. Whereas Cixous attended to the kinds of writing that occur vis-à-vis contact with the law, Derrida is more interested in the verbal structuring of the law as it is implied in Kafka's text, a structuring that turns out to be riddled with ambivalences. The first ambivalence concerns the title itself, where the preposition *before* can be understood either spatially or temporally. The very notion of *pre-position* appears to replicate Kafka's *Vor dem Gesetz* in that it is grammatically defined as coming "before" (*vor*) what is "posited" (*gesetzt*).

Pre-positions also suggest presuppositions, and Derrida alights on three legalistic axioms that generally determine how readers stand before *Before the Law*: 1, that the text has a fixed identity and that the original German text is the ultimate, legal authority; 2, that the text has a legally recognized author; and 3, that the text *Before the Law* is a literary narrative, governed by laws of genre (184–6). All three prejudgments or presuppositions are grounded in the logocentric system that Derrida aims to deconstruct, specifically by pressing the tensions that Cixous also detected: Between writing and the law, writing and living, literature and personal experience. How to respect and guard the singularity of the text vis-à-vis the generality of the law (187)? The system breaks down as soon as one moves from the title to the parable's opening sentence: "Before the law stands a doorkeeper." Identical words, with two distinct functions. Derrida emphasizes that the two phrases are homonyms rather than synonyms, pointing to two different referents (188–9). We could say that the title names the text as a *general* whole, while the sentence designates a *specific* situation, that the title is external in coming before the legend, while the sentence is internal to it. As for the law itself, Derrida reaches the same conclusion as Cixous: The law cannot be transmitted, it resists every "story" (*histoire*) and therefore transcends history. For the law to be law, it must state the general precept that operates above every specific case. "To be invested with its categorical authority, the law must be without history, genesis, or possible derivation. That would be *the law of the law*" (191).

Derrida's reading thus touches on the generality of the law, which is precisely what makes the law invisible. Derived from the Latin noun *genus*, which denotes a "tribe" or a "race," the general refers to an individual's origins, hence the figurative use of *genus* to mean "birth" or "origin." The term is cognate with the Greek noun *genos* ("tribe"), which in turn derives from the verb *gignesthai* ("to be born, to come into being"), related to our notions of *genesis* and *generation, engendering, gender,* and *genre.* In contrast to the invisibility of the *genus* is the stark visibility of the *species* ("that which is visible," from the verb *specere,* "to look"). We have returned, therefore, to the matter of *respect* and *regard,* back to the primal scene. Indeed, in Roman law, the act of engendering was ascribed to the father, whose contribution to procreation was hidden from public view, as opposed to the mother's childbearing, which was concretely visible. Accordingly, the father's role can only be imagined or instituted by law, never absolutely certain. As Freud often quoted: *Pater semper incertus est, mater semper certissima* ("the father is always uncertain, the mother always most certain"). Paternity, in other words, is upheld solely as a legal claim, and perhaps, as Joyce would say, only a legal fiction.

Although the law is said to exclude historicity and empirical narrativity, it invariably has recourse to narrative and fiction. Freud thus claimed, in *Totem and Taboo,* to have discovered the origin of the moral law in the "story" of the murder of the primal father. As Derrida points out, the fraternal horde felt remorse before the moral law was established—they were already acting in the law before the law (198). The crime, in other words, inaugurates nothing: For the deed to become effective, it must become a story, a *récit,* something recited, a text called to serve as witness, which is one of the meanings of the Latin verb *citare.* Hence, in *The Trial,* the priest *cites* the legend, which appears in quotation marks. And since stories have beginnings, they also have an end: The text, *Before the Law,* closes when the gate closes; "the man comes to his end without reaching his end" (210). Again and again, Derrida puts philosophy on trial by submitting its axioms to indefatigable investigation, reading the fine print, and forestalling any final verdict. Rather than overturn the exegetical tradition, he dismantles it, observes each of its verbal components, and thereby keeps the gate open. As he admits towards the end of the essay:

> This has hardly been a categorical reading. I have ventured glosses, multiplied interpretations, asked and diverted questions, abandoned decipherings in mid-course, left enigmas intact; I have accused, acquitted, defended, praised, subpoenaed.
> (216)

Derrida remains before *Before the Law* by maintaining respect for the literal meanings of the text, which is traditionally the lowest of the four types of scriptural exegesis. His own theoretical presupposition is one that resists the tug of allegorical, moral, or anagogical readings. The exegesis which should *lead* us *out* of the text's perplexities (*ex-ēgeisthai*) ends by leading us back in. Similarly, in Kafka's chapter, although K. insists on leaving to return to the bank, he asks the priest for the "main entrance" (*Haupteingang*) rather than the exit (KGW 3, 234/T 159).

The parable *Before the Law* readily recalls Hebraic, Talmudic, or kabalistic traditions, yet Kafka set the legend in a Catholic cathedral: *Im Dom*. According to manuscript evidence, the chapter appears to be the last text he wrote for *The Trial* before abandoning the project in January 1915.[30] While Kafka would instruct Brod to burn the manuscript, he personally saw the parable itself to publication, without the novelistic context, first in the New Year's Day number of the Prague Zionist weekly, *Selbstwehr* ("Self-Defense") and again in his 1920 collection, *Ein Landarzt* (*A Country Doctor*). *Before the Law* is therefore a text that was authorized by the living writer, yet also one that would soon be re-contextualized or even given a new home (*domus*) in a predominantly Catholic France.

Derrida, who like Cixous came from a Jewish-Algerian home, was arrested in Kafka's Prague—an experience that was either personal or literary, or literary because personal. The event was highly specific and visibly broadcasted, and therefore amounted to a primal scene that would inaugurate more written reflection, with further turns to Kafka's ghost, for example in the *Force of Law* (1990) and *Literature in Secret* (1999).[31] These readings once again consider Kafka in relation to the biblical Abraham and to Kierkegaard, analyzing, dissecting, and interrogating the repertoire of allusions that have sustained the French Kafka from the beginning: Kafka the *pharmakon*, the drug that is not there, the writing that either cures or poisons, aiding and destroying memory, including the memory of the writer whose absence is inscribed in the writing; or Kafka the *pharmakos*, the unique magician and scapegoat, tried before the law of general, invisible theories, which prosecute and execute, striving to make sense of the work left behind, summoning the writing as confirmation of a worldview, or enlisting the texts as strategies for unworking structures of authority and power—all chapters in the story that reflects and refracts the history of France/Kafka.

---

[30] For the chronology of the novel manuscript, see Kafka, *Historisch-kritische Ausgabe sämtlicher Handschriften, Drucke und Typoskripte*, vol. 3: *Der Prozess*, ed. Roland Reuß and Peter Staengle, (Basel: Stromfeld/Roter Stern, 1997).

[31] Derrida, "Force of Law: The 'Mythical Foundation of Authority,'" tr. Mary Quaintance, in *Acts of Religion*, ed. Gil Anidjar (New York: Routledge, 2002), 230–98; and "Literature in Secret: An Impossible Filiation" in *The Gift of Death*, 2nd Edition, tr. David Wills (Chicago: The University of Chicago Press, 2008), 119–58.

Works Cited

Adorno, Theodor W. *Prisms*. Translated by Samuel and Shierry Weber. Cambridge: The MIT Press, 1967.
Adorno, Theodor W. *Gesammelte Schriften*, vol. 10.1: *Kulturkritik und Gesellschaft* I. Edited by Rolf Tiedemann. Frankfurt: Suhrkamp, 1977.
Allan, Neil. *Franz Kafka and the Genealogy of Modern European Philosophy: From Phenomenology to Post-Structuralism*. Lewiston: Edwin Mellen Press, 2005.
Alt, Peter-André. *Franz Kafka: Der ewige Sohn*. Munich: Beck, 2005.
Anderson, Mark. *Kafka's Clothes: Ornament and Aestheticism in the Habsburg* Fin de Siècle. Oxford: Clarendon Press, 1992.
Badiou, Alain. *The Adventure of French Philosophy*. Translated by Bruno Bosteels. New York: Verso, 2012.
Barker, Andrew. "Giant Bug or Monstrous Vermin? Translating Kafka's *Die Verwandlung* in its Cultural, Social, and Biological Contexts." *Translation and Literature* 30 (2021), 198–208.
Barthes, Roland. *Critical Essays*. Translated by Richard Howard. Evanston: Northwestern University Press, 1972.
Barthes, Roland. *Œuvres complètes*. 4 vols. Edited by Eric Marty. Paris: Seuil, 2002.
Bataille, Georges. "Franz Kafka devant la critique communiste." *Critique* 41 (Oct. 1950), 22–36.
Bataille, Georges. *La littérature et le mal*. Paris: Gallimard, 1957.
Bataille, Georges. *Literature and Evil*. Translated by Alistair Hamilton. London: Calder & Boyars, 1973.
Bataille, Georges. *Essential Writings*. Edited by Michael Richardson. London: Sage, 1998.
Béal, François. *Vialatte, l'intemporel: Panorama de l'étrange échassier*. Paris: Harmattan, 2006.
Beauvoir, Simone de. *Prime of Life*. Translated by Peter Green. New York: Harper and Row, 1976.
Beauvoir, Simone de. *Journal de guerre: Septembre 1939–Janvier 1941*. Edited by Sylvie le Bon-de Beauvoir. Paris: Gallimard, 1990.
Beauvoir, Simone de. *Wartime Diary*. Translated by Anne Deing Cordero. Champaign: University of Illinois Press, 2008.
Beauvoir, Simone de and Bost, Jacques-Laurent. *Correspondance croisée (1937–1940)*. Edited by Sylvie le Bon-de Beauvoir. Paris: Gallimard, 2004.
Beauvoir, Simone de and Sartre, Jean-Paul. *Witness to My Life: The Letters of Jean-Paul Sartre to Simone de Beauvoir, 1926–1939*. Translated by Lee Fahnestock and Norman MacAfee. New York: Scribner's, 1992.

Works Cited

Beicken, Peter. *Franz Kafka: Eine kritische Einführung in die Forschung*. Frankfurt am Main: Athenäum Fischer, 1974.
Bernheimer, Charles. *Flaubert and Kafka: Studies in Psychopoetic Structure*. New Haven: Yale University Press, 1982.
Bertaux, Félix. *Panorama de la littérature allemande contemporaine*. Paris: Éditions de Sagittaire, 1928.
Bident, Christophe. *Maurice Blanchot: A Critical Biography*. Translated by John McKeane. New York: Fordham University Press, 2019.
Binder, Hartmut. *Kafka in Paris: Historische Spaziergänge mit alten Photographien*. Munich: Langen Müller, 1999.
Blanchot, Maurice. *L'Écriture du désastre*. Paris: Gallimard, 1980.
Blanchot, Maurice. *De Kafka à Kafka*. Paris: Gallimard, 1981.
Blanchot, Maurice. *The Space of Literature*. Translated by Ann Smock. Lincoln: University of Nebraska Press, 1989.
Blanchot, Maurice. *Infinite Conversation*. Translated by Susan Hanson. Minneapolis: University of Minnesota Press, 1993.
Blanchot, Maurice. *The Writing of Disaster*. Translated by Ann Smock. Lincoln: University of Nebraska Press, 1995.
Blanchot, Maurice. *The Work of Fire*. Translated by Charlotte Mandell. Stanford: Stanford University Press, 1995.
Blanchot, Maurice. *Friendship*. Translated by Elizabeth Rottenberg. Stanford: Stanford University Press, 1997.
Blanchot, Maurice. *Aminadab*. Translated by Jeff Fort. Lincoln: University of Nebraska Press, 2002.
Blanchot, Maurice. *Écrits politiques: Guerre d'Algérie, Mai 68, etc*. Paris: Lignes, 2003.
Blumenberg, Hans. *The Laughter of the Thracian Woman: A Protohistory of Theory*. Translated by Spencer Hawkins. New York: Bloomsbury, 2015.
Bogaerts, Jo. "Against Allegory: A Reappraisal of French Existentialism's Encounter with Franz Kafka." *Journal of the Kafka Society of America* 37 (2015), 27–44.
Blanchot, Maurice. Review: Sartre, *Situations*, vol. 3. *The Germanic Review* 90 (2015), 145–9.
Blanchot, Maurice. "Sartre's 'Guerre Fantôme': A Kafkaesque Subtext in the Postwar Writings." *The Germanic Review* 94 (2019), 57–74.
Bogain, Ariane. "Jules Romains' Vision of a United Europe in Interwar France: Legacy and Ambiguities." *Modern and Contemporary France* 21 (2013), 89–105.
Borges, Jorge Luis. *Selected Non-Fictions*. Translated by Eliot Weinberger. New York: Penguin, 1999.
Börhringer, Hannes. *Bernard Groethuysen: Vom Zusammenhang seiner Schriften*. Berlin: Agora, 1978.
Boschetti, Anna. *Sartre et 'Les Temps Modernes': Une entreprise intellectuelle*. Paris: Minuit 1985.
Bouju, Emmanuel. "Après quoi rien à dire: Délibération et réponse de Kafka." *Carnets* 6 (2016), 1–8.
Brentano, Franz. *Psychology from an Empirical Standpoint*. Translated by Antos C. Rancurello, D.B. Terrell, and Linda McAlister. New York: Routledge, 1995.
Breton, André. *Œuvres complètes*, vol. 1. Bibliothèque de la Pléiade. Edited by Marguerite Bonnet. Paris: Gallimard, 1988.
Breton, André. *Têtes d'orage*, Minotaure 10 (1937), 9, 17–19.
Breton, André. *Anthologie de l'humour noir*, 2nd ed. Paris: Sagittaire, 1950.

Brod, Max. "Frühling in Prag." *Die Gegenwart* (May 18, 1907), 316–17.
Brod, Max. "Kleine Prosa." *Die neue Rundschau* (July 1913), 1044–5.
Brod, Max. "Der Dichter Franz Kafka." *Die neue Rundschau* (November 1921), 1210–11.
Brod, Max. *Franz Kafka: A Biography*. Translated by Humphreys Roberts. New York: Schocken, 1960.
Butler, Judith. *Gender Trouble: Feminism and the Subversion of Identity*, 2nd ed. New York: Routledge, 1999.
Camus, Albert. *The Myth of Sisyphus*. Translated by Justin O'Brien. New York: Vintage, 1955.
Camus, Albert. *Essais*. Bibliothèque de la Pléiade, Paris: Gallimard, 1965.
Camus, Albert. *Essais II*. Bibliothèque de la Pléiade. Edited by Roger Quilliot and Louis Faucon. Paris: Gallimard, 1967.
Carrouges, Michel. "La Machine-Célibataire selon Kafka et Marcel Duchamp." *Mercure de France* 1066 (June 1952), 262–81.
Casanova, Pascale. *The World Republic of Letters*. Translated by Malcolm DeBevoise. Cambridge: Harvard University Press, 2007.
Charpentier, Pierre-Frédéric. *La Drôle de guerre des intellectuels français*. Panazol: Lavauzelle, 2008.
Cixous, Hélène. "The Laugh of the Medusa." Translated by Keith Cohen and Paula Cohen. *Signs* 1 (1976), 875–93.
Cixous, Hélène. *Readings: The Poetics of Blanchot, Joyce, Kafka, Kleist, Lispector, and Tsvetayeva*. Translated by Verena Andermatt Conley. Minneapolis: University of Minnesota Press, 1991.
Cohen-Solal, Annie. *Jean-Paul Sartre: A Life*. Translated by Anna Cancogni. New York: New Press, 2005.
Cohn, Dorrit. "Castles and Anti-Castles, or Kafka and Robbe-Grillet." *Novel* 5 (1971), 19–31.
Cohn, Dorrit. "Trends in Literary Criticism: Some Structuralist Approaches to Kafka." *The German Quarterly* 51 (1978), 182–8.
Corngold, Stanley. "Kafka and the Dialect of Minor Literature." *College Literature* 21 (1994), 89–101.
Corngold, Stanley. *Lambent Traces: Franz Kafka*. Princeton: Princeton University Press, 2006.
Cornick, Martyn. *The* Nouvelle Revue Française *under Jean Paulhan, 1925–1940*. Amsterdam: Rodopi, 1995.
Cornick, Martyn. "Jean Paulhan and the *Nouvelle Revue française*: Modernist Editor, Modernist Review?" *Romanic Review* 99 (2008), 9–26.
Cusset, François. *French Theory: How Foucault, Derrida, Deleuze & Co. Transformed the Intellectual Life of the United States*. Translated by Jeff Fort. Minneapolis: University of Minnesota Press, 2008.
Daniel-Rops. "L'univers désesperé de Franz Kafka." *Les Cahiers du Sud* (March 1937), 161–76.
Deleuze, Gilles and Guattari, Félix. *Kafka: Pour une littérature mineure*. Paris: Éditions de Minuit, 1975.
Deleuze, Gilles and Guattari, Félix. *L'anti-Œdipe: Capitalisme et schizophrénie*. Paris: Minuit, 1972.
Deleuze, Gilles and Guattari, Félix. *Anti-Oedipus*. Translated by Robert Hurley, Mark Seem, and Helen R. Lane. Minneapolis: University of Minnesota Press, 1983.

Deleuze, Gilles and Guattari, Félix. *Kafka: Toward a Minor Literature*. Translated by Dana Polan. Minneapolis: University of Minnesota Press, 1986.

Derins, Françoise. "A Lecture by Jean-Paul Sartre." Translated by Denis Hollier and Rosalind Krauss. *October* 87 (1999), 24–6.

Derrida, Jacques. *Acts of Literature*. Translated by Derek Attridge. New York: Routledge, 1991.

Derrida, Jacques. *Acts of Religion*. Edited by Gil Anidjar. New York: Routledge, 2002.

Derrida, Jacques. *The Gift of Death*, 2nd Edition. Translated by David Wills. Chicago: The University of Chicago Press, 2008.

Dubreuil, Laurent. *L'état critique de la littérature*. Paris: Hermann, 2009.

Duttlinger, Carolin, ed. *Franz Kafka in Context*. Cambridge: Cambridge University Press, 2017.

Eilittä, Leena. "Art as Religious Commitment: Kafka's Debt to Kierkegaardian Ideas and their Impact on his Late Stories." *German Life and Letters* 53 (2000), 499–510.

Ermarth, Michael. "Intellectual History as Philosophical Anthropology: Bernard Groethuysen's Transformation of Traditional *Geistesgeschichte*." *Journal of Modern History* 65 (1993), 673–705.

Espagne, Michel. "La fonction de la traduction dans les transferts culturels franco-allemands aux XVIIIe et XIXe siècles." *Revue de l'Histoire littéraire de la France* 3 (1997), 413–27.

Esslin, Martin. *The Theatre of the Absurd*. New York: Vintage, 2004.

Fauchery, Pierre. "Faut-il brûler Kafka?" *Action* 90 (May 31, 1946), 12.

Federici, Annalisa. "The *Transatlantic Review* and the *Nouvelle Revue Française*— Between Tradition and Modernity: The Ford-Larbaud-Joyce Connection." *International Ford Maddox Ford Studies* 15 (2016), 115–28.

Fló, Juan. "Jorge Luis Borges, traductor de *Die Verwandlung* (Fechas, textos, conjecturas)," *Anales de Literatura Hispanoamericana* 42 (2013), 215–40.

Flores, Angel, ed. *The Kafka Problem*. New York: New Directions, 1946.

Flynn, Thomas. *Sartre: A Philosophical Biography*. Cambridge: Cambridge University Press, 2014.

Fonsegrive, George. *"Kultur" et civilisation*. Paris: Bloud & Gay, 1916.

Foucault, Michel. *Language, Counter-Memory, Practice: Selected Essays and Interviews*. Edited by Donald Bouchard. Ithaca: Cornell University Press, 1977.

Frese Witt, Mary Ann. "Camus et Kafka." *La Revue des lettres modernes* 264 (1971), 71–86.

Gautier, Théophile. *Souvenirs de théâtre, d'art et de critique*. Paris: Charpentier, 1883.

Gautier, Théophile. "The Tales of Hoffmann." Translated by Anne E. Duggan. *Marvels & Tales* 23 (2009), 138–45.

Genette, Gérard. *Paratexts: Thresholds of Interpretation*. Translated by Jane E. Lewin. Cambridge: Cambridge University Press, 1997.

Gide, André. "Réflexions sur l'Allemagne." *Nouvelle Revue Française* (November 1921), 513–21.

Gide, André. *Journal*, vol. 1. Edited by Éric Marty. Paris: Gallimard, 1996.

Gide, André and Barrault, Jean-Louis. *Le Procès*. Paris: Gallimard, 1947.

Gillain, Nathalie. "Charlot, une source d'inspiration pour Henri Michaux: De la figuration de mouvements à la subversion des genres." *Études françaises* 55 (2019), 95–113.

Goebel, Rolf. "Paris, Capital of Modernity: Kafka and Benjamin." *Monatshefte* 90 (1998), 445–64.
Gordon, Daniel. "Bernard Groethuysen and the Human Conversation." *History and Theory* 36 (1997), 289–311.
Goth, Maja. *Franz Kafka et les Lettres françaises*. Paris: Corti, 1956.
Greenwood, Edward. "Literature: Freedom or Evil? The Debate between Sartre and Bataille." *Sartre Studies International* 4 (1998), 17–29.
Grégoire, Vincent. "Camus l'écrivain naissant face à la censure allemande." *Symposium* 63 (2009), 36–50.
Groethuysen, Bernard. *Die Entstehung der bürgerlichen Welt- und Lebensanschauung in Frankreich*, vol. 1. Halle: Niemeyer, 1927.
Groethuysen, Bernard. *Origines de l'esprit bourgeois en France*. Paris: Gallimard, 1927.
Heidsieck, Arnold. *The Intellectual Contexts of Kafka's Fiction: Philosophy, Law, Religion*. Columbia: Camden House, 1994.
Hollier, Denis. *The College of Sociology, 1937–1939*. Translated by Betsy Wing. Minneapolis: University of Minnesota Press, 1988.
Huffer, Lynn. "Blanchot's Mother," *Yale French Studies* 93 (1998), 175–95.
Hughes, Edward. *Albert Camus*. London: Reaktion, 2015.
Irigaray, Luce. *Speculum of the Other Woman*. Translated by Gillian C. Gill. Ithaca: Cornell University Press, 1985.
Jolas, Eugène. *Man from Babel*. Edited by Andreas Kramer and Rainer Rumold. New Haven: Yale University Press, 1998.
Jones, James. "Camus on Kafka and Melville: An Unpublished Letter." *The French Review* 71 (1998), 645–50.
Judt, Tony. *Past Imperfect: French Intellectuals, 1944–1956*. Berkeley: University of California Press, 1992.
Juliet, Charles. "La littérature et le thème de la mort chez Kafka et Leiris." *Critique* 126 (November 1957).
Kafka, Franz. *Das Schloß*. Munich: Kurt Wolff, 1926.
Kafka, Franz. "La Métamorphose." Translated by Alexandre Vialatte. *Nouvelle Revue Française* 172 (January 1, 1928), 66–84.
Kafka, Franz. "Bucéphale, et autres récits." Translated by Félix Bertaux, K.W. Körner, and Jules Supervielle. *Nouvelle Revue Française* 191 (August 1929), 205–11.
Kafka, Franz. *Le Verdict*. Translated by Pierre Klossowski and Pierre Leyris. *Bifur* 5 (July 1930).
Kafka, Franz. *Le Procès*. Translated by Alexandre Viallate. Paris: Gallimard, 1957.
Kafka, Franz. *The Metamorphosis*. Translated by Stanley Corngold. New York: Bantam, 1972.
Kafka, Franz. *Œuvres complètes*. Bibliothèque de la Pléiade, 2 vols. Edited by Claude David. Paris: Gallimard, 1976.
Kafka, Franz. *Historisch-kritische Ausgabe sämtlicher Handschriften, Drucke und Typoskripte*, vol. 3: *Der Prozess*. Edited by Roland Reuß and Peter Staengle. Basel: Stromfeld/Roter Stern, 1997.
Kafka, Franz. *The Office Writings*. Edited by Stanley Corngold, Jack Greenberg, and Benno Wagner. Princeton: Princeton University Press, 2009.
Klein, Rony. "Une rencontre autour de Kafka, Walter Benjamin, et Roland Barthes." *Études Germaniques* 283 (2016), 405–25.

Kuhn, Ira. "The Metamorphosis of *The Trial*." *Symposium* 26 (1972), 226–41.
Kundera, Milan. *Testaments Betrayed: An Essay in Nine Parts*. Translated by Linda Asher. New York: HarperCollins, 1995.
Lacouture, Jean. *Une adolescence du siècle: Jacques Rivière et la NRF*. Paris: Seuil, 1994.
Larbaud, Valéry. *Sous l'invocation de Saint Jérôme*. Paris: Gallimard, 1946.
Lecomte, Marcel. *Note sur Kafka et le rêve (La Métamorphose)*. In *Rêve*. Edited by André Breton. Paris, 1938.
Leiris, *L'Âge d'homme*. Paris: Gallimard, 1939.
Lloyd, Christopher. *Henri-Georges Clouzot*. Manchester: Manchester University Press, 2007.
Lottman, Herbert R. *The Left Bank: Writers, Artists, and Politics from the Popular Front to the Cold War*. Chicago: The University of Chicago Press, 1982.
Magny, Claude-Edmonde. *Les sandales d'Empédocle: Essai sur les limites de la littérature*. Neuchâtel: Baconnière, 1945.
Magny, Claude-Edmonde. "L'univers d'Henri Michaux et de Kafka." *La Revue internationale* (October 1946), n. p.
Mathieu, Jean-Claude. "Légère lecture de Plume." In *Ruptures sur Henri Michaux*. Edited by Roger Dadoun, 101–157. Paris: Payot, 1976.
Michaux, Henri. *Épreuves, Exorcismes*. Paris: Gallimard, 1949.
Michaux, Henri. *L'espace du dedans, Pages choisies, Poésie*. Paris: Gallimard, 1966.
Michaux, Henri. *Selected Writings: The Space Within*. Edited by Richard Ellmann. New York: New Directions, 1968.
Michaux, Henri. *Œuvres complètes*. Bibliothèque de la Pléiade, vol. 1. Edited by Raymond Bellour. Paris: Gallimard, 1998.
Michaux, Henri. *A Certain Plume*. Translated by Richard Sieburth. New York: New York Review of Books, 2018.
Milne, Anna-Louise. *The Extreme In-Between: Jean Paulhan's Place in the Twentieth Century*. London: Routledge, 2006.
Neesen, Peter. *Vom Louvrezirkel zum Prozess: Franz Kafka und die Psychologie Franz Brentanos*. Göppingen: Kümmerle, 1972.
Nizan, Paul. *Pour une nouvelle culture*. Edited by Susan Suleiman. Paris: Grasset, 1971.
North, Paul. *The Yield: Kafka's Atheological Reformation*. Stanford: Stanford University Press, 2015.
O'Neill, Patrick. *Transforming Kafka: Translation Effects*. Toronto: University of Toronto Press, 2014.
Paulhan, Jean. *Les Fleurs de Tarbes, ou la terreur dans les lettres*. Edited by Jean-Claude Zylberstein. Paris: Gallimard, 1990.
Paulhan, Jean and Suarès, André. *Correspondence: Jean Paulhan, André Suarès*. Edited by Yves Alain Favre. Paris: Gallimard, 1987.
Peeters, Benoît. *Derrida: A Biography*. Translated by Andrew Brown. Cambridge: Polity, 2013.
Plato. *Complete Works*. Edited by John M. Cooper. Indianapolis: Hackett, 1997.
Polatinsky, Stefan and Buys, Anthea. "Facing the Void: Primal Scenes in Maurice Blanchot and Hélène Cixous." *Arcadia* 46 (2011), 15–26.
Redfern, Walter. *All Puns Intended: The Verbal Creation of Jean-Pierre Brisset*. London: Taylor & Francis, 2017.
Rhein, Phillip. *The Urge to Live: A Comparative Study of Franz Kafka's* Der Prozess *and Albert Camus's* L'Étranger. Chapel Hill: The University of North Carolina Press, 1964.

Robbe-Grillet, Alain. *For a New Novel*. Translated by Richard Howard. New York: Grove, 1965.

Robert, Marthe. *Kafka*. Paris: Gallimard, 1960.

Robert, Marthe. "Kafka en France." *Mercure de France* 342 (May–Aug. 1961), 241–55.

Robert, Marthe. *As Lonely as Franz Kafka*. Translated by Ralph Manheim. New York: Harcourt Brace Jovanovich, 1982.

Robertson, Ritchie. "In Search of Historical Kafka: A Selective View of Research, 1980–1992." *Modern Language Review* 89 (1994), 107–37.

Rodlauer, Hannelore and Pasley, Malcolm, eds. *Max Brod, Franz Kafka: Eine Freundschaft*, vol. 1, *Reiseaufzeichnungen*. Frankfurt am Main: Fischer, 1987.

Roger, Jérôme. "Ponge, lecteur de Michaux: un différend sans merci." *Littérature* 115 (1999), 70–86.

Sandbank, Shimon. *After Kafka: The Influence of Kafka's Fiction*. Athens: The University of Georgia Press, 1989.

Sapiro, Gisèle. *La Guerre des écrivains*. Paris: Fayard, 1999.

Sartre, Jean-Paul. "À la Kafka." *Les Temps Modernes* 1:1 (October 1, 1945), 191.

Sartre, Jean-Paul. *Situations I: Essais critiques*. Paris: Gallimard, 1947.

Sartre, Jean-Paul. *Qu'est-ce que la littérature?* Paris: Gallimard, 1948.

Sartre, Jean-Paul. *What is Literature?* Translated by Bernard Frechtman. New York: Philosophical Library, 1949.

Sartre, Jean-Paul. *Que peut la littérature?* Edited by Yves Buin. Paris: L'Herne, 1965.

Sartre, Jean-Paul. *Situations X: Politique et autobiographie*. Paris: Gallimard, 1976.

Sartre, Jean-Paul. *Œuvres romanesques*. Bibliothèque de la Pléiade. Edited by Michel Contat and Michel Rybalka. Paris: Gallimard, 1981.

Sartre, Jean-Paul. *Lettres au Castor et à quelques autres, 1926–1939*. Edited by Simone de Beauvoir. Paris: Gallimard, 1983.

Sartre, Jean-Paul. *Les Mots et autres écrits autobiographiques*. Edited by Jean François Louette, Gilles Philippe, and Juliette Simont. Paris: Gallimard, 2010.

Sartre, Jean-Paul. *Situations*, vol. 3. Paris: Gallimard, 2013.

Sartre, Jean-Paul *Nausea*. Translated by Lloyd Alexander. New York: New Directions, 2013.

Sartre, Jean-Paul. *Critical Essays (Situations I)*. Translated by Chris Turner. London: Seagull, 2017.

Sartre, Jean-Paul. *Being and Nothingness: An Essay in Phenomenological Ontology*. Translated by Sarah Richmond. New York: Washington Square Press, 2018.

Schmeling, Manfred. "Das 'offene Kunstwerk' in der Übersetzung: Zur Problematik der französischen Kafka-Rezeption." *Arcadia* 14 (1979), 22–39.

Schmitz-Emans, Monika. "Kafka und die Weltliteratur," in *Kafka-Handbuch: Leben—Werk—Wirkung*. Edited by Bettina von Jagow and Oliver Jahraus, 271–92. Göttingen: Vandenhoeck & Ruprecht, 2008, 271–92.

Siepe, Hans. "André Gide et Franz Kafka." *Bulletin des Amis d'André Gide* 25: 114–15 (April–July 1997), 283–98.

Siess, Jürgen. "Bernard Groethuysen: Vers une anthropologie littéraire," *Raison présente* 68 (1983), 43–56.

Smith, Barry. "Brentano and Kafka." *Axiomathes* 8 (1997), 83–104.

Sokel, Walter. "Kafka und Sartres Existenzphilosophie." *Arcadia* 5 (1970), 262–77.

Stach, Reiner. *Kafka: The Early Years*. Translated by Shelley Frisch. Princeton: Princeton University Press, 2017.

Starkie, Enid. "Bouzingos and Jeunes-France." In *On Bohemia*. Edited by César Graña and Marigay Graña, 364–9. London: Taylor & Francis, 1990.

Stoekl, Allan. "Blanchot: Death, Language, Community and Politics." *Parallax* 12 (2006), 40–52.
Stratovsky, Yevgenya. "Agency and Political Engagement in Gide and Barrault's Post-war Theatrical Adaptation of Kafka's *The Trial*." *Comparative Literature and Culture* 20, no. 3 (2017): http://docs.lib.purdue.edu/clcweb/vol19/iss3/6, last accessed on June 15, 2022.
Surya, Michel. *Georges Bataille: An Intellectual Biography*. Translated by Krzysztof Fijalkowski and Michael Richardson. London: Verso, 2002.
Teboul, Margaret. "La réception de Kierkegaard en France 1930–1960." *Revues des sciences philosophiques et théologiques* 89 (2005), 315–36.
Vallejo, César. *Selected Writings*. Edited by Joseph Mulligan. Middletown: Wesleyan University Press, 2015.
van Rooden, Aukje. "Kafka Shared Between Blanchot and Sartre." *Arcadia* 55 (2020), 239–59.
Venuti, Lawrence. *The Translator's Invisibility: A History of Translation*. London: Routledge, 1995.
Viallate, Alexandre. *Kafka ou l'innocence diabolique*. Edited by François Béal and François Taillandier. Paris: Les Belles Lettres, 1998.
Wahl, Jean. *Études kierkegaardiennes*. Paris: Aubier, 1938.
Wahl, Jean. *Esquisse pour une histoire de l'existentialisme*. Paris: Éditions du club Maintenant, 1947.
Wetterwald, Denis, ed. *Alexandre Vialatte, Jean Paulhan, Correspondance, 1921–1968*. Paris: Julliard, 1997.
Zard, Philippe, ed. *Sillage de Kafka*. Paris: Éditions Le Manuscrit, 2007.

Index

Absurd, the 4, 89, 101–4, 105–7, 108–9, 116, 122
  Theater of the Absurd 137
Acéphale (journal) 81
Action (journal) 126, 129, 130, 132
Action française 27
Adorno, Theodor W., "Notes on Kafka" 3, 26, 151
  Notes to Literature 7
Ahlwardt, Hermann 46
Alain (Émile Chartier) 35
Alger républicain (newspaper) 101
Allan, Neil 12 n.13
Allégret, Marc 33
Alquié, Ferdinand 75
Anderson, Mark 14 n.18
Anouilh, Jean 120
anthroposophy 11
Apollinaire, Guillaume 30
Aragon, Louis 30
Aristotle 3
Arland, Marcel 98
Aron, Raymond 119
Augustine, Saint 8
Aux Écoutes (journal) 98, 118

Badiou, Alain 3 n.2, 153
Balthus (Balthasar Klossowski de Rola) 53
Balzac, Honoré de 54
Barbezat, Marc 105
Barrault, Jean-Louis 137–40

Barthes, Roland 5, 143–50, 155
  "Déliberation" 149–50
  "L'activité structuraliste" 147
  "La réponse de Kafka" ("Kafka's Answer") 143–8
  "Les deux critiques" 147
  "Qu'est-ce que la critique?" 147;
Bataille, Georges 5, 52, 81, 82, 117, 124, 125, 130, 136, 156
  Inner Experience 117
  La littérature et le mal (*Literature and Evil*) 133–6
Baudelaire, Charles 7
Bauer, Felice 10 n.10, 15, 17, 135
Baum, Oskar 68
Beauvoir, Simone de 85–90, 119
Benda, Julien 81
  La trahison des clercs 35, 128
Benjamin, Walter 81
  Arcades Project 7
Bergmann, Hugo 11
Bergson, Henri 61, 65
Bernheimer, Charles 151
Bertaux, Félix 49, 50, 51–2, 57, 70
  Panorama of Contemporary German Literature 49
Bifur (journal) 52–2, 57, 71
Bismarck, Otto von 43
Blanchot, Maurice 5, 6, 76, 87, 98, 108, 115–18, 124–6, 129–30, 132, 133, 147–8, 156, 158, 161, 164

Index

"Affirmer la rupture" 126
Aminadab 115–18
"Kafka et la littérature" ("Kafka and Literature") 135–6
"Kafka et l'exigence de l'œuvre" ("Kafka and the Work's Demand") 135
"La Lecture de Kafka" ("Reading Kafka") 121–3, 135
"La littérature et le droit à la mort" ("Literature and the Right to Death") 118, 124–6
La Part de feu (*The Work of Fire*) 135
L'Écriture du désastre (*The Writing of Disaster*) 161–3
"Le pont de bois (la répétition, le neutre)" ("The Wooden Bridge (repetition, the neuter)") 148–9
"Le tout denier mot" ("The Very Last Word") 8, 126
Thomas l'obscur (*Thomas the Obscure*) 76
Blei, Franz 13, 68
Blum, Léon 76
Blumenberg, Hans 6 n.5
Boese, Carl 57
Bogaerts, Jo 86, 87 n.5, 99 n.27, 132 n.22
Borges, Jorge Luis 29, 50, 72
  "Kafka and his Precursors" 151
Boschetti, Anna 118
Bost, Jacques-Laurent 89, 119
Bounoure, Gabriel 35, 70
Bouzingos, the 77
Brasillach, Robert 119–20, 121
Brentano, Franz 11, 12–14, 15, 60, 115, 136
Breton, André 5, 29, 30, 31, 36, 52, 54, 76–8, 82
  Anthologie de l'humour noir 77–8
  Nadja 75

Surrealist Manifesto 30, 52, 74, 75, 77
Têtes d'orage ("Storm Heads") 76
(with Philippe Soupault) *Les Champs magnétiques* 74–5
Brisset, Jean-Pierre 77
Brochier, Jean-Jacques 40
Brod, Max 11, 12, 15–17, 29, 36–7, 40, 52, 58, 67–70, 78, 79–80, 82, 107, 109, 124, 144, 149
Brod, Otto 16
Buber, Martin 68
Butler, Judith, *Gender Trouble* 5

Cahiers du Sud (journal) 102, 115
Caillois, Roger 81, 130–1, 132
Calvino, Italo 150
Camus, Albert 5, 9, 59, 82, 87, 97, 100–8, 120, 158
  Caligula 101
  "Hope and the Absurd in the Work of Franz Kafka" 59, 105–8
  La Peste (*The Plague*) 105
  Le Malentendu (*The Misunderstanding*) 105
  L'Étranger (*The Stranger*) 101, 102–4, 115–16
  Myth of Sisyphus 101–2, 105–8, 109
  Noces (*Nuptials*) 101
Carroll, Lewis 75, 110
Carrouges, Michel 75
Cassou, Jean 98
Céline, Louis-Ferdinand 98
Cendrars, Blaise 72
Ce Soir (newspaper) 96
Chaplin, Charlie 72–3, 88, 119, 121
Charpentier, Pierre-Frédéric 99–100
Cixous, Hélène 5, 12, 157–63, 165
  La Venue à l'écriture ("Coming to Writing") 158
  "The Laugh of the Medusa" 158

Claudel, Paul 120
Clouzot, Henri-Georges 120–1
  Le Corbeau 120
Cocteau, Jean 72, 120
Cohen-Solal, Annie 100
Collège de Sociologie 81, 130, 133
Collette 120
Combat (journal) 119
Commerce (journal) 27, 37
communism 4, 62, 76, 96–7, 98, 117, 133, 135
Corngold, Stanley 46 n.37, 136, 150, 155 n.20
Crevel, René 72
Criterion (journal) 27
Critique (journal) 124, 133
Cusset, François 5 n.3

Dada 30, 52
Daladier, Édouard 98
Daniel-Rops (Henri Petiot) 80
Däubler, Theodor, *Der Werwolf* 57
David, Claude 7–8, 10, 52
deconstruction 5, 9, 165
de Gaulle, Charles 119–20
Deleuze, Gilles 3, 5, 6, 12, 160
  (with Félix Guattari): *Anti-Oedipus* 153
  Kafka: Toward a Minor Literature 152–7
Derrida, Jacques 5, 6, 12, 104, 157, 164
  "Before the Law" 164–7
  Force of Law 167
  Literature in Secret 167
Descartes, René 17
Desjardins, Paul 61
Dial, The (journal) 27
Dickens, Charles 10
Dilthey, Wilhelm 60, 62, 65
Disque vert (journal) 72
Dostoevsky, Fyodor 10, 98, 102
Drieu la Rochelle, Pierre 81, 101

Duchamp, Marcel 52, *The Large Glass* (*La mariée mise à nu par ses célibataires, même*) 75
Dumesnils, René, *Flaubert: Son hérédité—son milieu—sa méthode* 17
Dunoyer, Jean-Marie 130
Duras, Marguerite 150

écriture féminine 157–8
Ehrenfels, Christian von 11, 60
Ellmann, Richard 73
Éluard, Paul 30, 75
Ernst, Max 75, 77
  Au Rendez-vous des amis 30
Esprit (journal) 97, 109
existentialism 4, 5, 7, 9, 10, 12, 67, 86–7, 117, 121, 132, 150, 151, 153
expressionism 26, 57

Fallada, Hans 86
Fantastic, the *see Littérature fantastique*
Fargue, Léon-Paul 27
Faucon, Louis 105
feminism 5
Fernandez, Ramon 35
Flaubert, Gustave 10, 98, 150–1, 159
  L'Éducation sentimentale 15–16, 17, 27, 161
Flynn, Thomas 92
Fonsegrive, George 38
formalism, Russian 12
Forneret, Xavier 77
Foucault, Michel 9, 153
Freud, Sigmund 7, 11, 12, 61, 65, 144, 153, 155, 161, 163, 166
  "From the History of an Infantile Neurosis" 158–9
  Totem and Taboo 166
Futurism 32

Gallimard, Gaston 27, 28, 30, 50, 58, 60, 61, 62, 70, 88, 96, 101, 119, 129
Gallimard, Michel 104
Gaullism 4
Gautier, Théophile 39, 51–2, 77
Genette, Gérard 58
George, Stefan 49
Gide, André 5, 25, 27, 28, 30, 32, 50, 61, 62, 76, 123
  Le Procès (stage adaptation) 137–40
  Les Faux-monnayeurs (The Counterfeiters) 53
  Sur le Logone 33–4, 35
Giraudoux, Jean 115
Gobineau, Arthur de 32
Goebbels, Joseph 58
Goebel, Rolf 34 n.17
Goethe, Johann Wolfgang von 10, 15
  Faust 33–4
Gogol, Nikolai 10
Gomperz, Heinrich 60
Goth, Maja 73 n.22, 75 n.27, 87 n.5
Grabbe, Christoph-Dietrich 77
Grenier, Jean 101
Groethuysen, Bernard 5, 12, 53, 58, 77, 82, 96, 116, 140, 144
  "À propos de Kafka" 59–67
Guattari, Félix 5, 12, 152–7
Guillain, Alix 62
Gullouin, René 35

Haas, Willy 29, 68, 70
Hamsun, Knut 10
Hegel, Georg Wilhelm Friedrich 3, 81, 125
Heidegger, Martin 7, 12, 80–1, 102, 118, 119, 123, 157
  Being and Time 61
Heidsieck, Arnold 12
Heine, Heinrich 6, 42
Hemingway, Ernest 102

Hesse, Herman 29
Hitler, Adolf 98, 100, 101
Hoffmann, E.T.A. 6, 10, 39, 51, 116
Hofmannsthal, Hugo von 49, 61
Hölderlin, Friedrich 42, 53, 61
Husserl, Edmund 7, 11, 12, 13, 14, 60, 61, 65, 87, 115, 157
Hyperion (journal) 13, 68

Ionesco, Eugène 5
  "Dans les armes de la ville" ("In the Arms of the City") 137
Irigaray, Luce 162

Jacob, Max 72
Jakobson, Roman 12
Jaloux, Edmond 98
Jan Hus Educational Foundation 164
Jaspers, Karl 7, 81
Je suis partout (journal) 119
Journal des Débats (journal) 76, 118, 129
Jouve, Pierre-Jean 53
Joyce, James 50, 52, 98, 157, 158, 161, 162
  Portrait of the Artist as a Young Man 159–60, 162
  Stephen Hero 159
  Ulysses 38
Joyce, Lucia 72
Jude, der (journal) 68

Kafka, Franz
  Beim Bau der chinesischen Mauer ("The Great Wall of China") 96, 156
  Betrachtung (Contemplation) 68
  Beschreibung eines Kampfes ("Description of a Struggle") 13–14, 72, 75, 94
  Blumfeld, ein älterer Junggeselle ("Blumfeld, an Elderly Bachelor") 75

Brief an den Vater ("Letter to His Father") 155
Das Schloß (*The Castle*) 17, 18, 28, 29, 43, 52, 58, 66, 69, 73, 79–80, 91, 93, 99, 105, 106–7, 109–10, 121, 130, 131, 146, 147–8, 154
Das Urteil (*The Judgment*) 18, 19, 52–4, 57, 66, 75, 135–6
Der Bau ("The Burrow") 66
Der Jäger Gracchus ("The Hunter Gracchus") 75, 122
Der Prozess (*The Trial*) 12, 18, 29, 40, 52, 58, 62, 65–7, 69–70, 71, 78, 79, 86, 91, 92–3, 94, 98, 99, 100, 103, 105, 107, 130, 137–40, 144, 146, 156, 157, 165–7
Diaries 17–18, 19–22, 78, 121–2, 149, 155, 160–1
Die Sorge des Hausvaters ("The Cares of a Family Man") 77, 152
Die Verwandlung ("Metamorphosis") 18, 25–6, 28, 29, 31, 34, 35, 36, 43, 45–9, 57, 71, 73, 75, 110, 146, 156
Ein Bericht für eine Akademie ("A Report to an Academy") 108
Ein Brudermord ("A Fratricide") 75
Ein Hungerkünstler ("A Hunger Artist") 66, 146
Ein Landarzt (*A Country Doctor*) 167
Ein Traum ("A Dream") 75
Forschungen eines Hundes ("Investigations of a Dog") 146
Gespräch mit dem Beter ("Conversation with the Supplicant") 94–5
In der Strafkolonie ("In the Penal Colony") 75, 98, 146, 156
Josefine, die Sängerin oder Das Volk der Mäuse ("Josephine the Singer or the Mouse Folk") 154–5, 156
Letters to Felice 10, 15, 17–18, 135
Vor dem Gesetz ("Before the Law") 5, 50–1, 67, 139, 158, 160–1, 163, 164–7
Kant, Immanuel 3
 Critique of Practical Reason 163
Kierkegaard, Søren 10, 11, 70, 79–81, 102, 106–8, 109, 110, 122, 132, 163, 167
 Fear and Trembling 79–80, 106–8
 Purity of Hope 107
Klossowska, Baladine 53
Klossowski, Pierre 5, 52–4, 57, 59, 71, 81
Knopf, Alfred 58
Kojève, Alexandre 81, 125
Körner, Karl Wilhelm 49–50, 52
Kundera, Milan 48–9

Lacomte, Marcel 75
L'Arbalète (journal) 105, 107
Larbaud, Valéry 27, 37–8, 72
L'Arche (journal) 121
Lautréamont (Isidore Ducasse) 50, 75, 80, 115
 Les Chants de Maldoror 108
Laval, Pierre 119
Lefebvre, Jean-Pierre 52
Leiris, Michel 5, 78–9, 81, 117, 128
 Aurora 78
 L'Âge d'homme 78–9
 La Règle du jeu 78
Les Temps Modernes (journal) 119, 123
Levinas, Emmanuel 115
Lévi-Strauss, Claude 147
Lévy, Pierre 52, 54
Leyris, Pierre 52–4, 71
Lichtenberg, Georg-Christoph 77

182 Index

L'Insurgé (journal) 76
Lispector, Clarice 158, 162
   Perto do coração selvagem (*Near to the Wild Heart*) 159–60, 163
Littérature fantastique 25–6, 39, 54, 57, 65, 116–18, 121
Loève-Veimars, François-Adolphe 39
Löwy, Jizchak 155
Lyotard, Jean-François 5, 153, 164

Macksey, Richard 150
Mac Orlan (Pierre Dumarchey) 42, 43
Magny, Claude-Edmonde (Edmonde Vinel) 26, 41, 73, 87, 108–11, 136, 138
Mallarmé, Stéphane 35, 115, 125
Malraux, André 61, 101
   La condition humaine 62
Manifesto of the 121 143
Mann, Heinrich 49
Mann, Thomas 29, 49
Marcel, Gabriel 61
Marty, Anton 11, 12, 60
Marx, Karl 7, 127
Marxism 4, 5, 62, 87, 117, 127–8, 150, 151, 153
Masson, André 81
Maulnier, Thierry 76
Mauriac, François 120, 128
Maurras, Charles 27, 76, 117
Maxence, Jean-Luc 76
Mercure de France (journal) 27
Merleau-Ponty, Maurice 119, 128
Mesures (journal) 96
Meyrink, Gustav, *Der Golem* 57, 59
Michaux, Henri 5, 28, 70–4, 85–6, 129
   "Clown" 88
   Drame des constructeurs 71–2
   Épreuves, Exorcismes 74
   Plume, précédé de Lointain intérieur 88–9

Qui je fus 35, 50, 70
Un certain Plume 71–4
Milton, John, *Samson Agonistes* 34
Minotaure (journal) 76
Monnier, Adrienne 30, 38
Morand, Paul, *Syracuse (U. S. A.)* 32–3, 35–6
Morel, Auguste 38
Mounier, Emmanuel 97, 109
Muir, Edwin and Willa 29, 37, 45–9, 58
Muschg, Walter 70

Nerval, Gérard de 19, 22, 64, 77, 115
   "El Desdichado" 36
Neue Rundschau, die (journal) 27, 6
Nietzsche, Friedrich 6, 7, 10, 11, 36, 67, 81, 97, 98, 153
Nizan, Henriette 100
Nizan, Paul 96–7, 100, 103
Nodier, Charles 116
Nora, Pierre, *Les Français d'Algérie* 104
North, Paul 80 n.39
Nouveau roman 5, 150–1
Nouvelle Revue Française (*NRF*) (journal) 25, 27–8, 29, 30, 31, 32, 35–6, 49, 50, 52, 54, 57, 59, 61, 62, 70, 96, 98, 101, 126

Ocampo, Victoria 50
Ollivier, Albert 119
Ortega y Gasset, José 29
OuLiPo (Ouvroir de littérature potentielle) 77, 150
Ovid 25
Ovide moralisé 25

Paris-Midi (newspaper) 85
Paris-Soir (newspaper) 101, 102
Parison, Henri 75
Parmenides 3
Pascal, Blaise 102

Paul, Saint 8, 41
Paulhan, Jean 5, 29–31, 32, 33, 36, 40, 50, 54, 61, 62, 75, 96, 98, 99, 101, 119, 128, 129
  Les Fleurs de Tarbes, ou la terreur dans les lettres 76
Perec, Georges 150
Péret, Benjamin 75
Personalism 97
Pétain, Philippe 102, 119
Phenomenology 5, 7, 11, 82, 87, 96, 157
Pia, Pascal 101
Picabia, Francis 52
Pick, Otto 68
Plato 15, 64
  Theaetetus 6
Pollak, Oskar 11
Ponge, Francis 72, 129, 130, 136
  Le Parti pris des choses 129
Poststructuralism 5, 7, 12, 14
Prassinos, Mario 75
Prévost, Jean 35
Proust, Marcel 7, 25, 28, 35, 109
psychoanalysis 11, 12, 144, 153
psychology, experimental 11
psychology, Gestalt 11, 60

Queneau, Raymond 101
Quincey, Thomas de 77

Rabbe, Alphonse, *Album d'un pessimiste* 77
Rabelais, François 98, 157
Revista de Occidente (journal) 29
Révolution surréaliste (journal) 78
Revue des Deux Mondes (journal) 27
Revue européenne (journal) 71
Revue rhénane (journal) 36, 42
Ribemont-Dessaignes, Georges 52, 54
Rilke, Rainer Maria 49, 53
Rimbaud, Arthur 64, 75, 80
Rivière, Jacques 27, 30

Robbe-Grillet, Alain 150–1
Robert, Marthe 11, 52, 143–9, 150, 152, 158
  Kafka 143–4, 146–7
  L'ancien et le nouveau: de Don Quichotte à Franz Kafka 147
Robertson, Ritchie 40 n.29, 161 n.24
Robin, Armand 97
Romains, Jules 34, 38, 61, 77
  La vie unanime 32
  L'homme blanc 31–2, 35, 96
Ronsard, Pierre de 129
Roubaud, Jacques 150
Roussel, Raymond 77
Rowohlt, Ernst 68

Sarraute, Nathalie 150
Sartre, Jean-Paul 3, 5, 12, 61, 65, 82, 85–90, 102–3, 115–21, 122–6, 127, 129, 132, 133–4, 136, 143, 150, 151, 158
  La legende de la vérité (*Legend of Truth*) 97
  L'être et le néant (*Being and Nothingness*) 93–4, 115
  La nausée (*Nausea*) 14, 88, 90–2, 94–8, 100–1, 102, 103, 110, 118
  Réflexions sur la question juive (*Anti-Semite and Jew*) 132
  Que peut la littérature? 88
  What is Literature? 123, 132–3
Saurès, André 31
Saussure, Ferdinand de 144, 147
Selbstwehr (journal) 167
semiotics 5, 153
Schiller, Friedrich 6
Schocken, Salman 68
Shakespeare, William 53
Sheikevitch, Marie 35
Shestov, Lev 81, 107, 108
Sieburth, Richard 72–3

Index

Simmel, Georg 60, 62
Simon, Claude 150
sociology 5
Sokel, Walter 87 n.5
Sollers, Philippe 150
Soupault, Philippe 52, 72
Spinoza, Baruch de 131
Stalinism 127, 132
Steiner, Rudolf 11
Strakovsky, Yevgenya 137
Strindberg, August 10
structuralism 5, 12, 147–8, 149, 153, 154
Stumpf, Carl 11, 12, 60
Supervielle, Jules 49–50, 52, 70
  Débarcadères 50
Surrealism 4, 26, 27, 29, 30, 31, 36, 42, 50, 63–4, 74–5, 110, 144
Sussman, Henry 150
Swift, Jonathan 77
Symbolism 61, 130

Tel Quel (journal) 149, 150, 157
Thales 6
Thérive, André 98
Thibaudet, Albert 35
Thorez, Maurice 127
Tolstoy, Leo 10
Trubetzkoy, Nikolai 12
Tulchosky, Kurt 29

Utitz, Emil 11

Valéry, Paul 25, 27, 28, 50, 120
  Petits Textes 34, 35
Vallejo, César 52 n.46
Védrine, Louise 98
Venuti, Lawrence 37
Vialatte, Alexandre 25, 26, 29, 36–8, 40–1, 42–9, 50–2, 53–4, 57–9, 78, 79, 80, 144
  Battling le ténébreux 36
Volontaires, les (journal) 98
Voltaire 38

Wagenbach, Klaus 12
Wagner, Richard 6
Wahl, Jean 5, 81, 82, 107–8, 109, 110, 122
Wegener, Paul 57
Wells, H.G., *The War of the Worlds* 26
Weltsch, Felix 68
Weltsch, Robert 68
Werfel, Franz 61, 68
Whitman, Walt 32
Williams, William Carlos 52
Wolff, Kurt 25, 29
Wölfflin, Heinrich 60

Zhdanovism 127

Volumes in the series:

1. *Improvisation as Art: Conceptual Challenges, Historical Perspectives*
by Edgar Landgraf

2. *The German Pícaro and Modernity: Between Underdog and Shape-Shifter*
by Bernhard Malkmus

3. *Citation and Precedent: Conjunctions and Disjunctions of German Law and Literature*
by Thomas O. Beebee

4. *Beyond Discontent: 'Sublimation' from Goethe to Lacan*
by Eckart Goebel

5. *From Kafka to Sebald: Modernism and Narrative Form*
edited by Sabine Wilke

6. *Image in Outline: Reading Lou Andreas-Salomé*
by Gisela Brinker-Gabler

7. *Out of Place: German Realism, Displacement, and Modernity*
by John B. Lyon

8. *Thomas Mann in English: A Study in Literary Translation*
by David Horton

9. *The Tragedy of Fatherhood: King Laius and the Politics of Paternity in the West*
by Silke-Maria Weineck

10. *The Poet as Phenomenologist: Rilke and the* New Poems
by Luke Fischer

11. *The Laughter of the Thracian Woman: A Protohistory of Theory*
by Hans Blumenberg, translated by Spencer Hawkins

12. *Roma Voices in the German-Speaking World*
by Lorely French

13. *Vienna's Dreams of Europe: Culture and Identity beyond the Nation-State*
by Katherine Arens

14. *Thomas Mann and Shakespeare: Something Rich and Strange*
edited by Tobias Döring and Ewan Fernie

15. *Goethe's Families of the Heart*
by Susan E. Gustafson

16. *German Aesthetics: Fundamental Concepts from Baumgarten to Adorno*
edited by J. D. Mininger and Jason Michael Peck

17. *Figures of Natality: Reading the Political in the Age of Goethe*
by Joseph D. O'Neil

18. *Readings in the Anthropocene: The Environmental Humanities, German Studies, and Beyond*
edited by Sabine Wilke and Japhet Johnstone

19 *Building Socialism: Architecture and Urbanism in East German Literature, 1955–1973*
by Curtis Swope

20. *Ghostwriting: W. G. Sebald's Poetics of History*
by Richard T. Gray

21. *Stereotype and Destiny in Arthur Schnitzler's Prose: Five Psycho-Sociological Readings*
by Marie Kolkenbrock

22. *Sissi's World: The Empress Elisabeth in Memory and Myth*
edited by Maura E. Hametz and Heidi Schlipphacke

23. *Posthumanism in the Age of Humanism: Mind, Matter, and the Life Sciences after Kant*
edited by Edgar Landgraf, Gabriel Trop, and Leif Weatherby

24. *Staging West German Democracy: Governmental PR Films and the Democratic Imaginary, 1953–1963*
by Jan Uelzmann

25. *The Lever as Instrument of Reason: Technological Constructions of Knowledge around 1800*
by Jocelyn Holland

26. *The Fontane Workshop: Manufacturing Realism in the Industrial Age of Print*
by Petra McGillen

27. *Gender, Collaboration, and Authorship in German Culture: Literary Joint Ventures, 1750–1850*
edited by Laura Deiulio and John B. Lyon

28. *Kafka's Stereoscopes: The Political Function of a Literary Style*
by Isak Winkel Holm

29. *Ambiguous Aggression in German Realism and Beyond: Flirtation, Passive Aggression, Domestic Violence*
by Barbara N. Nagel

30. *Thomas Bernhard's Afterlives*
edited by Stephen Dowden, Gregor Thuswaldner, and Olaf Berwald

31. *Modernism in Trieste: The Habsburg Mediterranean and the Literary Invention of Europe, 1870–1945*
by Salvatore Pappalardo

32. *Grotesque Visions: The Science of Berlin Dada*
by Thomas O. Haakenson

33. *Theodor Fontane: Irony and Avowal in a Post-Truth Age*
by Brian Tucker

34. *Jane Eyre in German Lands: The Import of Romance, 1848–1918*
by Lynne Tatlock

35. *Weimar in Princeton: Thomas Mann and the Kahler Circle*
by Stanley Corngold

36. *Authors and the World: Modes and Models of Literary Authorship in 20th and 21st Century Germany*
by Rebecca Braun

37. *Germany from the Outside: Rethinking German Cultural History in an Age of Displacement*
edited by Laurie Johnson

38. *France/Kafka: An Author in Theory*
by John T. Hamilton